S0-AEU-318

Black Politics
in Philadelphia

Black Politics in Philadelphia

EDITED BY
Miriam Ershkowitz
AND
Joseph Zikmund II

BASIC BOOKS, INC., Publishers

NEW YORK

Library of Congress Catalog Card Number: 72-89284
SBN 465-00698-1
Manufactured in the United States of America
Designed by Vincent Torre

73 74 75 76 77   10 9 8 7 6 5 4 3 2 1

To our sons
William Geoffrey Ershkowitz
Brian Joseph Zikmund

Contents

PART THREE
THE POLITICS OF BLACK PARTICIPATION IN
COMMUNITY-CONTROLLED ANTIPOVERTY PROGRAMS

PART FOUR
EPILOGUE

Foreword

Black Politics in Philadelphia represents a pioneering effort to present a comprehensive picture of the role of the Blacks, past and present, in one of America's major cities, based on a combination of existing sources and new research. In line with the new trends in the study of American minority groups and the Blacks in particular, it shows the Black community as both political actor and the victim of political action, revealing its growing role as one part of the mosaic that makes up the contemporary American city. In focusing on the political life of Black city dwellers, it opens up a new view of the political consequences of the urbanization of the Black community in America and sets the pattern for the examination of the political life of other minorities in the urban setting.

This volume also reflects the convergence of several scholarly fields and civic interests. In the first place, it is a prime example of the convergence of the two fields of urban politics and Black studies whereby the techniques and questions devised for the former over the past eighty years are used to illuminate the concerns of the latter, a field that has gained recognition more recently. By doing so, it helps reveal the necessarily intimate relationship linking both fields.

This book is also a significant example of the convergence of the concerns of scholarship and public affairs. The articles included in this volume were all prepared according to the canons of scholarship by men committed to the pursuit of truth in the scientific spirit, but all speak to one of the great concerns of public affairs today—in Philadelphia and in the United States as a whole. Moreover, they speak directly to that concern and are most helpful in putting it in proper focus for those who wish to actively respond to the challenges it has set before us all. At a time when the intellectual and rational dimensions of civilization are everywhere under assault in the name of "relevance," it is good to be reminded that, in social research, a good theoretical question has good practical implications and a good practical question raises proper theoretical questions.

Beyond these convergences, this volume also introduces us to some truths about the Black condition in a major American city (that was—and is—neither as bad nor as good as the mythologies would have us believe). As the studies included in this volume reveal, Blacks have not only been a "presence" in Philadelphia since its founding nearly 300 years ago, but have been a political presence in one way or another for nearly 200 years. The "ups and downs" of the Black community in the political arena parallel its experiences in the social and economic arenas but, whatever their social or economic state, Blacks have not been the political "non-persons" that they were in the South or have been in some Northern cities as well.

This book also tells us something about the level of attention paid to their condition by Blacks and others over the years. The search of the literature for materials to include in this book uncovered few items written before the 1960's but, relative to the materials available on other ethnic or racial groups, the Philadelphia Blacks have attracted considerable attention. Indeed, more studies of the kind included here are precisely what are needed for us to develop a proper understanding of American cities and the American people in all their diversity.

It has been assumed for too long that American cities are all the same, that their problems are all the same and that, accordingly, the solutions to those problems are bound to be the same. One of the major tasks of urbanists today must be to dispel that assumption, to clarify the uniquenesses of American communities as well as to uncover the commonalities that they share. For, in fact, the best responses to the problems of the cities and their peoples are likely to be those generated locally in response to the unique local conditions found in each city rather than those imposed from "on high" on the basis of erroneous assumptions about the uniformity of local conditions across the United States. Books such as this one should help us to better understand those local conditions and to develop appropriate strategies to respond to them.

This book, accordingly, has the secondary purpose of encouraging similar efforts for other cities and other minorities—ethnic, racial, or religious. The Center for the Study of Federalism will itself sponsor additional volumes dealing with both in the future as part of its own concern for the "ecology" of American federalism—the environmental framework in which the American political system must function. As an arm of Temple University, one of the country's great urban universities, the Center recognizes its special obligation to explore those aspects of that environment that bear most directly upon the great American cities and most particularly upon the city in which it is located.

It is doubly gratifying then that this, the first book of its kind to be sponsored by the Center and the third in its series of publications under the imprint of Basic Books, was so ably edited by two scholars who have been closely associated with the Center since its establishment in 1967 and that half of the books chapters are by Temple authors, three of whom have also been closely associated with the Center.

Daniel J. Elazar

Philadelphia
1973

Acknowledgments

We gratefully acknowledge the assistance and encouragement provided by Professor Daniel J. Elazar of the Temple University Center for the Study of Federalism. We also want to thank Mrs. Darla Glendening of the Center and Miss Linda Scherr and Mrs. Doris Shinn of the Temple University Department of Political Science for their help with many aspects of this project including the typing of the manuscript. We are indebted to the authors of the studies included here and to the publishers who permitted us to reprint work previously printed elsewhere.

For any errors in the introductory analytic materials, we assume full responsibility.

M. B. E.
J. Z. II

In Part One:

"Urban Blacks and Irishmen: Brothers in Prejudice," by Dennis Clark. Printed by permission of the author.

"The Black Vote of Philadelphia," by W. E. Burghardt Du Bois. Reprinted from *Charities* 15 (October 7, 1905), 31-35. Copyright 1905 by the Charity Organization Society.

"The Movement for the Betterment of the Negro in Philadelphia," by John T. Emlen. Reprinted from *The Annals of the American Academy of Political and Social Science* 49 (September, 1913), 81-92, by permission of the American Academy of Political and Social Science. Copyright 1913 by the American Academy of Political and Social Science.

In Part Two:

"Recent Negro Ballots in Philadelphia," by Oscar Glantz. Reprinted from the *Journal of Negro Education* 28 (Fall, 1959), 430-38 by permission of the author and the Bureau of Educational Research of Howard University. Copyright 1959 by Howard University.

"The Negro Vote in Philadelphia Elections," by William J. McKenna. Reprinted from *Pennsylvania History*, 32 (October, 1965), 406-15, by permission of the author and the Pennsylvania Historical Association. Copyright 1965 by the Pennsylvania Historical Association.

"The Electoral Politics of Reform and Machine: The Political Behavior of Philadelphia's 'Black' Wards, 1943-1969," by Charles A. Ekstrom. Printed by permission of the author.

"Blacks and Philadelphia Politics: 1963-1966," by John Hadley Strange. Printed by permission of the author.

"Cecil Moore and the Philadelphia Branch of the National Association for the Advancement of Colored People: The Politics of Negro Pressure Group Organization," by Paul Lermack. Printed by permission of the author.

In Part Three:

"Poverty, Politics and Administration: The Philadelphia Experience," by Harry A. Bailey, Jr. Printed by permission of the author.

"Articulateness, Political Mobility and Conservatism: An Analysis of the Philadelphia Antipoverty Election," by Elliott White. Printed by permission of the author.

In Part Four:

"A Final Word," from *The Philadelphia Negro*, by W. E. B. Du Bois (Philadelphia: University of Pennsylvania, 1899).

Black Politics
in Philadelphia

Introduction

To assert that a book on Black politics in a major American city is relevant to crucial issues in our time is to belabor the obvious. Students of American history and political science in general, particularly those specializing in Black history or Black studies, contemporary public policy, ethnic politics, local history, urban history, or urban politics, all should be interested. The important question is, What does this particular collection of articles and essays offer each of its potential publics?

Black Politics in Philadelphia is a book of edited selections about three narrowly defined, yet interrelated, subjects—Blacks, politics, and the city of Philadelphia. In one sense, this is a specialized book and its appeal or usefulness would seem limited only to those interested in its tightly-defined subject matter or its rather narrow geographic focus. On the other hand, the political experiences of Blacks in Philadelphia differ very little from the experiences of Blacks in large cities throughout all of the (nonsouthern) United States. For example, is W. E. B. Du Bois' classic study of *The Philadelphia Negro* during the 1890's important to the sociological world because it provides an in-depth exploration of the conditions of his people in one city—Philadelphia—or because it contains insights about the plight of urban Blacks generally? Clearly, the answer to our question is, both. Students of Philadelphia, *qua* Philadelphia, gained a tremendously valuable description of their city. At the same time, Du Bois makes a significant contribution to the general field of sociology. The editors of *Black Politics in Philadelphia* hope that this book, in its own way, can make a similar dual contribution.

Chronologically, the book concentrates on the twentieth century, providing only background commentary for the period 1682-1900. Thus, for the historically-minded, the book's unique advantage must come from Dennis Clark's fascinating original study of Black-Irish relations and from the reprinting of such a fugitive selection as Du Bois' little-known "Black Vote of Philadelphia" from *Charities* (1905). For the political scientist or urbanologist, *Black Politics in Philadelphia* offers a broad introduction to the contemporary Black urban political scene. In each of the sections, available articles are presented along with original essays to give a meaningful picture of Black politics in the city of Philadelphia.

In any collection of materials such as this which draws upon the works of several disciplines, it is inevitable that a wide range of methodologies and technical sophistication will be represented. The selections in *Black Politics in Philadelphia* are no exception. Some of the reprinted articles, of course, were written before our present level of methodological concern had begun to develop. Others come from the more descriptive traditions within history and political science. In all cases, however, the primary concern of the editors has been to provide the reader with the fullest and most meaningful picture of the Black man in Philadelphia politics, even where methodology had to be sacrificed to achieve that substantive completeness.

PART ONE

FROM SETTLEMENT
THROUGH
THE FIRST
WORLD WAR

Introduction

Black people have been a significant part of Philadelphia life since the city began in the early seventeenth century. Initially, of course, Negro slaves were treated much the same as white indentured servants. Only after 1700 were laws passed in the city to distinguish the African slave from all other kinds of people. In 1726 interracial marriages were prohibited. At this time a 9:00 P.M. curfew and travel restrictions were put into effect against Negroes in Philadelphia. However, when compared to conditions elsewhere in the colonies, Negro slavery in Pennsylvania, generally, and in Philadelphia, particularly, was relatively mild. Moral and ethical objections to slavery were expressed from the time of William Penn's first arrival and the creation of the Quaker settlement. As early as 1700, slavery traders had been required to pay the colony twenty shillings for every Negro imported, and the rate was progressively increased in 1705, in 1715, and in 1761. By 1750, however, the importation of Africans into Pennsylvania had virtually ceased, although formal prohibition of the slave trade did not come until 1780. The Black population of Philadelphia at the middle of the eighteenth century was estimated to be about 6,000.[1]

Paralleling the decreased importation of slaves into the Quaker colony during this period was the gradual increase in the number of free Negroes. Just as the medieval city provided liberty and opportunity for runaway peasants, Philadelphia drew escaped slaves. By the middle of the eighteenth century most Quakers had shifted from opposition to the slave trade to opposition to slavery itself. Influential Philadelphians such as Benjamin Franklin, Benjamin Rush, and Anthony Benezet openly worked for the abolition of the slave system.[2] In 1780 Pennsylvania made provision for the gradual end of slavery. As John Hope Franklin notes, "The law provided that no Negro born after that date should be held in bondage after he became twenty-eight years old, and up to that time he was to be treated as an indentured servant or apprentice."[3] At the time of the first national census in 1790, freedmen outnumbered Negro slaves in Philadelphia by almost eight to one.[4]

Freedom, however, did not bring political power to most Blacks. W. E. B. Du Bois describes conditions during this period as follows:

> The first result was widespread poverty and idleness. This was followed, as the number of freedmen increased, by a rush to the city. Between 1790 and 1800 the Negro population of Philadelphia County increased from 2,489 to 6,880, or 176 percent, against an increase of 43 percent among whites. The first result of this contact with city life was to stimulate the talented and aspiring freedman; and this was the easier because the freedman had in Philadelphia at that time a secure economic foothold; he performed all kinds of domestic service, all common labor and much of the skilled labor. The group being thus secure in its daily bread needed only leadership to make some advance in general culture and social effectiveness. . . . Especially, however, to be noted are Richard Allen, a former slave of the Chew family, and Absalom Jones, a Delaware Negro. These two were real leaders and actually succeeded to a remarkable degree in organizing the freedman for action.[5]

Another of these early Black leaders in Philadelphia was James Forten. Born of freedman parents in 1766, Forten served first as apprentice and then as foreman at Robert Bridges' Sail Works on the south wharves of the city. When Bridges died in 1798, Forten took control of the entire establishment. Wealth and civic leadership soon followed. During the War of 1812 Forten mobilized Negro volunteers for the defense of the city. In 1813, 1817, 1830, 1832, and 1836 he organized Philadelphia Blacks for political action at the state and national level. Throughout this period Forten was active in the Abolition Movement.[6] Although individuals such as Allen, Forten, and Jones did wield considerable power both within and without the Black community, freedman in general were impotent in city politics. The reason was simple: they seldom voted.[7]

By 1830 only thirteen of Philadelphia's 14,460 Negroes were still slaves.[8] Yet, the living conditions of most of the city's Blacks were poor. Socially, Philadelphia had become a southern city, and life would become even worse after the anti-Negro riots of 1834. For five successive years, Philadelphia Blacks suffered severely at the hands of racist white mobs. Although runaway slaves still flocked to the city, many native freedmen fled for their lives. Again in 1842-1843 and, finally, in 1849 mob violence was directed against the Negro. As a consequence of this persecution and the economic depression which hit the city during this decade, Philadelphia's Black population declined slightly from 1840 to 1850. However, after mid-century, conditions improved. The rise of the abolitionist movement, a revived economy, and the civic spirit engendered by the outbreak of the Civil War all worked to make the 1850's and 1860's a time of relative prosperity and political influence for Philadelphia Blacks.[9] W. E. B. Du Bois sees the Negro spirit at the end of the Civil War as optimistic—unfortunately, too optimistic:

> After the war and emancipation great hopes were entertained by the Negroes for rapid advancement, and nowhere did they seem better founded than in Philadelphia. The generation then in its prime had lived down a most intense and bitter race feud and had gained the respect of the better class of whites. They started with renewed zeal, therefore, to hasten their social development.[10]

The 1870's opened with events of tremendous symbolic importance for the Philadelphia Negro: the murder of a local Black leader and the rapid creation and collapse of the Freedman's Bank. After the war Philadelphia Negroes, following the direction of a national Black leader such as Frederick Douglass, moved in large numbers into the Republican Party. The rapid increase in GOP support within the city threatened to overthrow the long-established Democratic machine and to destroy the new-found political power of the European immigrants. In the spring of 1871 election disorders were so common and police protection so poor that U. S. Marines had to be called in to preserve order. The next fall's election produced even more violence, culminating in the murder of

9

Octavius V. Catto, a young Negro teacher of considerable city-wide reputation, by a gang of Irish thugs. The city was openly shocked, and Catto's funeral ". . . was perhaps the most imposing ever given to an American Negro . . ." up to that time.[11] (See Chapter 1.) The loyalty that Blacks displayed toward the Republican Party played no small part in the rise to power and continued successes of the new Quay political organization in the city. Though never a large percentage of the city's electorate, Negro voters regularly supported the party of emancipation, often without receiving the political rewards expected by other voting blocs in machine politics.[12]

Even so, the legal barriers that prevented the Blacks' advance to full citizenship in Philadelphia were gradually discarded. In their place stood the informal, though no less effective, forces of race prejudice—again primarily, but not exclusively, concentrated among white ethnics. One example of these informal and often uncontrollable factors is the story of the rise and demise of the Freedman's Bank. Begun in 1865 under the sponsorship of the national government, the bank's services were confined to members of the Negro race. A branch soon opened in Philadelphia. Due in part to the inexperience of some of its employees and to the financial manipulations of men like Jay Cooke, the bank closed in June of 1874.[13] As John Hope Franklin notes:

> Thousands of Negro depositors suffered losses they could ill afford. Negro leaders, some of whom were blameless, were castigated by their fellows, while the Cookes and others who benefited most escaped with out public censure.[14]

To the average American, both white and Black, this important first venture in Black capitalism was a dismal failure and provided those advocating Negro inferiority with a useful example for their polemics.[15] It would be a small step from racial inferiority in the 1880's and 1890's to race prejudice in the twentieth century.

The Philadelphia which W. E. B. Du Bois studied in the 1890's contained 40,000 Negroes—about 3.8 percent of the city's total population.[16] The largest portion of these were crowded into the Center City area between the Delaware and Schuylkill Rivers. Despite efforts at political reform the Quay machine still controlled the city and would continue to do so until 1904. Du Bois concentrated his investigation on the Seventh Ward, a small slice of Center City running from Seventh Street on the east, to the Schuylkill on the west, and from Spruce Street on the north to South Street. More Blacks lived there (8,861) than anywhere else in the city; still they made up less than 30 percent of the local population. Of these 12 percent were classified as totally illiterate, and virtually all were employed in common laboring or servant jobs.[17]

The politics of the Seventh Ward during the 1890's was not atypical of city politics generally during this period.[18] Black precinct workers, kept loyal through city patronage jobs, used white money to buy Black votes for the Republicans. Besides the more crass forms of bribery, a common device of machine control was the political club. Du Bois describes the activities of these organizations as follows:

> A political club is a band of eight or twelve men who rent a club house with money furnished them by the boss, and support themselves partially in the same way. The club is often named after some politician—one of the most notorious gambling hells of the Seventh Ward is named after a United States Senator—and the business of the club is to see that its precinct is carried for the proper candidate, to get "jobs" for some of its "boys," to keep others from arrest and to secure bail and discharge for those arrested. Such clubs become the center of gambling, drunkeness, prostitution and crime. . . .
>   The leader of each club is boss of his district; he knows the people, knows the ward boss, knows the police; so long as the loafers and gamblers under him do not arouse the public too much he sees that they are not molested.[19]

Anyone familiar with city politics during the last decades of the nineteenth century will find here a description of the urban machine common to numerous ethnic populations at that time. Du Bois also knew that the Philadelphia Negro differed little in his politics from other minority peoples; yet he was disappointed that his own people did no better.[20] Du Bois' general findings concerning the status of the Black man in Philadelphia politics at the turn of this century are summarized in his article "The Black Vote of Philadelphia."[21] (See Chapter 2.)

Though the politics of the nation became significantly more progressive after 1900, Philadelphia remained much as before. When Matthew Quay died in 1904, Republican leadership passed to George Vare and his brothers, Edwin and William, and to Boise Penrose. Penrose led the dominant faction in the city Republican organization; the Vares often led the intraparty opposition.[22] Negro voters continued to support the machine, and their socioeconomic condition remained virtually as it was in the 1890's. John T. Emlen summarizes the situation in his article "The Movement for the Betterment of the Negro in Philadelphia," published in 1913.[23] (See Chapter 3.) Black politicians in the second and third decades of this century preserved many of the patterns noted by Du Bois several years earlier. The way to get ahead in the Republican machine was to produce the votes on election day. One of those who found success in this manner was Tom Gibson. Gibson's control over his territory was so strong that even in 1933 after virtually all of the city of Philadelphia had repudiated the Republicans, the parts of the city under his personal leadership still went to the GOP by heavy margins.[24]

The social conditions of Philadelphia Blacks during the 1920's and 1930's became even worse than before. Although the city did not suffer a major race riot in 1919, when many other cities were seriously hit, minor outbreaks did occur. Historian Sam Bass Warner argues that increased residential segregation may have served to dampen racial tensions during these years. With both Blacks and white ethnics bound more tightly to clearly defined areas in the city, the opportunity for accidental clashes between people "looking for a fight" decreased. Yet, as Warner points out, these segregated residential patterns were direct causes of the "Philadelphia Negro crisis today."[25] One of the most important factors leading to this increased residential segregation and, ultimately, to the creation of our present Black ghettos was the tremendous migration of Blacks out of the South and into northern cities during the First World War. Before that time the movement had been slow, but steady, with the greatest concentrations of Negroes developing in such border cities as Baltimore and St. Louis. After 1916 the northward flow of southern Blacks radically increased in volume and changed markedly in character. Allen Spear describes these differences:

> The largest influx of Negroes between 1916 and 1919 occurred in the key northern industrial states—Pennsylvania, Illinois, Ohio, New

York, and Michigan, in that order—while the southern black belt states—Mississippi, Georgia, South Carolina, Alabama, and Louisiana —experienced the greatest Negro emancipation. Although Negroes continued to move from the Lower South to the Upper South and from the Upper South to the North, a large portion of the World War I migrants went directly from the Gulf and South Atlantic states to the North. Generally, they followed the meridians of longitude: Negroes from the Carolinas and Georgia moved to New York and Pennsylvania; Negroes from Alabama, Mississippi, and Louisiana followed the Illinois Central and Gulf, Mobile, and Ohio railroads to Chicago, Detroit and Cleveland.[26]

As a consequence, the Negro population in Philadelphia increased 59 percent from 1910 to 1920. By 1930, 222,504 Blacks lived in the city, more than twice as many as any single foreign-born ethnic group. Still, they constituted only 11 percent of the city's total population.[27] In the decade of the Great Depression the number of Negro people in Philadelphia expanded by less than 15 percent, the smallest ten-year increase in the twentieth century.[28] It is little wonder; economic hard-times always seemed to hit the city's Negroes the hardest.

During the 1930's Philadelphia celebrated its 300th birthday. The city had grown in those three centuries from wilderness to established metropolis. Those same years had seen the Philadelphia Negro progress very gradually from indentured servant to ghetto freedman. The next thirty years would produce Philadelphia's new-style Black politics.

NOTES

1. John Hope Franklin, *From Slavery to Freedom* (New York: Alfred A. Knopf, 3rd ed., 1967), pp. 96-98. Franklin suggests that twentieth century estimates would put the figure closer to 3,000. The total Philadelphia population in 1750 must have been somewhere between 15,000 and 20,000. Carl Bridenbaugh, *Cities in Revolt* (New York: Capricorn Books, 1964), p. 5.

2. Franklin, *From Slavery . . .* , pp. 98 and 126-27. See also W. E. B. Du Bois, *The Philadelphia Negro* (Philadelphia: U. of Penn., 1899), pp. 15-17.

3. Franklin, *From Slavery . . .* , p. 140.

4. *Ibid.,* p. 146. Du Bois, *Philadelphia Negro,* pp. 17-24, implies that one of the reasons that the Negro population dropped in the city from 1750 to 1790 might have been the sale of slaves out-of-state after the passage of the 1780 emancipation law.

5. Du Bois, *Philadelphia Negro,* pp. 17-18.

6. Ray Allen Billington, "James Forten: Forgotten Abolitionist," *Negro History Bulletin* 13 (November, 1949). Reprinted in August Meier and Elliott Rudwick, *The Making of Black America* (New York: Atheneum, 2 vols., 1969), vol. 1, 289-301.

7. Sam Bass Warner, Jr., *The Private City* (Philadelphia: University of Pennsylvania, 1968), p. 87.

8. *Ibid.,* p. 127. Total population for Philadelphia County at this time was 161,271.

9. *Ibid.,* pp. 125-57, and Du Bois, *Philadelphia Negro,* pp. 25-39.

10. Du Bois, *Philadelphia Negro,* p. 39.

11. *Ibid.,* pp. 39-45. See also Leslie H. Fishel, Jr., "The Negro in Northern Politics," *Mississippi Valley Historical Review* 42 (December, 1955). Reprinted in Meier and Rudwick, *Black America,* vol. 2, 56-74.

12. Du Bois, *Philadelphia Negro,* pp. 372-73. For a general description of Pennsylvania and Philadelphia politics during this era see Sylvester K. Stevens, *Pennsylvania* (New York: Random House, 1964), pp. 253-69, and on the relative power of Black leaders in Philadelphia and other northern cities see Allen H. Spear, *Black Chicago* (Chicago: University of Chicago, 1967), p. 191.

13. Franklin, *From Slavery . . . ,* pp. 314-15.

14. *Ibid.,* p. 315.

15. On the doctrine of Negro inferiority and its prevalence after the Civil War see Charles H. Wesley, *The Quest for Equality* (Washington: United Publishing Corp., 1968), pp. 67-73. On race prejudice also see Du Bois, *Philadelphia Negro,* ch. XVI.

16. Du Bois, *Philadelphia Negro,* pp. 50 and 53.

17. *Ibid.,* pp. 58, 59, 91, and 100-108.

18. For other examples of Negroes and machine politics see Gilbert Osofsky, *Harlem: The Making of a Ghetto* (New York: Harper Torchbooks, 1968), ch. XI, and Spear, *Black Chicago,* chs. VI and X.

19. Du Bois, *Philadelphia Negro,* pp. 378-79.

20. *Ibid.,* p. 375.

21. W. E. B. Du Bois, "The Black Vote of Philadelphia," *Charities* 15 (October 7, 1905), pp. 31-35.

22. Stevens, *Pennsylvania,* pp. 270-82.

23. John T. Emlen, "The Movement for the Betterment of the Negro in Philadelphia," *Annals* 49 (September, 1913), pp. 81-92.

24. J. T. Salter, "Tom Gibson vs. Public Opinion," *National Municipal Review* 24 (July, 1935), pp. 385-90

25. Warner, *Private City,* pp. 168-75, and Arthur I. Waskow, *From Race Riot to Sit-In* (Garden City, N. Y.: Doubleday Anchor, 1967), pp. 12 and 305.

26. Spear, *Black Chicago,* pp. 138-40.

27. Warner, *Private City,* pp. 161 and 182.

28. E. Digby Baltzell, "Introduction to the 1967 Edition" in Du Bois, *Philadelphia Negro,* p. xxix.

1

URBAN BLACKS AND IRISHMEN: BROTHERS IN PREJUDICE

DENNIS CLARK

Dennis Clark, executive assistant to the director of the Samuel S. Fels Fund, Philadelphia, offers an analysis of Black versus Irish antagonism in Philadelphia. Clark emphasizes the influence of the urban environment in exacerbating the hostility between the two groups. Dr. Clark's essay was written expressly for this volume.

Of all the ethnic antagonisms that have arisen in the turbulence of American social development, few have such a distinctively rancorous history as that between Black man and Irishman. Only the white vs. Indian and English vs. French antagonisms have a longer span of intergroup hostility. Indeed, the enmity between Blacks and Irishmen has become sufficiently proverbial in historical reference that its patent acceptance has served to discourage analysis.[1]

It is important to examine somewhat more closely this long-standing minority conflict, for unlike the other ethnic duels that have plagued this country, it has distinctive features. It has largely been an internal conflict lodged in the centers of national life, not an external one located on the periphery or frontier. It has for most of its course involved two ethnic minorities, not a dominant majority group and an ethnic subgroup. Much of the interpretive literature on our sorry racial history deals with the latter kind of adversary relationship. The Irish-Black conflict has also been an almost exclusively urban phenomenon. In a period when we are devoting increasing attention to our urban situation, past and present, this persistent tradition of group strife should be of special interest to us. As an intraurban contention, much of the hostility has political implications in a time of rising Black political aspirations. The Irish have been an avidly political group, and the rise of Black power now impinges with climactic force upon a system of political organization that the Irish had a big part in constructing.[2]

Any attempt to gain insight into a problem with such a lengthy history demands some limitation of the topic. This article will deal with Black-Irish conflict in only one city, Philadelphia. Such a restriction of the topic is resorted to in the hope that it may prompt broader inquiries merited by the scope of the subject.

To understand the social realities underlying and contributing to the legacy of Black-Irish antagonism, one must first identify the similarities and differences between the two groups. Both have long traditions of minority status in Philadelphia. Free Blacks were present in the city before the American Revolution, and Irishmen were a part of the colonial population as laborers, indentured servants and refugee political exiles.[3] Both groups spoke English, a fact that did not help them to surmount ethnic barriers as might have been expected. Both Blacks and Irishmen came to Philadelphia from distinctively rural backgrounds, for the slave-holding South and rack-rented Ireland were each dominated by agriculture. Blacks and Irishmen entered the industrial city largely as unskilled labor, and this fact had important consequences for their social development. Both had a deep tradition of having been exploited by hereditary overlords, and the psychological results of this similarity have added to their respective histories of alienation and minority consciousness. Both were stigmatized as violence-prone by nature. Indeed, both were viewed as separate races, for in the nineteenth century the Irish were viewed as "Celts," and so considered themselves. However, the attribution was not so damaging in America as that of being Black.[4]

The histories of the two groups diverge in a number of significant respects. The Irish were pioneers in mass ghetto living and could be said to have founded the ghetto as a Philadelphia urban residential institution under the pressure of Nativist discrimination. After a period of initial social disorganization due to emigration in the 1840's, the Irish stabilized family life in conformity with the authority-centered pattern set forth in Roman Catholic teachings. The Irish had as a resource, and used with prodigious energy, the elaborate juridical and institutional structure of the Catholic church. Teachers, leadership, funds and designs for self-improvement were obtained through this medium. Finally, this group handily attached itself to government and utilized public jobs, programs and processes for its advancement.[5]

In contrast, Blacks, traditionally segregated, came to full fledged ghetto status in great number after the Irish influx. The Irish ghettos formed before the Civil War, while the Black population did not begin to increase heavily until after the Civil War. Black family life, evolving within the rural culture of the South after the depredations of slavery, was disrupted again in the migrations to the Northern cities. Its adaptations to urban conditions were not strongly shaped by any highly codified and supervised system of religious teaching. A looser structure with more matriarchal influence developed. Black churches, though pervasive in Negro life, were not coordinated and were more democratic than the Catholic structure. With respect to government, the record of repression by public authorities in the South and the disfranchisement and intimidation of Blacks in the North even after the Civil War prevented the use of government for Negro advancement until well into the twentieth century. This was 100 years after the Irish infiltrations into the political processes had produced swift naturalization, patronage and public contracts. In addition, the factor of skin color was ineradicable and worked to reinforce minority status despite any gains in social or economic mobility for Blacks.[6]

Within the framework of the economic and social growth of the city, the histories of the two minorities represent courses of development that are different chronologically and demographically, but which involve engagement with many of the same problems of urban life. The Irish Catholics began to increase substantially in the city's population in the 1830's. The great wave of Irish immigration in the 1840's constituted a profound shock to the Philadelphia social order, since it was the largest single concentrated influx of strangers the city had known since its foundation. By 1850 there were 72,000 Irish-born residents in Philadelphia County. In 1860 this group had increased to 95,000. Four major areas on the outer edges of the city were heavily Irish: Southwark-Moyamensing and Grays Ferry-Schuylkill in South Philadelphia; lower

17

Kensington and Port Richmond in North Philadelphia. The entry of Irish immigrants continued throughout the nineteenth century, and the Irish remained the largest foreign-born group in the city between 1860 and 1910, composing about 15 percent of the total population. After World War I the group began to decline until by 1960 Irish-born Philadelphians numbered only 58,000 in a population of over two million. Throughout this long cycle of minority status, the Irish experienced notable shifts in residential and occupational life. Their original mid-nineteenth century areas of concentration persisted until the 1890's. Steady accessions of new Irish immigrants replaced those dispersing to newer residential areas with the momentum of the social mobility of the expanding city. The original Irish areas also received influxes of Jews, Italians and Eastern Europeans during the "New Immigration" after 1880. The Irish dispersion was broad, extended over the second half of the nineteenth century, and included penetration of upper- and middle-class areas. The erosion of the old Irish areas continued in the twentieth century until the group lost any real residential focus in the city.[7]

Blacks in Philadelphia numbered only a few thousand at the beginning of the nineteenth century, but by 1840 there were over 20,000 in the county. This total remained fairly stable until after the Civil War, when it began to rise with migration from the South. By 1890 there were 40,000 Philadelphia Negroes. In the succeeding decades there was a dramatic increase from 84,000 in 1910 to 134,000 in 1920. The massive increases of the Negro population during and after World War II led to the present vast concentration that all but dominates the inner city in a configuration surrounding the central business district. From a tiny ghetto at the eastern edge of South Philadelphia in the early nineteenth century, Blacks moved west behind Cedar (now South) Street, forming the axis for the later enlarged black area across the southern edge of the downtown district. From a nucleus around Tenth Street and Columbia Avenue in North Philadelphia, Blacks moved west along Columbia Avenue and then obliquely northwest along Ridge Avenue, thus extending a residential angle that served as the arms to embrace a large area of that section of the city. In the 1890's middle-class Blacks moved to West Philadelphia, north of Market Street, in a concentration forecasting a

18

greater Black residential shift in this direction after the 1940's.[8]

With respect to the growth of the city, the development of the two minorities offers some fundamental contrasts. The Irish increased their numbers swiftly and heavily between 1830 and 1860 when the industrial character of Philadelphia was being formed. They were thus able to become part of the railroad, metals, and textile industries that were central to the urban economy. This fact, plus Irish small-business activity in an age of expanding free enterprise, permitted large numbers to participate in the outward residential expansion of the city and to achieve a flexible social position within it. Blacks increased less rapidly in relation to Philadelphia's total population. They confronted a post-Civil War economy that was moving beyond the take-off stage to a more rigid composition. When great tides of Black workers entered the city during the periods of the two world wars, the need for unskilled labor, though strong in wartime, was not nearly so consistent as during the early period of industrialization. To the difference of economic mobility was added the difference of color with all the superstitions attached to it. These two factors restricted Black penetration of the broader urban fabric, resulting in an intensive segregation more thorough and more enduring than that which the white immigrants experienced.[9]

Sam Bass Warner in one of the few historical articles that attempts to provide more than a chronological framework for the city's past gives a convenient typology for viewing Philadelphia development. Three major periods may be discerned: a preindustrial period that yielded to industry as the nineteenth century unfolded; a period of rapid industrialization after 1830, consolidating in the Victorian era; and a time of extension and dispersion of economic and residential life leading to the current pattern. It is helpful to consider the interaction of Blacks and Irishmen against this three-phase background.[10]

In the preindustrial city Negroes were a minority that, like German-speaking Philadelphians and the Irish, lived in a position of clustered subordination in the British-dominated city. The situation was not one of continuous tension. The American Revolution and then the French Revolution disseminated ideas of liberal civil practices that functioned within a class system and a Whiggish economic hegemony. The scattered residential make-up of the city somewhat insulated one group from the other. Free Blacks developed a number of skilled pursuits and businesses, but their numbers were limited and poor Negroes made up the majority of those populating the alley dwellings near South Street. The strong personality of Richard Allen created the Bethel African Methodist Episcopal Church at Sixth and Lombard Streets, and later the Zoar African Methodist Episcopal Church at Fourth and Brown Streets. The location of these churches is significant, for it indicates an early propinquity of Blacks and Irishmen. The Irish immigrants were concentrated near both of these locations in the early nineteenth century.[11]

The Irish of the eighteenth and early nineteenth centuries were composed of two groups, the poor, including the indentured, and an articulate cadre of liberal leaders, many of whom were political exiles. The poor lived on the margin of the city's life, socially and economically. The leadership group took a vigorous and at times flamboyant part in local affairs. Regarded with hostility or skepticism by the dominant families of British lineage, the Irish nevertheless thrust themselves into prominence and controversy. In addition to leaders of the revolutionary period, such as Thomas Fitzsimons, Stephan Moylan, John Barry, and George Meade, the early nineteenth century had such gifted men as Mathew Carey, the political economist, and the literateur Robert Walsh. These men were Catholic, but the city also contained a host of fiery and democratic Irish Protestants. Such a group established the Irish as a distinctively active public influence in the city in a way that was not paralleled for the Black population. Some of the Irish leadership were part of the pioneer abolitionist opinion in the city. Robert Walsh was a strong advocate of such sentiment, and such abolitionist agitators as Thomas Brannagan became well known antislavery controversialists. Irish attachment to the ideals of the French Revolution disposed educated figures toward an antislavery view.[12]

Within the loose fabric of the preindustrial city, Blacks and Irish shared a disadvantaged position, but they could coexist with one another without consistent friction. In addition, the libertarian political stance of prominent Irishmen permitted a sympathetic view of Black aspirations of freedom. This period of estranged coexistence, relative tolerance, and mutual subordination, broken only occasionally by hoodlum elements, did not produce any definite pattern of relationships between Blacks and Irishmen. Both were largely excluded from political life, and both were accorded only grudging tolerance by the dominant elements of the city.

The period of rapid industrialization that began in the Jacksonian years produced severe strains within Philadelphia. Dislocation of traditional institutions, increased economic competition, depression and massive immigration taxed the capacity of the city to maintain order and stability.[13] While the Black population grew, it did not grow rapidly enough to make a dramatic impact upon the social geography of the city in the way that the incoming tide of Irishmen did. The Irish influx of the 1840's caused a broad challenge to Anglo-Saxon domination of the city. The Irish slum areas proliferating along the southern and northern edges of the city seemed to threaten to surround it. The tumultuous Irish identification with the Democratic party identified them with proslavery opinion. The Irish immigrants, jammed into overcrowded housing, laboring under a memory of oppression in Ireland, and confronted by Nativist hostility in the city, were appropriate tinder for intergroup conflagration. The anti-Catholic riots of 1844 only heightened their restiveness. Jostling with Blacks who competed for slum space and menial jobs prompted an antagonism toward Blacks among the Irish that was stimulated by their own insecurity.

In the turbulence of the industrializing city, clashes between gangs of unemployed or competing workmen were not unusual. There were Black vs. Irish race riots in 1832 and again in 1842 in Southwark and Schuylkill, and in 1849 near Sixth and Lombard Streets.[15] Later, political rivalry set Irish Democrats against abolitionist Republicans.[16] An urban folk tradition of Black-Irish antagonism grew up, marked by street fighting and countless bloody encounters in the dim half-world of the slums.

There were some Irishmen who still adhered to the libertarian principle. John B. Colohan, a lawyer married to a Quaker, was an officer of the Irish Repeal Association's auxiliary in Philadelphia. This group was dedicated to aiding Daniel O'Connell's campaign to separate Ireland from British parliamentary control. The organization in Philadelphia was torn apart in 1843 by a bitter dispute over remarks O'Connell made expressing his opposition to slavery. O'Connell's espousal of universal liberty was rejected by the majority of his followers, but John B. Colohan and a few others stood firm.[17]

The furious debates of the Civil War period found the city deeply split over the issues that the conflict symbolized. Negroes won sympathy from some, aid via the "Underground Railway" from a few, and finally wartime support from the overwhelming majority when an antislavery attitude became synonymous with the defense of the Union. The Irish, largely anti-Negro, still volunteered to fight for the Union in great numbers under St. Clair Mulholland, James O'Reilly and Thomas Francis Meagher.[18] Their wartime response helped to dispel the suspicions about their loyalty to the country that Nativist prejudices had propagated. Daniel Dougherty, a lawyer and orator, was a founding member of the Union League and a favorite speaker on the Union cause.[19] The Irish Democrats, however, fell into a permanent limbo because of the identification of their party with the South. They did not recover for generations. The Republican party became so powerful in the city and state that its sovereignty went unchallenged for decades. Blacks had lost the franchise in the state as a result of court decisions in 1838. In the wake of the Civil War, as their numbers grew due to in-migration from the South, they regained it. This sparked murderous election brawls in the 1870's as the Irish sought to keep Blacks from voting in areas they controlled. As W. E. B. Du Bois wrote, "As the Irishman had been the tool of the Democrats, the Negro became the tool of the Republicans."[20]

The Irish-Black vendetta that grew between 1830 and 1870 practically amounted to an accepted communal pathology. Like so much of the mid-nineteenth century experience of the Irish, it was strongly determinant. Unable themselves to gain control of the city politically, they treated with resentment the attempts of others to gain power. Though politically hamstrung, they were able to make social and economic advances.[21] One of the chief media for their educational and social rise was the Roman Catholic network of schools and self-help organizations that the Irish built with impressive energy and then dominated.[22] The Catholic church, by definition an interethnic and transcultural entity in the scope of its mission, sponsored various activities in behalf of Negroes. St. Peter Claver Church was built in 1891 at Twelfth and Lom-

22

bard Streets. The heiress Katherine Drexel, daughter of one of the city's wealthiest families, founded an order of nuns to work with Negroes and Indians, and devoted her life and fortune to institutions she set up, several of which served Philadelphia. Additional bequests from Irishmen like Patrick Quinn and the conduct of missionary work by Irish priests and nuns did not alter the deep cleavage between the Irish and Blacks. Protestant Negroes caught in a static web of urban privation and discrimination were rarely compatible with Irish Catholics, more mobile, more accepted, but themselves still alienated from many channels of social life by the memory and persistence of religious and ethnic barriers. As the city entered its mature period of industrialized metropolitan status, Black segregation increased as Irish concentration diminished.

In 1880 Philadelphia Negroes briefly deserted the Republicans in a hotly contested mayoralty campaign. William Still, Robert Purvis and James Forten led the Black revolt, tempted by police jobs held out to them by Democrats. As the nineteenth century closed, Blacks had built a political redoubt in the Seventh Ward between Spruce and South Streets in South Philadelphia. From this ward came the first Black Common Council members, and Harry Bass won a seat in the Pennsylvania Assembly from the ward. The center of Black political activity was the Citizens Republican Club founded by Andrew Stevens, a caterer, in 1895. Such men as Dr. N. P. Mossell launched much of their early civil rights work from it. Eventually the Negro politicians moved their influence into the Thirtieth Ward between South and Christian Streets west of Broad Street. With the aid of a newspaper, *The Philadelphia Tribune,* founded in 1887, the Black community finally began to navigate politically in the 1890's.[24]

The Irish, split between those who remained doggedly loyal to the hapless and outnumbered Democrats and those who sought their fortunes in the Republican party, contested Black inroads into their traditional South Philadelphia territory. Democratic ward bosses resisted every inch of encroachment. The most notable Irish leader to emerge in Republican circles was James P. "Sunny Jim" McNichol, a contractor-politico who headed the Republican City Committee and wielded enormous power in the early twentieth century. In a more liberal city, McNichol would probably have gone on to become mayor, but in a

Republican city in an imperiously Republican state, he rose only to the state Senate.[25]

The friction in the South Philadelphia area continued for decades. At the time of World War I the increase in the Black population in the area's Thirtieth and Thirty-Sixth Wards caused acute tension. In 1917 the use of Blacks as "scab" labor during strikes caused racial brawls. Competition for housing, entry of Blacks into "white" occupational categories, and neighborhood resentments set the stage for violence. In the summer of 1918 a mob rioted outside a house newly occupied by a Negro woman on Ellsworth Street. Disorder spread. The *Philadelphia Tribune* alleged that Irish police and rioters worked together against Negroes. The other Philadelphia papers displayed littler tolerance of Negro complaints in the aftermath of the rioting. The political fortunes of numerous ward bosses and party chieftains were deeply threatened by the growth of the Black population from 84,000 in 1910 to over 134,000 in 1920.[26]

As the Black population swelled in the twentieth century, it covered ever greater areas in the inner city in South, North and West Philadelphia. The Irish, continuing the residential dispersion they had begun so early, gradually evacuated the older areas. Paradoxically, however, their political prominence increased as they lost any definable residential base for themselves as a group. They achieved in Philadelphia, as they had elsewhere, a special identification with political roles, assuming a generalized political function as intermediaries, monitors, and strategists. Upon the basis of political experience begun in representation of their own ghetto interests, they built a broader framework of urban political aptitude based upon interethnic alliances and professionalized political leadership. On this basis, long after they had lost demographic concentration, the Irish broke through in the twentieth century to achieve their political aspirations of the nineteenth century in Philadelphia.[27]

The city's Blacks under J. C. Asbury were vassals of the powerful machine of William S. Vare until 1928. The Democrats made little or no effort to capture their allegiance for decades. The memory that it was the Republicans who had restored the franchise to Negroes and the facts that Democrats ruled the racist South and were ineffectual in Philadelphia bound Blacks to the G.O.P. But in 1928 the Black vote became

24

fluid, with Al Smith getting more Black votes than any previous Democrat in the city. In 1932 the Democrats were rallied at last by the handsome and popular John B. Kelly, who lost by a narrow margin. In 1932 the Democrats got 30 percent of the Black vote, while getting 42 percent of the city-wide vote. The next year the Democrats went out to register Black voters in earnest. Thus, the shift of the Negro vote, once begun, increased.[28] Still, in 1937 2,500 Negroes were reportedly employed in city and county government jobs under the Republicans, a powerful patronage hold that retarded Democratic progress.[29]

The break in the Republican hold on the city did not really come until 1951, when Joseph S. Clark and Richardson Dilworth, two socialite reformers, led a Democratic surge into City Hall, the first Democratic municipal administration in the city in sixty-seven years. Behind it was a keenly managed ward-level effort tended by James Finnegan and Congressman William J. Green, two unabashedly professional Irish politicians. Blacks, who then represented over one fourth of the city's population, shared in the victory after returning solid Democratic majorities in their wards.[30] As something of an anticlimax, the first Irish Catholic was elected mayor in 1962, when James H. J. Tate took office as a Democrat. Under the reform administration and the Tate regime, Blacks moved into numerous high city posts, becoming deputy mayor, department heads and heads of antipoverty and urban improvement programs. Irishmen and Blacks collaborated in city government and politics after generations of estrangement.

The racial crisis of the 1960's, however, fiercely tested the new alliance. Blacks were attempting to penetrate beyond their ghetto areas, and intermittent neighborhood disorders accompanied housing changes. Black rioting and militancy in the ghetto produced bitter confrontations with the police, a portion of the municipal service still strongly Irish in personnel and spirit. As the reform glow faded from the Democratic machine, racial polarization increased.[31] Many white neighborhoods where the Irish had lived changed their population in a few years and became totally black. Portraits of John and Robert Kennedy might appear beside that of Martin Luther King in ghetto windows, but the sneering racism of hard-hat Irish blue-collar workers left little room for interethnic sentimentality in the age of the Black Panthers.

25

A "new breed" of younger Irish Democrats arose, including Congressman William Green, Jr., son of the William Green who had been the architect of the Democratic machine that underlay the reform of the 1950's. These men, such as housing coordinator Gordon Cavanaugh and School Board member Gerald Gleeson, held fast to political careers despite the intense pressures of urban problems and Black militancy. The Republicans, headed by William Meehan and William Devlin, also showed younger Irish leadership. Although far removed from the old ward-heeler image, these men still had to contend with ever-growing demands from Blacks for patronage and control. By the end of the 1960's there were three Black City Councilmen out of seventeen, a share that did not match the fact that Blacks constituted almost one-third of the city's population. With Black mayors appearing in Cleveland, Gary and Newark, the possibility of a Black mayor for Philadelphia was widely discussed. The prospect for an Italian mayor seemed real also. An eclipse of Irish power that had been so long in the making by a Black political power that had been kept in the wilderness for an even longer period offered an anomalous situation in the distinctive ethnic history of the city.

The Irish had long maintained their vigorous anti-Negro posture despite such influences of liberal Catholicism as were exercised upon them in a notably conservative Archdiocese. The Catholic Interracial Council under Judge Gerald Flood, Robert Callahan and Mrs. Anna McGarry was unequal to the glacial prejudice that prevailed.[32] These leaders tried to ameliorate such conflicts as the race violence accompanying integration of the transit system operators during World War II, when the transit workers were a heavily Irish group. Matthew McCloskey, the powerful Democratic National Finance Chairman and Philadelphia contractor, might set up a Martin de Porres Foundation to provide Blacks with scholarships, but the curse could not be taken off the old tradition. Politics was a more expedient and successful meeting ground than religion, but the rising militancy of Blacks, decrying "the system" and repudiating the gradualism of electoral politics, threatened to undermine Black political leadership.[33]

What seems evident from this review of Black-Irish relations over an extended period is that urban conditions constituted an exacerbating background for this minority conflict. Beginning with industrialization, what Seymour Lipset has termed "working class authoritarianism" infected the Black-Irish relationship.[34] The insecurity and resentment generated by a harsh industrial system played upon both minority groups, with Blacks suffering most. Their raucous and intolerant prejudice undercut counsels of civic, religious and political prudence for generations. It was the primary force in a long ethnic duel. Second, the marginal and subservient status of both Blacks and Irishmen within the broader framework of the city's politics and social structure made each group mutually uncertain and highly protective of their political vested interests in the wards and public offices.[35] Neither group could work with the other without feeling tainted. Negro Republicans saw Irish Catholics as intractable foes dating from before the Civil War, even if they could not state this view safely. The Irish saw the Blacks as rivals for political control over the bottom of the city's society, a control that could be lucrative and lead to higher things. Third, the spatial and social ecology of the city placed the groups in adjacent positions where they were bound to clash given the circumstances of their competition for housing and facilities. When two groups live along borders of rigidly segregated territory under conditions of mutual hostility, conflict is to be expected.[36] The Irish outnumbered Blacks and were strongly represented in police work after the 1880's, and this added to their propensity for aggression toward Blacks. Negroes occupied older areas as their population swelled and responded with their own cult of violence.

The aggravating influences of urban life that beset these two groups formed a troubled subculture of conflict underlying political life in Philadelphia. The assumptions of mutual respect and justice required for democratic intercourse were simply absent amid the poverty, struggle and cynicism of lower-class life in the city. When the opportunity for political interaction for positive goals did present itself in the twentieth century, the legacy of past injury was still intimidating. Black men and Irishmen had each survived the ravages of ghetto life and industrial cruelty, but each was scarred and seared in the spirit.

NOTES

1. Carl Wittke devotes a chapter to early Black-Irish conflict in *The Irish in America* (Baton Rouge, La.: Louisiana State University Press, 1952), pp. 125-134. John Higham in *Strangers in the Land* (New York: Atheneum, 1970), p. 26 notes the combative conditions of immigrant life. The persistence of traditions of competition and conflict have belied earlier assumptions of rapid assimilation and have escaped thorough analysis. See Lawrence H. Fuchs, ed., *American Ethnic Politics* (New York: Harper and Row, 1968), i.

2. The prominence of the Irish in American politics is summarized well by Bruce M. Stave, *The New Deal and the Last Hurrah* (Pittsburgh: Pittsburgh University Press, 1970), pp. 7-8. Also Fuchs, *American Ethnic Politics, p. 6.*

3. This article deals almost exclusively with Irish Catholics. Irish Protestants, the "Scotch-Irish" so active in the eighteenth century in Pennsylvania, occupied a social position that made them more rural and less exposed to conflict with Blacks, although their epic battles with Indians were terrible. See James Leyburn, *The Scotch-Irish: A Social History* (Chapel Hill, N.C.: University of North Carolina Press, 1962), i.

4. For background on Black Philadelphians see Thomas J. Woofter, *Negroes in Cities* (New York: Doubleday and Company, 1928), Carter G. Woodson, *A Century of Negro Migration* (Washington, D.C.: Association for the Study of Negro Life and History, 1918), Richard B. Sherman, ed., *The Negro and the City* (Englewood Cliffs, N.J.: Prentice-Hall, Inc., 1970), and W. E. B. Du Bois, *The Philadelphia Negro* (Philadelphia: University of Pennsylvania Press, 1899).

Background on Irish immigrants is contained in William Forbes Adams, *Ireland and the Irish Emigration to America* (New Haven: Yale University Press, 1932), Marcus Lee Hansen, *The Atlantic Migration* (Cambridge: Harvard University Press, 1940), Wittke, *Irish in America,* William A. Shannon, *The American Irish* (New York: Macmillan Co., 1963) and L. P. Curtis, *Anglo-Saxons and Celts* (New York: New York University Press, 1968).

5. Irish adaptation to Philadelphia is detailed in Dennis Clark, "The Adjustment of Irish Immigrants to Urban Life: The Philadelphia Experience" (Ph.D. diss. in history, Temple University, 1970).

6. Negro life in the city is reflected in Du Bois, *Philadelphia Negro, passim,* and George F. Simpson, *The Negro in the Philadelphia Press* (Philadelphia: University of Pennsylvania Press, 1936), and James Erroll Miller, "The Negro in Pennsylvania Politics" (Ph.D. diss. in Political Science, University of Pennsylvania, 1945), pp. 69-78.

7. Irish population figures are presented in Irwin Sears, "Growth of Population in Philadelphia: 1860-1910" (Ph.D. diss. in history, New York University, 1960), pp. 67-68, and Clark, "Adjustment of Irish Immigrants," pp. 29-30. Figures for 1960 are from the *Eighteenth Census of the United States, Census of Population,* Part 40, Pa., Table 79 (Washington, D.C.: Government Printing Office, 1963), pp. 40-437. Figures are rounded to the nearest thousand. See also Sam Bass

Dennis Clark

Warner, *The Private City: Philadelphia* (Philadelphia: University of Pennsylvania Press, 1968), Table VII, p. 55.

8. Black population figures are given in Miller, "Negro in Pennsylvania Politics," pp. 57, 77, 86, Leonard Blumberg, *Negroes in Metropolitan Philadelphia* (Philadelphia: The Urban League of Philadelphia, 1959), pp. 31-33, *Philadelphia's Non-White Populations, Report No. 1* (Philadelphia: City Commission on Human Relations, 1961), p. 3.

9. Irish job and residential mobility is described in Clark, "Adjustment of Irish Immigrants," pp. 39-45 and 75-81, and Warner, *Private City,* pp. 55-58.

10. Sam Bass Warner, "If All the World Were Philadelphia: A Scaffolding for Urban History," *American Historical Review* 74, no. 1 (October, 1968), 26-43.

11. Clark, "Adjustment of Irish Immigrants," pp. 54-58, and J. T. Scharf and Thompson Westcott, *History of Philadelphia: 1609-1884,* 3 Vols. (Philadelphia: L. H. Everts Co., 1884), vol II, p. 1397, and Works Progress Administration, *Philadelphia: A Guide to the Nation's Birthplace* (Philadelphia: William Penn Association, 1937), p. 107.

12. George O'Brien, *A Hidden Phase of American History* (New York: Dodd-Mead Co., 1920) and John Tracy Ellis, *Catholics in Colonial America* (Baltimore: Helicon Press, 1965), p. 398. For post-Revolutionary Irishmen see Edward C. Carter II, "A Wild Irishman Under Every Federalist's Bed," *Pennsylvania Magazine of History and Biography* 94, no. 3 (July, 1970), 342. Lewis Leary, "Thomas Brannagan: An American Romantic," *Pennsylvania Magazine of History and Biography* 78, no. 3 (July, 1953), 332-380. For Robert Walsh see M. H. Rice, *American Catholic Opinion and the Anti-Slavery Controversy* (New York: Columbia University Press, 1944), p. 111.

13. Warner, *Private City,* pp. 125-160. See also Michael Feldberg, "The Philadelphia Riots of 1844" (Ph.D. diss. in history, University of Rochester, 1970).

14. Warren F. Hewitt, "The Know Nothing Party in Pennsylvania," *Pennsylvania History* 2, no. 2 (April, 1935), 69-85, and Ray Allen Billington, *The Protestant Crusade: 1800-1860* (Chicago: University of Chicago Press, 1964), p. 183.

15. Elizabeth M. Geffen, "Violence in Philadelphia in the 1840's and 1850's," *Pennsylvania History* 34, no. 4 (October, 1969), 381, and Woodson, *Negro Migration,* pp. 45-48.

16. Irwin Greenberg, "Charles Ingersoll: the Aristocrat as Copperhead," *Pennsylvania Magazine of History and Biography* 93, no. 2 (April, 1969), 194.

17. Accounts of this dispute are in the *Public Ledger* (Philadelphia) for June 3, 6, 12, 15, 23, 28 and July 20, 1843.

18. John H. Campbell, *History of the Friendly Sons of St. Patrick and the Hibernian Society* (Philadelphia: Hibernian Society, 1892), pp. 273-274, 493, and Ella Lonn, *Foreigners in the Union Army and Navy* (Baton Rouge, La.: Louisiana State University Press, 1951), pp. 124-125, 253, 257.

19. *Biographical Encyclopoedia of Pennsylvania in the Nineteenth Century* (Philadelphia: Galaxy Publishing Co., 1874), p. 276.

20. Du Bois, *Philadelphia Negro,* p. 373, and pp. 38-39.

21. Dennis Clark, "Hamstrung Hibernians" in *Greater Philadelphia Magazine* (March, 1960). The resistance of Philadelphia class structure to change is explored

in Nathaniel Burt, *The Perennial Philadelphians* (Boston: Little Brown and Co., 1963) and E. Digby Baltzell, *The Protestant Establishment* (New York: Random House, 1964).

22. Thomas McAvoy, *History of the Catholic Church in the United States* (Notre Dame, Ind.: University of Notre Dame Press, 1969), pp. 226-265.

23. Daniel J. Mahony, *Historical Sketches of Catholic Churches and Institutions in Philadelphia* (Philadelphia: Daniel J. Mahony, 1895), pp. 146-147 and 211.

24. WPA, *Philadelphia: A Guide,* p. 107, and Miller, "Negro in Pennsylvania Politics," pp. 77 and 84-86.

25. Edward Morgan, *City of Firsts* (Philadelphia: City of Philadelphia, 1919), p. 291.

26. I am indebted to Irwin Greenberg of Temple University for making available to me data on this period. For newspaper accounts of the rioting see the *Inquirer,* the *Evening Bulletin* (Philadelphia) for July 29, 1918 and the *Record* (Philadelphia), July 29, 1918.

27. Edward Levine, *The Irish and Irish Politicians* (Notre Dame, Ind.: University of Notre Dame Press, 1966), pp. 188-189. See also Milton Barron, "Intermediacy: Conceptualization of Irish Status in America," *Social Forces,* 27, no. 3 (March, 1949), pp. 256-263, and Daniel P. Moynihan and Nathan Glazer, *Beyond the Melting Pot* (Cambridge, Mass.: MIT Press, 1970), pp. 250-274.

28. Miller, "Negro in Pennsylvania Politics," pp. 195-210.

29. WPA, *Philadelphia: A Guide,* p. 107.

30. James Reichley, *The Art of Reform* (New York: Fund for the Republic, 1959), *passim* and Edward C. Banfield, *Big City Politics* (New York: Random House, 1967), pp. 107-120.

31. Dennis Clark, "Post-Kennedy Irish: The American Decline," *Hibernia* (Dublin, Ireland: March, 1967). Black resentment against the Irish, especially the Irish police, became fully expressed in the 1960's. Anti-Irish sentiment erupted even in the Catholic church. See Rev. Lawrence Lucas, *Black Priest, White Church* (New York: Random House, 1970), pp. 98-99 and 240.

32. William Osborne, *Segregated Covenant* (New York: Herder and Herder, 1967), pp. 152-179.

33. As Philip Foner writes: "Blacks, unlike immigrant groups, are achieving local power at a time when the cities are bankrupt, and effective political power, not to mention tax revenues, has shifted from localities to Washington." "In Search of Black History," *New York Review of Books* 15, no. 7 (October 22, 1970), 14.

34. Seymour Lipset, *Political Man* (Garden City, New York: Doubleday and Company, 1960), pp. 109-113.

35. The tension between Black unity goals and the *quid pro quo* of politics is indicated by James Q. Wilson, *Negro Politics* (Glencoe, Ill.: Free Press, 1960), p. 169, where Black goals are seen as a continuing theme, and Sherman, *The Negro in the City,* p. 159, where expedient machine politics are seen as the tradition.

36. Alan D. Grimshaw, ed., *Racial Violence in the United States* (Chicago: Aldine Publishing Co., 1969), pp. 289-298.

2

THE BLACK VOTE OF PHILADELPHIA

W. E. BURGHARDT DU BOIS

The late W. E. Burghardt Du Bois, one of the most important sociologists of the century, first published this article in the October 7, 1905 issue of *Charities*. In this study, he analyzes the close relationship of the Blacks in Philadelphia to the city's corrupt political machine. He points out that the Negroes' poverty and lack of voting experience were two significant factors that led to their manipulation by political leaders. Du Bois concludes that no substantial municipal governmental reform will occur in Philadelphia until the city's Blacks are educated as to the nature of the political process.

The typical Philadelphia colored man is a young immigrant from the South, from twenty to forty years of age, who has come to the city to better his fortune, as he conceives fortune. His conception of government, as he comes into a great modern world city, is extremely crude. He knows practically nothing of the actual work of any typical government,—local government in the South is a Chinese puzzle to the average citizen; the Negro sees it only in its repressive and harrying functions, and he is allowed to take little or no part in it. The chances are, then, that the young immigrant to Philadelphia has no adequate idea of his duty or privilege as a citizen and has thought little about them, save perhaps in a more or less theoretical way. He comes to find work and freedom—and by freedom he means a chance for expansion, amusement, interest, something to make life larger than it has been on the lonely country plantation, or in the Negro quarter of a southern town. His contact with the new world, then, is as wage-earner and seeker after the goods of life—knowledge and amusement; with this goes the untrammelled right to vote—a right he has never before had, and which his brothers in Philadelphia have not always had.

The laws of 1682 for the new state of Pennsylvania made property holders voters and made the qualifications for freedmen less than those for others. Negro electors undoubtedly helped to adopt the constitution, as the right of suffrage after 1776 was given to "every freeman of the full age of twenty-one years, having resided in this state for the space of one whole year." When the new state constitution of 1790 was framed, it was proposed to limit the suffrage to "free white citizens"; but Albert Gallatin helped to defeat this proposition, and Negroes in the state had the legal right to vote for a half century thereafter. Still public opinion in many cases was against Negroes voting, and in Philadelphia "the colored man could not with safety appear at the polls." One Negro man named Fogg, having been denied the right to vote in Luzerne County, took the case to the courts in 1837. He won in the lower courts but the Supreme Court in a curious decision upheld the exclusion, claiming that a Negro though free could never be a "freeman." The next year the constitutional convention met. The qualifications for suffrage came up and an attempt was made to restrict voting to "free white male" citizens. The amendment was lost by a vote of 61 to 49. This aroused the Negro haters and they began the same sort of campaign of vilification and detraction that the black men of America so often have suffered. Petitions for and against Negro suffrage poured in, but only the latter were printed and published, and Bucks County, where once a Negro nearly had been elected to the legislature, outdid itself in working for exclusion. The result was a protracted fight, and a final adoption of the white suffrage plank by a vote of 77 to 45. The Negroes of Pennsylvania were thus disfranchised for thirty-two years, until the passage of the war amendments.

About 5,500 Negroes were eligible to vote in Philadelphia in 1870. In 1900 there were 20,000 Negro voters and in 1905 there are perhaps 25,000 voters.

Nothing in the Negro immigrant's earning of a living is apt to direct his attention to government unless, of course, he is employed by the city. He is usually employed as servant or laborer by private parties and sees little more of government than when he was in the South. When, after work, and on Sundays and holidays, he starts out for recreation he is apt in the denser parts of the city to run upon two and only two rival claimants for his interest: the church and the club. Parks and out-of-door sports do not attract him, for he has the country-bred indifference to raw nature and his daily work is largely physical. He is not welcome at the white Young Men's Christian Association, while the Negro branch is a sickly sort of thing constituted largely of prayer meetings and cant. All the ordinary amusements of a great city are either unknown and un-appreciated by this new-comer, or he feels by word or glance that he is not wanted. There is left, as I have said, the club and the church. Now the church he knows and knows well: it has been the center of his com-munity from the days his fathers landed in America until now. The chances are, however, that this young man has tired of the monotony of church services and their lack of adaptability to his newer needs and de-mands; in the South, he has loafed outside the door to laugh and joke and escort his girl home; and he does not take the church seriously—he is rather tired of it.

The Political Club

As he saunters up Lombard street, then, of evenings, he may drop into the church if it is Sunday, and other days he stands lonesomely about, gaping and longing for a fellow soul. But he finds soon that at one place he is welcome and that is at the club. He may be introduced to the club accidentally or by design, through the medium of the saloon or corner pool-room, or by chance companions. At any rate he finds here and there throughout the city ten or fifteen little groups of good fellows— gay young blades, roystering tellers of doubtful tales, well-dressed con-noisseurs of the town's mysteries, and they welcome the newcomer cordially and make him feel at home. No where in Philadelphia is there such a welcome for the friendless, homeless black boy, no where is so much consideration shown for his feelings, his wants, his desire for pleasure. He easily joins therefore the crowd of loafers and idlers and laborers who circle and congregate about these clubs.

What is a "club?" He finds that it is a suite of rooms more or less elaborately furnished where a crowd of men can always be found smoking and talking and drinking. Usually, too, they play cards for small stakes and sometimes gamble with various devices for sums mounting up to $25 or more. Here one may make all kinds of acquaintances from honest laborers to drunken debauchees—and the clubs grade from semi-criminal haunts to respectable well-furnished quarters. Nearly all of them, however, and particularly the lower grades, are above all "political," and they give our young immigrant his first introduction into "politics"; He comes to know gradually that these pleasant quarters where his friends meet and enjoy themselves are furnished through "politics"; that if it were not for "politics" they could not have beer to drink or play cards in peace. Moreover, there is poor John So and So arrested last week—he'll get clear by "politics." Is the new Philadelphian willing to help along the folks who are doing these kindnesses to him and his? Why, certainly. And when election day comes he receives a bit of printed paper with unknown names and deposits it in a place indicated.

It may be now that he becomes one of the constituent members of the club, being invited by the president. This president selects his own membership of tried and true men warranted to do as he says: he keeps his hold over them by furnishing them amusement if they are honest laborers, or by giving them money if they are poor laborers out of a job, or loafers, or by protecting them if they fall afoul of the police. The newcomer soon sees that he is in a network of intrigue, influence and bribery. The policeman on his beat, the magistrate, the criminal, the prostitute, the business man, all fit in their little circle in the great "machine," and this is "politics";—of certain questions as to the ownership of gas works, the payment for franchises, the reform of the civil service —of these things he has never heard; he is submerged in a sea of mud and slime called politics which the great and good and wise city of Philadelphia has prepared for him; he has never seen its shores or surface, and of its clearer, sweeter waters he has never heard.

Other Groups

Of the 25,000 Negro voters in Philadelphia from one-half to two-thirds fall into the class I have described. There are, of course, other Negro voters in the city—or rather men eligible to vote. There is, first, the native Philadelphian of Negro descent—member of an educated and well-to-do group of people. There are the better class of immigrants from the country districts of the state, Maryland, and Virginia. These men come into politics from a different angle. A large number of them, especially of the better class of immigrants, neglect to vote—the campaign of contempt for civic duties and civic privileges has been preached to them assiduously. They have seen those of their number who preached political suicide for the Negro vociferously applauded and they have come to think it a virtue to neglect the exercise of the right of suffrage. Thus the result of the foolish campaign against the Negro in politics has been simply to drive out of political life the very class of Negroes needed most, and to deliver political life and activity into the hands of the political clubs and their ignorant or debased followers.

Then, too, the Negro voter even of the better class feels no civic pride. Philadelphia is not his city; it grants him nothing in particular save what he struggles for in sweat. It shows him no kindness unless he be a criminal or pauper, and under the political organization preceding the recent upheaval, it did not need his vote or seek it. The Negro feels in Philadelphia and in America few promptings of patriotism, and he looks upon all local questions from the standpoint of his social and individual interests. His greatest hardship is difficulty of employment; his characteristic, poverty. This is due to present and past conditions, *i. e.,* prejudice and lack of skill and application. Both these handicaps can be overcome, but it takes hard work. To such a class the direct or indirect bribery of money is a tremendous temptation. Direct distribution of money to Negro voters at the polls is therefore considerable, but this does not touch the upper half or third of the voting population. This part is influenced by the indirect methods of bribery. There are in the employ of the city to-day, approximately:

1	member of the common council.
3	clerks in the city service.
10	or more messengers.
65	policemen.
30	school teachers.

These persons on the whole represent the better class of Negroes and with a few exceptions have given first-class service; but so far as the office-holders themselves are concerned these are the best jobs they could get; probably in no other way could these people get employment that would give them half their present incomes. Their jobs are "in politics," and their holders must and do support the "machine." Moreover, such civic pride as the Negro has is naturally expended on these representatives of his race in public life and they support the party that puts these men in office. Thus office holding is both a direct and indirect bribe to the Negroes and to the better class of them.

The Treatment of the Good-Government Negro

It happens, however, that the political hold of the "machine" in Philadelphia has been so great and far-reaching, their majorities so overwhelming, and the white citizens so supine in their bondage, that the "machine" cares little for the 25,000 Negro votes and has cut down their patronage lately in some respects; Negroes used to have three counsellors: now they have one, and Boss Durham before his fall said that this "would be the last one." "There are some Negroes in my division," said a ward politician, "and they've been coming to me and telling me what they want, but I tell 'em to go to hell. We don't need their votes." If on finding their support not sought or needed, perhaps the better class do not vote. This makes little difference for the ward bosses having the registration lists vote the names of all who do not appear at the polls. A colored man, headwaiter at a large hotel, went down to the polls; pretty soon he came back. "Did you vote?" he was asked. "No," he said, "I find that I had already voted—I'd like to know which way!"

Suppose now one of the better class of Negroes should determine to go into politics with a view to better conditions. Has this ever happened? Colonel McClure in his *Reminiscences* does not know of any case, but it has been pointed out to him since that he was mistaken. Men of Negro blood like Henry L. Philips, one of the most public-spirited of Philadelphia's citizens, white or black, and Walter P. Hall, a member of the present reform Committee of Seventy, have continually and repeatedly sided with reform movements. And others have, too. Yet it is true that no large mass of colored voters have followed reform movements hitherto. Nor is the reason for this far to seek. Under the machine an honest man interested in politics had no place. A young friend of mine offered his services in his ward. "See the ward Boss" was the answer. And the ward Boss—"What do you want?" he said, and he meant: "Do you want protection to run a bawdy house, or to sell liquor without a license or to get somebody out of jail? And if so, are you willing in return to falsify voting lists, round up repeaters, etc." My friend saw nothing attractive in this career and he is consequently "out of politics." When now a reform movement like that of the Municipal League has come, it has invariably made the mistake of supposing that because there are few of the better class of Negroes in politics, there is no better class worth appealing to. Moreover, if a few of the leading Negroes were appealed to what could they say to the masses: could they promise that Negroes would be retained in civil service, or on the police force, or as teachers? No, the reformers were not promising jobs. But this matter was more than the question of a simple job—it was a question of economic opportunity. It was really the same question of earning a living that is the main motive in the political action of the whites. Why are Philadelphia politics dirty? Because the most influential and respected citizens of the town are using public business for private gain. White citizens find that franchises, concessions, and favorable administration furnish them the most money. Negroes, being barred from business, largely find the actual salaries of office not only the greatest attraction, but an actual matter of bread and butter. Thus the Negroes have always been suspicious that the reform movements tended not to their betterment but to their elimination from political life and consequently from the best chance of earning a living. And the attitude of some of the reformers and their contempt for Negroes has not improved this race opinion.

It might be asked,—Could not the better element of Negroes outvote the worse element and support an independent movement? This has been tried and the machine beat it. A few years ago a clean young colored lawyer, Harry W. Bass, revolted against the machine and ran for the legislature. He made a good run in the seventh ward, receiving a large vote but not a majority. A little later he ran again and the machine was alarmed. Immediately they nominated another Negro of fairly respectable character on another independent ticket and finally nominated a white candidate on the regular ticket. The result of this three-cornered fight was that Bass received but 400 votes, the white machine candidate was elected, and the other "independent" candidate was given a political job at Harrisburg.

In the present latest upheaval the Negroes are represented on the Committee of Seventy by a business man, Walter P. Hall. In a few of the wards they have organized under the new city party of reform. In the great Negro ward, the seventh, there is one Negro member of the ward committee. While it is uncertain how far the Negro will support reform at present, yet it is certain that an influential part of the better class will co-operate and that there is a great opportunity to give 70,000 Negroes the best chance of education in politics that they have ever had.

The Reconstruction Situation Repeated

What now is the wrong and right of this situation? It is manifestly this: If you wish democratic government to be successful you must strive to inculcate into the humblest citizen a conception of its duties and its rewards. There is no democratic government in Philadelphia, and has not been for a generation. There is an oligarchy of ward politicians and business men using public office for private gain. Into this system a new mass of untrained Negro voters were cast and they followed their leaders, as was perfectly natural. As a mass they went into politics for what they could get out of it and in this respect Lombard and Walnut streets joined hands and made common cause. We have an exact repetition here of the reconstruction difficulties in the South on a smaller scale. The brother thieves of the *Credit Mobilier,* the Tweed ring, and the other northern tricksters, began the looting of the newly reconstructed southern states. They used the ignorant Negroes for their tools. The result was that the Negroes followed their leaders and stole and looted too. Yet this experience is put into history as a classic example of the unfitness of Negroes to exercise political power. Philadelphia needs to go back to the very a b c of government—to teach its citizens, white or black, the duties and rewards of good citizenship, to open its civil service on equal terms to all and to show the 25,000 Negro voters what government means.

3

THE MOVEMENT
FOR THE BETTERMENT OF
THE NEGRO IN PHILADELPHIA

John T. Emlen, Secretary and Treasurer of the Armstrong Association of Philadelphia, analyzes the socioeconomic condition of Philadelphia's Blacks in this article, which was first published in the September, 1913 issue of *The Annals of
the American Academy of Political and Social Science.* After evaluating the
public and private institutions that served the Black community, he concludes
that private groups were more sensitive to Negro needs.

Philadelphia has a Negro population according to the 1910 census of
84,459. Four other cities in the United States have larger Negro populations: Washington, 94,446; New York, including Manhattan, Bronx,
Queens, Richmond and Brooklyn, 91,709; New Orleans, 89,262; and
Baltimore, 84,749. No other cities in the United States have Negro populations at all approaching these in numbers.

At the present rate of increase, New York will probably in the next
ten years be the leading Negro city, and Philadelphia, second. This may
be seen by the fact that in the past ten years New York increased about
31,000; Philadelphia, about 22,000; Washington, about 12,000; New
Orleans, about 11,500; and Baltimore, about 5,500.

The accompanying maps indicating the distribution of the total population and of the Negro population by wards show how the Negroes
are spread over the city. Map A on page 41 shows by wards the distribution of the total population in 1910, each dot indicating a population
of 5,000 persons. The chief business section of the city centers about
Market and Chestnut Streets, and between the Delaware and Schuylkill

MAP A

Distribution by Wards of Negro Population of Philadelphia, both White and Negro, 1910

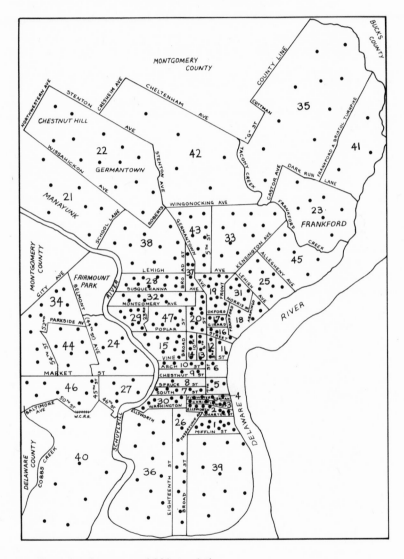

Note: One dot to every 5,000 population.

MAP B

Distribution by Wards of Negro Population
of Philadelphia, 1890

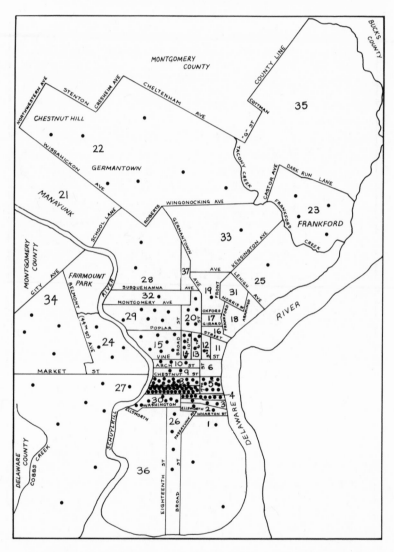

Note: One dot to every 250 Negroes. No Tabulation for Wards 35, 36, and 37.

Rivers, so that this district shows less congestion of dwellings than those immediately surrounding it on both sides. In the surrounding districts or wards, the population is the thickest, but is fairly evenly distributed, becoming, however, less concentrated in the outlying and suburban wards. Map B on page 42 shows the Negro population of Philadelphia, in 1890, each dot indicating 250 persons. Map C, on page 44 shows similarly the Negro population of 1910. In noting the map of 1890,[1] one sees the largest concentration of the Negro population in the 7th ward, and the next largest in the 4th, 5th, 8th and 30th, which are adjoining.

In 1910, the Negro population has, to some extent, shifted and spread. In the central 5th and 8th wards, it is very much smaller than in 1890, and, while the 7th is larger by about 2,700, it has not increased in proportion to the increase in some other parts of the city. The 30th ward, to the southwest of the 7th, has increased over five-fold, and further to the south, in the 26th and 36th wards, and to the west in various parts of West Philadelphia, and to the north in the 14th, 15th, 20th, 47th and 32d, and in Germantown, the increase has been very great. The Negro population, therefore, has a very large concentrated nucleus, but has increasingly spread in large numbers over two-thirds of the city.

In studying the bettering of conditions among such a population, one must inquire about the greatest needs and the practical opportunities for meeting them. There should be sufficient opportunities for religious and educational instruction, for recreation, for the amelioration and improvement of social and of economic conditions, and for the improvement of conditions of health and of housing.

Scattered through the wards to meet the religious needs of this population are about 105 churches of about 12 different denominations, mostly Baptist, or of some form of Methodist Episcopal. These churches are, apart from their function as centers of religious inspiration, centers for social entertainment and intercourse to a much larger extent than are the churches of the white people, yet very few of them are able at the present time to meet the needs of the population in some of the educational and recreational ways in which social centers should meet them. Accordingly, social centers in various sections have grown up. These with playgrounds in the city are indicated in Map D on page 45.

MAP C

*Distribution by Wards of Negro Population
of Philadelphia, 1910*

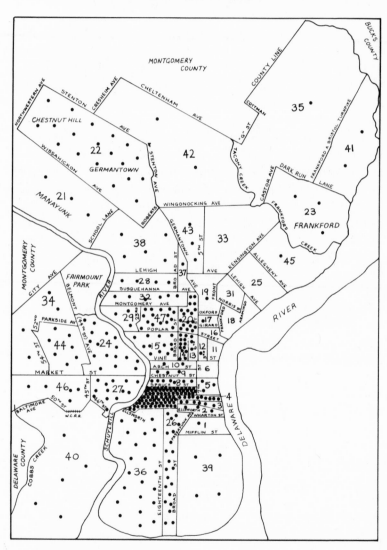

Note: One dot to every 250 Negroes.

MAP D

*Playgrounds, including Parks used as Playgrounds
and Social Centers, Available to Negroes, 1913*

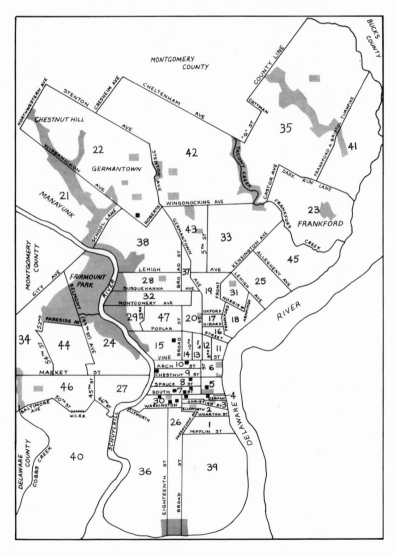

Note: ■ *Indicates a Social Center.*

Two playgrounds are available for the thickly populated center of the 7th and 30th wards—one on the extreme lower edge of the colored population and one which is well located for the 30th, and the upper part of the 7th. Unfortunately, the latter will probably soon be abolished and the ground used for other purposes, and if no other ground is secured, this will be a serious loss to the community. A ground is also especially needed in the neighborhood of the 40th and 27th wards.

A number of the social centers are at the present time doing very good work, but as a group they are in number and equipment very inadequate to meet the present needs. The things that are needed throughout the city to make the proper recreational facilities are playgrounds and the increased use of the school yards and buildings. On account of the great financial difficulties in securing sufficient money for social centers, adequate provisions can usually be made only at the schools. It will, however, be of no special value to have these unless, when they are opened, they can have the proper supervision. The use of such facilities with good sympathetic supervision is one of the greatest needs of the colored people at the present time. The Thomas Durham school building, in the 7th ward, is becoming an increasingly valuable social center of the kind needed. There are now, as may be seen on the map, a number of centers in the central section, noteworthy among which will be the Y. M. C. A., with its new $100,000 building, and the Y. W. C. A., with its new plant.

Some of the institutions and agencies for relief and for social betterment are for both white and colored and some for colored only. In some organizations purporting to work "without distinction of color" it is very difficult to get attention for a colored case. On the whole, however, in most lines a fair proportion of colored cases receive attention. Some of the activities and opportunities of such institutions and agencies may be briefly summarized. The day nurseries receiving colored children are fairly adequate for the different sections where there are large colored populations, except in the neighborhood of the 47th and 20th wards, where one is much needed. Four of them are in or near the central section where there is the largest population, one in West Philadelphia, and one in Germantown. Most of the hospitals receive colored cases in large numbers, and in two hospitals courses are given for the training of

46

colored nurses. Lying-in charities afford shelter and protection. One agency meets colored immigrants from the South at the wharves, and affords them needed protection. Dependent children are provided for through a number of institutions in many of which there is coöperation, the cases being distributed through the children's bureau. Many of these institutions have a long history and between them furnish quite as good facilities as are afforded to white children.

The report of the committee on municipal charities[2] says that ten institutions care for both white and colored, with a capacity of 2,567, and ten for colored children only, with a capacity of 567. It is sometimes necessary to send more children to these institutions than would normally be sent, because of the extreme difficulty in finding proper kinds of homes in the country near Philadelphia in which to place them. In spite of thorough and continual investigation by the Children's Aid Society, the number of such homes seems to be very small in proportion to the need. Provisions additional to those made by the municipality for the aged and infirm are furnished by one institution, with accommodations for 140, and by one small home. The state reformatories are for both white and colored. In addition to the facilities by the municipality, two private institutions for the blind, two for the deaf, and two for the feeble-minded and epileptic admit Negroes. The number of Negroes about one year ago in these institutions, according to investigation, were, respectively, 10, 21 and 31. General agencies for charity organization, children's aid, protection of children from cruelty, etc., and other agencies of outdoor relief, should be and are run under general organizations for both races.

Negroes have much more difficulty in securing good houses in good neighborhoods than members of the other races have. Various building and loan associations have helped them much to overcome this handicap. Under the Housing Commission of Philadelphia, several committees of colored people have, from time to time, been organized to care for the needs of their own communities, but very little interest has been shown by the committees and not much has been done. Through such committees the colored people could, with entire protection to themselves, rid many communities of filth, bad drainage, and overcrowding, and could much improve health conditions. Most of the agencies for the improvement of health—namely, hospitals with their social service departments, dispensaries, anti-tuberculosis society, etc.—give their interest and attention to colored and white.

Economic opportunities for the majority of Negroes are limited. They can work in but few trades, though one may find in census reports that there are Negroes in almost all kinds of work that do not require large capital. The figures in such reports do not always reveal real conditions. If one hundred carpenters, for example, are recorded, so many of these are unskilled that the figures do not represent real conditions, and seem to show a larger number of workmen in this occupation than actually exists. The women are restricted chiefly to domestic service, and though this restriction is unfortunate and resented by them, they do quite as well economically as white girls of similar efficiency and training. To men, however, the restrictions are more serious. Unskilled Negro men through faults partly their own, and partly those of the other race, are limited in the kinds of work open to them, and the Negro boys are restricted in the kinds to which through skill and training they may rise.

Vocational training, and training in the qualities of character necessary to success, are needed. Ample facilities for academic training but not for vocational are available. Courses at the University of Pennsylvania are open to those desiring to enter. Good courses may be obtained by a limited number in private institutions in dressmaking, sewing and cooking. Several private schools give trade courses, and at the Philadelphia Trade School several courses are open, but in training in trade and business courses and in the lines of work in which the majority enter, there are not, and can not be, sufficient facilities except through the public school system. Public schools are the means through which, not only the educational, but, to a large extent, the economic needs must be met.

The historical development of the agencies and institutions, some of them dating from long before the time of emancipation, may be sketched briefly. As early as 1770, a school house was built by members of the Society of Friends for the education of the colored people, and a number of such educational institutions were established, from time to time, but gradually the public school system has come to fill the function for which these pioneers planned. Two institutions for dependent colored children, started in 1822 and 1855, are still existent and perform an important work for dependent children. In more recent times other institutions for dependent children have been established. In 1864, a home for aged and infirm colored persons was founded. A trade school started in 1837 was, in 1902, made a normal school for academic and industrial training of Negro teachers. The majority of these institutions founded fifty years ago, or more, are supported by endowment, and the control of the management is, to a large extent, in the hands of members of the white race. Many of them are very well conducted and are an invaluable help in meeting the present needs. Most of the organizations treating chiefly colored cases, however, have started within the past twenty years. They include hospitals, schools, homes, social centers, etc. In some of these, the institutions in both their work and oversight are carried on largely by colored people. Some are supported by voluntary contributions, but some receive a considerable amount of their support from state appropriations.

In any large city there should be an organization to work in a general practical way for the interest of the colored people, supplementing at any time the community needs which are not being met by the other institutions. This the Armstrong Association of Philadelphia has for five years increasingly endeavored to do in Philadelphia.

Several general activities for such an organization are obvious: (1) A bureau of record of various institutions both within and outside of the city, to help the various agencies in the treatment of individual cases. (2) An occasional investigation in a field in which improvement seems possible. (3) Education of the white members of the community to make them feel a sympathy with and responsibility to the other race. (4) Education of the colored members of the community to make them feel a practical interest in the progress of their people. (5) Practical work in fields needing temporarily special attention.

A large amount of data relative to a bureau of record has been obtained and a bureau partially completed. Three careful investigations have been made and printed. Literature is sent annually to over 10,000 white persons in Philadelphia. Much of this is merely in circular form but it gains the attention of many who otherwise would not hear of the Negro problem from a sympathetic point of view. In this, of course, work somewhat similar is done by others. Lectures have been held in schools and churches. Recently the meetings at which these lectures have been held have been well attended. At each of the recent meetings an expert has given an address on a special phase of social work.

In addition to the above, the Armstrong Association has given a great deal of attention and effort to two subjects of especial importance at the present time: First, the economic situation, which a worker of the charity organization reports is the greatest handicap of the colored people; second, the public schools as an agency for help.

To aid in solving the difficulty of the economic situation, the Armstrong Association established an office with a department for employment which has grown steadily. The chief purpose of the employment work is: (1) To help skilled Negroes to get work, and (2) to help Negroes into new kinds of work. During the past year it has helped in securing five hundred jobs and placements for colored men and women. These placements were made through the office at which opportunities were looked up, references secured, and often investigations made of how the work was done. This five hundred does not, however, represent the actual number assisted, because a number of men who were helped to get work several years ago, have since then dealt directly with their customers without the necessity of using the Armstrong Association as an intermediary, and have consequently each year obtained positions which are not credited to us. Our purpose among mechanics has been to increase the number of workers and to help those who are already working. Three associations among the mechanics were formed, covering different branches, and two others have affiliated with us, namely—the stationary engineers and the portable engineers. Among the stationary engineers there has been considerable appreciation of the importance of continued organization, but among the others the advantages of mutual coöperation do not seem to be yet appreciated. Mechanics have been helped by us in the drawing of contracts and specifications and, sometimes, in their accounts, with the result that one man increased his work from a very small amount to about $7,000, in one year, and in the next year to about $25,000. The progress of the men has been handicapped through their lack of capital and through their inability to secure loans at reasonable rates of interest. But such loans would be of little value without training on their part in being able to handle the financial side of large operations. A remedial loan association would, however, be of great value to them. The association was instrumental in helping more than a hundred shirt waist workers to secure places in shirt waist factories. Different individuals among these changed so frequently from year to year that any organization among them to increase their numbers and efficiency proved to be impossible. Over a hundred track workers for the Pennsylvania Railroad were found places, and thus introduced into a kind of work which was new to them in the neighborhood of Philadelphia.

The association is planning to continue to increase the industrial possibilities among the men by further study of openings, and by following up individual cases to see in each case whether the difficulty is prejudice, improper supervision, or inefficiency, and whether this difficulty can be remedied.

To help the public schools experimentally, the Armstrong Association employs a trained worker in two important school centers, under the direction of the principals. The worker gives her whole time to the two schools where the largest number of colored children attend. Through her there has been established a point of contact between the home and the school, and by visits in the homes and studies of the needs and possibilities of each individual child, by meetings of parents, by treatment of special cases, and by vocational guidance the parent and the child both become more interested in the school and the child is helped. A social center is promised in one of these schools which already has an evening school, and in the other it is hoped that an evening school will soon be established. In both it seems as if progress is being made and new possibilities shown. In the actual handling of the work, Negro social workers are usually the best, and they will be of increasing importance. Nothing can be more important at the present time than the thorough training and guidance of such workers, who with proper oversight, increasing from time to time, will make their work more efficient. Through such workers there should be an improvement in general in the conditions among the colored people.

The work just outlined of an organization for the systematic study and betterment of conditions of Negroes living in cities, is comparatively new, starting five years ago, but we are convinced that it has done good and that such work has possibilities for good. Similar work is being undertaken in New York and several other cities, and will be increasingly recognized as an important part of the program of social work of an American city.

NOTES

1. These maps give the population accurately by wards, but of course as they do not show the relative distribution of population in different parts of the ward, the results in a few wards are a trifle misleading. For example, in the 26th and 36th wards, the greater part of the Negro population is toward the northern ends.

2. Report of Sub-Committee on "Dependent Children" in the *Report of the Committee on Municipal Charities,* 1913.

PART TWO

FROM THE
NEW DEAL THROUGH
THE CIVIL
RIGHTS MOVEMENT

Introduction

The Great Depression and Roosevelt's New Deal destroyed the seventy-year alliance of Philadelphia Negroes with the city's Republican machine. In the brief four-year period from 1932 to 1936 Philadelphia Black neighborhoods moved from solidly Republican to solidly Democratic majorities. At no time since 1936 have the Republicans seriously threatened this new found power base of the Democratic Party. However, the loss of this one voting bloc did not fundamentally alter Republican control over city politics until after World War Two, for even in 1940 Negroes constituted only thirteen percent of the city's population. At the same time, the escape from the strong organizational authority which the Republican machine had provided in previous years led to a marked decrease in Negro voter turnout after 1936.[1] (See Figures 1 and 2.)

Perhaps national political issues during the Thirties were not the only factors leading to a shift in the partisan allegiance of Negroes at this time. James Reichley reports the following incident, which certainly must not have been an isolated case:

> The Republican organization in Philadelphia treated . . . [the Negroes] with about as much consideration as their "safe" voting habits required. According to Raymond Pace Alexander, only about fifty of the approximately 500 Negro Republican committeemen were given political jobs. Marshall Shepard, a Negro clergyman in Philadelphia in the Thirties, recalls once when he and other Negro spokesmen traveled to the Atlantic City summer home of the great

William Vare to request Negro representation on the GOP ticket for that year. The great man replied, according to Shepard: "Never! Never! The people of Philadelphia would never stand it." The young minister returned to Philadelphia, enlisted in the hard-to-find Democratic party, and made his church the site of the first meeting in the city to support the candidacy of Franklin D. Roosevelt for President of the United States.[2]

FIGURE 1

*Percent of Registrants Voting in
Philadelphia Elections, 1924-1946*

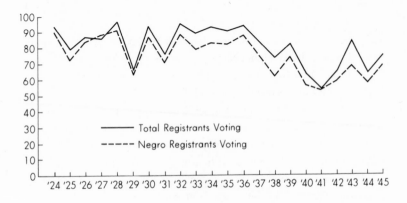

Despite this loss of Negro support the Republican organization remained in power until the end of the 1940's, and in the end it was political reform, not partisan realignment, which destroyed the Republican power base in Philadelphia.

Hit by serious scandal and divided by new factional conflicts, the Republicans held on to city control until the municipal elections of 1949. Then, confronted with a reform-minded Democratic ticket headed by Joseph Clark and Richardson Dilworth, the old system folded. Although not necessarily motivated by the reform spirit itself, Negroes supported the Clark-Dilworth team overwhelmingly. Reichley notes:

> The entrance of Dilworth and Clark into city politics finally completed the job of converting the great majority of Negroes to the

FIGURE 2

*Percent of Vote Given Head of Democratic Ticket
in Philadelphia, 1928-1946*

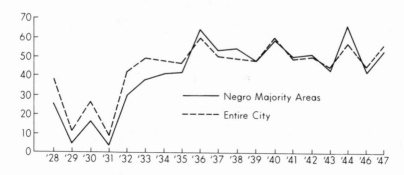

Source: Annual Reports (Philadelphia) Registration Commission, 1928-1946.

Democratic party, and in 1949 Marshall Shepard was elected to the office of recorder of deeds, a position that had once been held by William Vare himself. Since then, the Negro vote has remained almost four-fifths Democratic.[3]

During the 1950's when Dilworth replaced Clark at the top of the reform ticket, Negroes continued to back Democratic candidates for city office. Again, James Reichley suggests two reasons:

> Clark is liked because his strict enforcement of civil service regulations made it possible for large numbers of Negroes to find jobs for the first time in the city administration. . . . Dilworth is liked because he has eloquently and effectively sought to relieve the simmering racial tensions within the city.[4]

However, one must also remember that the Democratic organization, not the Republican, now controls the several thousand patronage jobs which are still left to the city's dominant political party.[5] (For three related studies of Negro voting in Philadelphia during those years see Oscar Glantz, "Recent Negro Ballots in Philadelphia," William J. McKenna, "The Negro Vote in Philadelphia Elections," and Charles A. Ekstrom, "The Electoral Politics of Reform and Machine: The Political Behavior of Philadelphia's 'Black' Wards, 1943-1969." See Chapters 4, 5, and 6.)

The reform era in Philadelphia politics lasted until 1963 when Mayor Dilworth retired. Actually, the reform movement at the practical level of city politics began to die as early as 1953, when Mayor Clark and the regular Democratic organization split on the questions of taxation and of control over city jobs. In 1957 the regulars defeated a reform candidate for district attorney.[6] During the second Dilworth administration political power moved into the hands of a new Democratic machine. The nomination and election of James H. J. Tate as mayor in 1963 and his stunning reelection victory four years later meant the end of political reform in Philadelphia. Although the slogans of reform zeal still echo throughout the city on occasion, machine politics has returned to the city.

As already indicated, the most direct consequences of the reform movement for Negroes in Philadelphia was access to public employment. In 1963 Negroes held more than 11,000 of the estimated 28,000 city positions (about thirty-nine percent). In addition, more than 30 percent of the public school teachers were Black. Unfortunately, in both the school and civil service systems Negroes tended to predominate in manual jobs and at the bottom of the pay and tenure scales.[7]

Despite these gains in public employment, the Philadelphia Negro has not developed an active role in city politics over the past two decades. One reason is that Negro voting is overwhelmingly and indiscriminately Democratic. While the white ethnics often split their partisan vote to avoid supporting a Negro, Philadelphia Negroes do not effectively bolt the straight Democratic ticket to help Republican blacks.[8] Thus, the city Democratic machine, like its Republican predecessor, finds little need to consider the special interests of the Black community or to offer special political rewards to Black leaders or voters.

Because the Negro voter casts a predictable, straight Democratic ballot, Negro leaders have had to remain under the unsympathetic domination of white, ethnic political bosses. No distinct Negro machine has emerged. Thus, the lot of the Black ward leader and potential office-holder has been none too happy. John Strange has summarized these conditions in his study of the Negro in recent Philadelphia city politics. (See Chapter 7.)

After exploring the benefits which Philadelphia Negroes have achieved through the usual political processes, Strange turns to the quasi-political activities of such groups as the NAACP. He concludes that direct action has produced some results, but it has not altered the basic condition of Negro life in the city.[9] Active in the *Girard College* Cases and in numerous protest demonstrations, the local chapter of the National Association for the Advancement of Colored People has come to reflect the splits within the Black community as well as the strengths. Perhaps the most divisive force in the Philadelphia NAACP chapter was Cecil Moore, a Black activist typical of a new breed of local Negro leaders. (Paul Lermack describes the style of Cecil Moore and the problems he created in Chapter 8.)

The pent-up frustration from over 300 years of servitude and mistreatment exploded into riots during the summers of 1963 and 1964.[10] There can be little doubt that political impotency and the poor success of demonstrations and other quasi-political activities also contributed to the social and economic climate in the Philadelphia ghetto. The city police have kept the city quiet over the past five years, but one must ultimately ask whether curfews and extended police shifts can ever really substitute for meaningful political participation. Perhaps this is simply a different way of asking whether a modern American city can afford to be governed by yet another white, ethnic-oriented urban machine.

NOTES

1. James E. Miller, "The Negro in Present Day Politics with Special Reference to Philadelphia," *Journal of Negro History* 33 (July, 1948), 323 and 330.

2. James Reichley, *The Art of Government* (New York: Fund for the Republic, 1959), p. 69.

3. *Ibid.*

4. *Ibid.,* p. 70.

5. *Ibid.,* pp. 24 and 71.

6. Edward C. Banfield, *Big City Politics* (New York: Random House, 1965), pp. 110-112.

7. John H. Strange, "The Negro in Philadelphia Politics: 1963-1965" (Ph.D. diss., Princeton University, 1966), pp. 133-137.

8. *Ibid.,* pp. 96-106.

9. *Ibid.,* pp. 162-163.

10. *Report of the National Advisory Commission on Civil Disorders* (New York: Bantam Books, 1968), pp. 35 and 37.

4

RECENT NEGRO BALLOTS IN PHILADELPHIA

OSCAR GLANTZ

Oscar Glantz, professor of sociology at Brooklyn College of the City University of
New York, analyzes Black voting patterns in four presidential elections—1944,
1948, 1952, and 1956—in this article which was first published in the Fall,
1959 issue of the *Journal of Negro Education*. Glantz notes that Black voters
in Philadelphia aligned themselves with the Democrats as they had done in
other cities. In Philadelphia, the Democrats increasingly came to depend upon
the Black vote.

The Problem

It is well recognized that Negro voters have been expressing a majoritarian preference for the Democratic party since 1936, by contrast to the overwhelming support which had been returned to the Republican party during the long years from reconstruction through 1932.[1] Moreover, it is evident that this majority preference for the Democratic party had increased steadily from 1936 through 1952, when Mr. Stevenson received approximately three-fourths or four-fifths of the Negro vote in a number of Northern cities, particularly in the largest centers of Negro population.[2] In Cincinnati, for example, the Democrats received the following percentages of the total vote in the 16th Ward (where the Negro proportion of the total population was 92.1 percent in 1940 and 94.5 percent in 1950): 65.1 in 1936—66.9 in 1940—67.7 in 1944—75.0 in 1948—81.2 in 1952.[3] However, there is no question about the fact that Mr. Stevenson was the recipient of decreasing Negro support in

1956, in Cincinnati and elsewhere.[4] Available data indicate that this decrease varied considerably in Northern cities, from one to approximately 21 or 22 percentage points.[5]

According to Henry Lee Moon, the Democratic loss in Philadelphia was less than one percentage point, but it should be noted that his estimate may be too imprecise for the historical record.[6] Accordingly, one of the purposes of the current paper is to present a revised estimate of Negro voting behavior in Philadelphia, not only for the two Eisenhower-Stevenson elections but also for the presidential contests of 1944 and 1948.

In addition, it is the purpose here to measure the extent to which Negroes had participated in these four elections, and further to compare both the voting and participation statistics with similar data for white persons in the city. Inasmuch as the Democratic party was victorious in Philadelphia in all four elections, the comparison between the two groups of voters will reveal the extent to which Negroes had contributed to the Democratic margin of victory in each election. Needless to say, a metric of this sort has political significance for the future aspirations of the two major parties, both locally and nationally.

Procedure

To obtain the best measure of Negro political behavior in Philadelphia, the writer selected every political division (precinct) in which Negro registrants represented more than 90 percent of the total registration throughout the successive election years of 1944, 1948, 1952 and 1956. During those years, there were 44 such precincts in three different parts of the city, namely five in West Philadelphia, 14 in South Philadelphia and 25 in North Philadelphia.[7] When this cross-sectional group of 44 divisions is viewed as a single sample, the data show the following percentages of Negro registrants for the four election years in the series: 94.0, 96.0, 96.9 and 96.6 (Table 4-1).

The utility of the sample is threefold. Given such large percentages of Negro registrants from representative sections of the city, it is not at

TABLE 4-1

*Electoral Participation Data, 44-Division
Area of Philadelphia*

	REGIS-TERED VOTERS (1)	NEGRO REGIS-TRANTS (2)	PERCENT-AGE OF NEGROES (3)	NUMBER VOTING (4)
1944	32,817	30,856	94.0	23,399
1948	33,671	32,311	96.0	25,546
1952	31,947*	30,952	96.9	24,846
1956	28,544*	27,572	96.6	22,122

The loss of registrants from 1948 to 1952 and thence to 1956 is largely a result of de-population in some of the divisions included in the sample area, and should not be taken as an indication of decreasing Negro participation in presidential elections.

TABLE 4-2

Electoral Participation Data, Philadelphia

	REGIS-TERED VOTERS (1)	WHITE REGIS-TRANTS (2)	NEGRO REGIS-TRANTS (3)	NEGROES AS PERCENT-AGE OF ALL REG-ISTRANTS (4)	NUMBER VOTING (5)
1944	1,005,396	873,488	131,908	13.1	845,644
1948	1,050,417	888,711	161,706	15.4	885,297
1952	1,096,345	917,980	178,365	16.3	954,226
1956	1,039,959	844,490	195,469	18.8	890,703

all indiscriminate to refer to the voting record in the sample as the voting record of the Negro people in Philadelphia.[8] Secondly, given the same sample for successive election years, it is possible to gain a more precise measure of the changes in Negro voting behavior which have occurred through time. Further, it is possible to utilize the behavioral data in the 44 divisions as a basis for estimating the participation and voting performances of both Negro and white registrants in the entire city, so that the political records of the two groups can be compared from one election to the next. The procedure for estimating the extent of Negro and white participation in each election can be illustrated as follows (1956 data):

(1) *Percentage of voters among Negro registrants, Philadelphia:*
(This is the same as the percentage of voters among registrants in the sample area.)

$$\frac{22,122 \text{ (No. of voters, sample area: Table 4-1, col. 4)}}{28,544 \text{ (No of registrants, sample area: Table 4-1, col. 1)}}$$

$= \quad 77.5$

(2) *Number of Negro voters in Philadelphia:*

195,469 (No. of Negro Registrants, Phila.:
X   77.5 Table 4-2, col. 3)
_____
= 151,488

(3) *Number of white voters in Philadelphia:*

890,703 (No. of voters, Phila.:
− 151,488 Table 4-2, col. 5)
_____
= 739,215

(4) *Percentage of voters among white registrants, Philadelphia:*

$$\frac{739,215}{844,490 \text{ (No. of white registrants, Phila.: Table 4-2, col. 2)}}$$

$= \quad 87.5$

In this manner, the turnout of Negro and white registrants in each election can be compared. Moreover with these data at hand, it is possible to estimate the percentage of Negro voters among all voters, thereby providing a figure which can serve as a comparison to the percentage of Negro registrants among all registrants (available in Table 4-2, column 4).

(5) *Percentage of Negro voters among all voters:*

$$\frac{151,488 \text{ (Estimated no. of Negro voters, Phila.)}}{890,703 \text{ (No. of voters, Phila: Table 4-2, col. 5)}}$$

$= \quad 17.0$

Continuing with 1956 data, the procedure for estimating the percentage of Democrats among Negro and white participants can be illustrated as follows:

(6) *Percentage of Democrats among Negro voters, Philadelphia:*

16,275 (No. of Democrats, sample area:

——— Table 4-3, col. 2)

22,122 (No. of voters, sample area:

= 73.6 Table 4-3, col. 1)

(7) *Number of Democrats among Negro voters in Philadelphia:*

151,488 (Estimated no. of Negro voters,

X 73.6 Phila.)

= 111,495

TABLE 4-3

Voting Data, 44-Division Area of Philadelphia

	NUMBER VOTING (1)	DEMO-CRATIC (2)	REPUB-LICAN (3)	OTHER (4)
1944	23,399	15,719	7,574	106
1948	25,546	14,937	9,856	753*
1952	24,846	19,831	5,015	—**
1956	22,122	16,275	5,847	—**

Primarily Progressive party (508).
**None listed.

TABLE 4-4

Voting Data, Philadelphia

	NUMBER VOTING (1)	DEMO-CRATIC (2)	REPUB-LICAN (3)	OTHER (4)	DEMO-CRATIC MARGIN (5)
1944	845,644	496,373	346,380	2,891	149,993
1948	885,297	432,699	425,962	26,636*	6,737
1952	954,226	557,352	396,874	—**	160,478
1956	890,703	507,289	383,414	—**	123,875

*Primarily Progressive party (20,745).
**None listed.

(8) *Number of Democrats among white voters in Philadelphia:*

507,289 (No. of Democrats, Phila.:

— 111,495 Table 4-4, col. 2)

= 395,794

(9) *Percentage of Democrats among white voters, Philadelphia:*

$$\frac{395,794}{739,215} \text{ (Estimated no. of white voters, Phila.)}$$

$$= 53.5$$

With this procedure, it is possible to compare the strength of the Democratic party among Negro and white voters in each election. There is also an opportunity here to estimate the contribution of Negro voters to the toal Democratic margin. By subtraction, the number of Republicans among Negro voters can be calculated as 39,993 (151,488 voters minus 111,495 Democrats), so that the Democratic margin among Negro voters can be calculated as 71,502 (111,495 Democrats minus 39,993 Republicans). Thus:

(10) *Percentage of Democratic margin contributed by Negro voters:*

$$\frac{71,502 \text{ (Estimated Dem. margin among Negro voters, Phila.)}}{123,875 \text{ (Dem. margin among all voters, Phila.: Table 4-4, col. 5)}}$$

$$= 57.7$$

Election Participation

Presidential elections regularly call forth a large proportion of Philadelphians to engage in political battle. For example, at least 84 percent of all registrants participated as voters in the four elections under review: 84.1 percent in 1944, 84.3 percent in 1948, 87.0 percent in 1952 and 85.6 percent in 1956. The peak in 1952 is particularly impressive when one considers that the total number of registered persons that year represented "87.7 per cent of the potential maximum registration."[9] It should be noted, however, that the potential maximum registration does not refer to the total population of voting age, but only to those persons who are eligible to register (or to remain on the registration rolls) in any given election year.

A large number of persons are ineligible each year because they cannot satisfy the citizenship or residence requirements. Newcomers to the city and citizens who move frequently from one division to another are principally affected by the residence requirements, and Negro citizens probably account for a disproportionate share of persons in these categories.[10] For this reason, it is important to limit any comparative examination of election participation to those individuals who were on the registration rolls at the time of the election. Otherwise, an excess of political ineligibility in a given group can easily be mistaken as an excess of political apathy.

In the current comparison of Negro and white participation, the data in Table 4-5 are concerned exclusively with persons who were registered to vote. Within this context, it can be noted initially that the proportion of Negro registrants who went to the polls in 1944, 1948 and 1952 increased from 71.3 percent to 75.9 and thence to 77.8, suggesting thereby that an upward trend was well under way when the stakes included the presidency. However, the increments of 1948 and 1952 were

TABLE 4-5

Participation Differences Between White and Negro Registrants in Philadelphia

	PERCENT VOTING OF WHITE REGIS- TRANTS	PERCENT VOTING OF NEGRO REGIS- TRANTS	NEGROES AS PER- CENTAGE OF ALL REGIS- TRANTS	NEGROES AS PER- CENTAGE OF ALL VOTERS
1944	86.0	71.3	13.1	11.1
1948	85.8	75.9	15.4	13.9
1952	88.8	77.8	16.3	14.5
1956	87.5	77.5	18.8	17.0

not augmented in 1956, a year of decreasing participation in Philadelphia on the part of all voters. With a turnout of 77.5 percent, there was more stability from 1952 to 1956 among Negroes than among whites (the latter group accounted for almost all of the decrease in 1956), but this can hadly be regarded as a solid achievement in view of the continuing gap between the two groups. Observe in Table 4-5 that Negro registrants were less active than white registrants in all four elections. The only improvement occurred between 1944 and 1948, when a 15 percentage-point disparity was narrowed to 10 points. In 1952 and 1956, the difference remained at 10 points.

Another way of looking at electoral participation is to compare the percentage of Negro registrants to the percentage of active Negro voters. These data are included in Table 4-5, where it can be observed that the proportion of Negro registrants among all registrants increased regularly from 1944 through 1956; that the proportion of Negro voters increased as well; but that Negroes did not exercise their registered strength in any of the four elections. As 13.1 percent of the registrants in 1944, they accounted for only 11.1 percent of the voters. By 1956, they represented 18.8 percent of the registrants but could muster only 17.0 percent of the voters. Part of this failure to match their registered weight is probably a reflection of disenchantment with the leadership of both parties in Congress, where civil rights legislation has been betrayed over and over again.

Voting Preferences

To comprehend the full significance of recent Negro ballots in Philadelphia, it is necessary to place the voting record of Negroes within the larger context of the voting record of the general population. Accordingly, the purpose here is not only to examine the majority-minority distribution of Negro preferences, but also to measure the impact of this distribution upon the margin of the leading party.

The pertinent data are presented in Table 4-6, where it can be observed that the Democratic party gained a majority of Negro ballots in all four elections. These majorities varied considerably from one election to the next, but particularly in relation to the Truman-Dewey contest of 1948. Note that Roosevelt received 67.2 percent of the Negro vote in 1944, but that this percentage dropped to 58.5 percent for Truman in 1948, leaving a defection of 8.7 percent. While not overwhelmingly large, this defection is nonetheless difficult to understand, especially in view of Mr. Truman's unequivocal position that year on the general question of civil rights. A small part of the explanation can be

67

TABLE 4-6

Voting Differences Between White and Negro
Participants in Philadelphia

	PERCENT OF DEMO- CRATIC WHITE VOTERS	PERCENT OF DEMO- CRATIC NEGRO VOTERS	DEMO- CRATIC MARGIN AMONG ALL VOTERS	DEMO- CRATIC MARGIN AMONG NEGRO VOTERS	PERCENT OF MARGIN CONTRIB- UTED BY NEGRO VOTERS	NEGRO VOTERS AS PERCENT OF ALL VOTERS
1944	57.6	67.2	149,993	32,730	21.8	11.1
1948	47.3	58.5	6,737	24,424	100.0*	13.9
1952	54.8	79.8	160,478	82,706	51.5	14.5
1956	53.5	73.6	123,875	71,502	57.7	17.0

*For white voters alone, there was a Republican margin of 17,687.

seen in Table 4-3, where the data indicate that two percent of the Democratic vote went to the Progressive party (508/25,546), but the total explanation requires the type of information which is not available in a purely statistical study.[11] At the same time, the statistics demonstrate that in 1948 the Republican party continued to receive less than 40 percent of the Negro vote, additional adherents notwithstanding. It can be noted also that the downward shift in Democratic preference was reversed dramatically in 1952. That year, the candidacy of Stevenson appealed to 79.8 percent of the Negro voters in Philadelphia, thereby providing the Democratic party with an increase of 21.3 percentage points over 1948. However, when Mr. Stevenson posed as a moderate in his second campaign, some of this bountiful subscription was lost to the Republican party. Even so, there was less alienation than one might have expected, for the data in Table 4-6 indicate that he retained the better part of the Negro vote in 1956. As the reader may observe, he received 73.6 percent of the Negro ballots that year, thereby losing 6.2 percentage points from his 1952 majority.[12]

It can be noted also that in all four elections the Democratic preference among Negro voters was substantially larger than it was among white voters, ranging from approximately 10 percentage points in 1944 and 1948 to no less than 25 in 1952 and 20 in 1956. As a consequence, the Negro contribution to the Democratic margin in each election was greater than the proportion of Negro voters among all voters. As 11.1 percent of all voters in the Roosevelt-Dewey election of 1944, they accounted for 21.8 percent of the total Democratic margin. As 13.9 percent of all voters in the Truman-Dewey election of 1948, they were responsible for the entire margin, and as well, contributed enough votes to overcome a lead of 17,687 which the Republican party had obtained among white voters. In the Stevenson-Eisenhower election of 1952, Negro voters continued to lend disproportionate weight to the Democratic party by contributing 51.5 percent of the margin which enabled Stevenson to carry the city by 160,000 votes. In 1956, as 17 percent of all voters (and despite a decrease of 6.2 percentage points in Democratic preference), Negro participants gave Mr. Stevenson 57.7 percent of his total margin in Philadelphia.[13]

When the Negro contribution to a margin-of-victory exceeds the 50 percent mark, as it did in Philadelphia in the last three presidential elections, it has to be characterized as an *indispensable* contribution. This is to say that the opposition party would have gained the citywide victory in each of these elections if the Negro vote had been reversed. For example, if the Republicans had received 73.6 percent of the Negro vote in 1956, rather than the Democrats, Mr. Eisenhower would have carried Philadelphia with a margin of approximately 19,000 votes. As it happened, he received only 26.4 percent of the Negro vote and thereby lost the city by approximately 123,000 votes. Here, in these data, is a striking example of the strategic position of the Negro vote as a balance of power. Insofar as purely local elections are concerned, it can be noted that "Mayor Richardson Dilworth of Philadelphia credits the Negro vote with having installed him in City Hall" in 1955.[14]

Summary

By employing official registration and voting data for all political divisions in which Negro registrants represented more than 90 percent of the total registration in 1944, 1948, 1952 and 1956, it was possible to gain a precise accounting of major statistical aspects of Negro political behavior in Philadelphia during those years. In summary, the following observations and comments may be recorded:

1. In presidential elections from 1944 through 1952, the proportion of Negro registrants who went to the polls increased from 71.3 percent to 77.8 percent. This increase suggests that Negro registrants are reaching new levels of political consciousness, and perhaps a new sense of political efficacy.

2. In 1956, a year of decreasing turnout for white voters, the Negro turnout levelled off at 77.5 percent.

3. In all four elections, however, Negro registrants did not exercise their political strength to the same degree as white registrants, with disparities between the two groups ranging from 15 percentage points in 1944 to 10 points in the three presidential elections subsequent to 1944. This gap serves to illustrate the continuing need for political education at the grass roots.[15]

4. In each election, the Democratic party received a majority of Negro ballots, but these majorities varied considerably from one election to the next. In the first three elections under review, 67.2 percent, 58.5 percent, and 79.8 percent of the Negro vote went to Roosevelt, Truman, and Stevenson, respectively. The last figure is undoubtedly a record high for Democratic preference on the part of Philadelphia's Negro voters.

5. In 1956, Stevenson retained the biggest part of his old majority, receiving 73.6 percent of the Negro ballots in his second campaign for the presidency.

6. In all four elections, the Democratic preference among Negro voters was substantially larger than it was among white voters, ranging from approximately 10 percentage points in 1944 and 1948 to no less than 25 points in 1952 and 20 in 1956.

7. Negro voters accounted for varying disproportionate percentages of the total Democratic margin-of-victory in Philadelphia. For example, in the two Eisenhower-Stevenson elections, Negroes represented 14.5 percent of all voters in 1952 and 17 percent in 1956, but contributed 51.5 percent of Stevenson's margin in the first contest and 57.7 percent of his margin in the second contest. These contributions can be taken as excellent examples of political strength. If Negro in-migration to Philadelphia continues at a relatively high rate, and if the Negro people

Oscar Glantz

enhance their strategic position by a further upturn in political participation, the Negro body politic is likely to become a permanent balance
of power in the future of Philadelphia politics.

NOTES

1. Previous studies of Negro political behavior indicate that the Democratic
party had received scant support from Negro voters in the 1932 election. For
example, Franklin D. Roosevelt obtained approximately 23 percent of the Negro
vote in Chicago and 29 percent in Cincinnati, while the gubernatorial candidate
in Michigan that year obtained slightly less than 37 percent of the Negro vote in
Detroit. See Harold F. Gosnell, "The Negro Vote in Northern Cities," *National
Municipal Review,* Vol. 30, 1941, pp. 264-267 and 278; Ernest M. Collins, "Cincinnati Negroes and Presidential Politics," *Journal of Negro History,* Vol. 41,
1956, pp. 131-137; and Edward H. Litchfield, "A Case Study of Negro Political
Behavior in Detroit," *Public Opinion Quarterly,* Vol. 5, 1941, pp. 267-274.

2. For Negro voters in 1952, Henry Lee Moon reports Democratic percentages
of 70.5, 72.5, 74.6, 75.9, 76.0, 79.0, 79.1 and 85.8, respectively, in Chicago, Philadelphia, Kansas City, St. Louis, Brooklyn, Harlem, Pittsburg and Detroit. "The
Negro Voter in the Presidential Election of 1956," *Journal of Negro Education,*
Vol. 26, 1957, pp. 219-230 (data from Table I, p. 221 and Table II, p. 222).

3. Collins, *op. cit.,* Table 1, p. 133.

4. For Cincinnati, the writer would estimate that the Negro vote for Stevenson
dropped nine percentage points, from 81.2 in 1952 to 72.2 in 1956. The comparative figure for 1956 was supplied by the Hamilton County (Ohio) Board of Elections; the figure for 1952 was taken from Collins' report.

5. Moon, *op. cit.,* Table I and II. It should be noted that Negro voters in the
South, by contrast to the North, abandoned the Democratic party to a much
larger extent. In some Southern cities, the Democratic loss was greater than 50
percentage points. *Ibid.,* Table III, p. 224.

6. Moon utilized the voting returns from 14 complete wards in Philadelphia,
which suggests that his political area was too heterogeneous to provide us with a
precise account of Negro preferences. In some of these wards, the size of the
white population is roughly equal to the size of the Negro population. This is not
to say that Moon's data are valueless, but merely to suggest that they are subject
to some error.

7. These included the following divisions: 9th (of the 4th Ward); 14th (of the
7th Ward); 9th and 10th (of the 14th Ward); 14th, 15th, 27th and 30th (of the
20th Ward); 27th (of the 24th Ward); 14th (of the 28th Ward); 1st, 2nd, 4th and
6th (of the 29th Ward); 2nd through 11th (of the 30th Ward); 8th, 9th, 10th,
11th, 13th, 14th, 16th and 17th (of the 32nd Ward); 1st and 2nd (of the 36th
Ward); 1st and 2nd (of the 36th Ward); 1st (of the 44th Ward); 13th, 14th, 16th,
17th, 18th and 19th (of the 47th Ward) and 13th, 15th and 20th (of the 52nd
Ward).

8. For an earlier study of Negro voters in Philadelphia, see J. Erroll Miller, "The Negro in Present Day Politics with Special Reference to Philadelphia," *Journal of Negro History,* Vol. 3; 303-343, 1948. Professor Miller gauged the Negro vote by employing a sample of 11 combined Wards (Negro majority Wards) in which Negro registrants represented 67.8 percent of the total registration.

9. Registration Commission of Philadelphia, *47th Annual Report,* 1952, p. 4.

10. In the voluminous literature on political participation in a democracy, much of it exhortative in nature, the problem of residence requirements has received very little attention. Yet, in every section of the country large numbers of citizens are prevented from voting merely because they have not resided in one place for three months or six months or one year, as the local law may require. Such restrictions effectively disfranchise certain segments of the working class in particular, *e.g.,* migrant farm laborers and construction workers who need to move from one locality to another. As well, they impinge upon the political participation of Negro migrants from Southern states to such areas as Philadelphia.

11. That the explanation must be sought in local political affairs is apparent when one compares the Negro vote in Philadelphia and Cincinnati. For the two cities, the Democratic percentage was roughly identical in 1944 (67.2 and 67.7), in 1952 (79.8 and 81.2) and in 1956 (73.6 and 72.2), but not in 1948 (58.5 vs. 75.0). *See* footnote 4.

12. By contrast with the data for Negro voters in the current study, Henry Lee Moon's data for Philadelphia show smaller Democratic preferences of 72.5 in 1952 and 71.6 in 1956, thereby pointing to a negligible decrease of 0.9 percentage point. Moon, *op. cit.* Table I, p. 221.

13. It should be emphasized that these percentages represent Negro contributions to the net Democratic margin in each election. Certain sub-groups within the white group, *e.g.*, unionized factory workers, also contribute heavily to the Democratic party, but when the white group is treated as a single group, these sub-group contributions are partially cancelled (or completely cancelled, *e.g.*, in 1948) by Democratic deficits among other sub-groups.

14. Quoted in Robert Bendiner, "The Negro Vote and the Democrats," *The Reporter,* 14:8, May 31, 1956.

15. "Politicians count influence in terms of ballots in the box. If the ballots are not there, a city can have a million Negroes for all the clubhouse boys care." Roy Wilkins, "The Future of the Negro Voter in the United States," *Journal of Negro Education,* 26; 427-28, Summer 1957.

5

THE NEGRO VOTE IN
PHILADELPHIA ELECTIONS

WILLIAM J. McKENNA

William J. McKenna is a political scientist and economist on the faculty of Temple University. In this article, which first appeared in the October, 1965 issue of *Pennsylvania History*, he traces Black voters' influence on the rise to local dominance of the Democratic Party. McKenna feels that beginning with its initial local victory in the 1951 mayoralty race, the Democratic Party could count on a solid bloc of Black voters.

Bloc voting[1] has been evident in the pattern of Philadelphia politics for many years. The strength of the Democratic party in Philadelphia has been concentrated in the Italian, Polish, Jewish, and Negro blocs in most of the elections since the election of President Franklin D. Roosevelt in 1932.[2] Religion,[3] economics, and political philosophy[4] have been important factors in the bloc voting pattern of Philadelphia.

The foundation of the strength of the Democratic party in Philadelphia, however, is in the voting behavior of the seventeen so-called Negro wards. This paper will examine this pattern and discuss the factors that have influenced the pattern.

The Negro Population of Philadelphia

Since 1940 the Negro population of Philadelphia has increased by 303,620–from 250,880 in 1940 to an estimated 554,400 in 1963.[5] The Negro population of Philadelphia is largely concentrated in the areas immediately east and west of the Schuylkill River. This area is one of overcrowded housing, inadequate schools, and industrial plants. It contains many of the families who are on relief and other assistance programs. The rate of unemployment in this area is more than double that of the rest of the city. Public housing has been built in the area but this has not greatly lessened the concentration of Negro population in the region.[6]

The Political Pattern of Philadelphia

Prior to the election of President Franklin D. Roosevelt in 1932, Philadelphia was definitely a one-party Republican city. As late as 1931 the Democratic candidate for mayor received a total vote of only 30,821 compared to a Republican total of 367,344—a Republican landslide majority of 336,523 or 90.1% of the total vote.[7] In 1932, however, the Republican candidate for President carried the city by only 70,766 votes. The subsequent elections witnessed a further weakening of the strength of the Republican party in Philadelphia for all city, state, and national offices. In Philadelphia the Republican party barely won the elections for United States Senator in 1934 and 1938, and has lost all such elections since 1940 with the exception of the national Republican swing of 1946.[8] Since 1950 the Republican party has lost every election for Governor by substantial margins. Again, since 1932 the Republican party has suffered defeat in all Presidential elections. The climax in the Republican decline in Philadelphia occurred in the Presidential election of 1960, when that party was defeated by 331,544 votes. A similar pattern of Republican decline is evident in all local elections in Philadelphia since 1932. Although the Republican party won the mayoralty elections in 1935-1947, the majorities were far from impressive,[9] when compared with the pre-1935 majorities.[10] Since 1951 the Democrats have won every mayoralty election.[11]

The principal architects of the rise of the Democratic party in Philadelphia were two unusual men: Joseph S. Clark and Richardson Dilworth. In 1947 these two former Republicans spearheaded the reform movement in Philadelphia. Dilworth ran for mayor in 1947 but was defeated by a Republican ward leader, Bernard Samuel, by 91,622 votes. In 1949 Clark was elected city controller by a Democratic majority of 112,000 votes.[12] The history of the Democratic party since 1947 has largely been the history of these two men. They were reformers. They were both graduates of "Ivy League" colleges (Harvard and Yale), and each was wealthy in his own right. Both men were committed to the elimination of political corruption and political bossism which had characterized Republican politics in Philadelphia for many years. In 1951 Clark was elected mayor by 125,000 votes. Since that date the Democratic party has dominated practically all elections in Philadelphia.[13]

The Negro Vote in Philadelphia

For the purpose of this study the term "Negro Ward" is applied to those wards which in 1960 had a total Negro population of 50% or more. There are sixteen of these wards. The 38th Ward has also been included in this study because in 1960 it had a Negro population of 24,505 (33.3%), and it is contiguous with the other heavily populated Negro wards.

These seventeen wards in 1960 had a total Negro population of 414,864, or 78.4% of the 529,239 Negro population of Philadelphia. Sixteen of these wards had a 1960 Negro population varying from approximately 50.0% to 95.8% (see Table 5-1).

Even before the Democratic party succeeded in winning municipal elections in Philadelphia, these seventeen Negro wards had provided a significant basis of support for the Democratic party. For example, in the Presidential elections of 1940-1948, these wards had provided a Democratic majority that was 44.3%, 52.6%, and 457.5% of the total city-wide Democratic majority.[14] A similar trend prevailed in the elections for the United States Senator and Governor in 1950.[15]

Since 1952 the seventeen Negro wards in Philadelphia have consistently given a still heavier percentage of their votes to the Democratic party. The percentages for each of the seventeen Negro wards for the three presidential elections since 1952, the three gubernatorial elections

TABLE 5-1

Negro Population: 17 So-Called Negro Wards, City of
Philadelphia, 1950 and 1960

| | NEGRO POPULATION | | | |
| | 1950 | | 1960 | |
WARD	TOTAL	PERCENT	TOTAL	PERCENT
4	4,294	42.7	4,055	58.2
13	7,859	59.3	5,070	70.2
14	9,604	67.8	8,560	82.7
20	25,559	58.3	24,110	74.4
24	36,741	58.0	45,666	80.8
28	20,040	39.6	46,230	91.3
29	12,594	41.2	23,095	81.3
30	23,789	87.4	21,587	91.4
32	44,872	73.7	52,191	95.8
36	22,623	43.0	23,542	52.0
37	4,372	20.2	11,284	60.2
38	6,132	8.7	24,505	33.3
44	23,398	56.3	28,598	78.0
46[1]	2,297	2.6	40,171	50.0
47	27,690	76.5	28,173	90.2
52	20,059	35.4	27,975	53.6
17 Wards*	291,923	77.6	414,864	78.4
City	376,041		529,239	

*In 1961 the 46th ward was divided into the new 46th and 60th wards.
Source: Greater Philadelphia Facts, Chamber of Commerce of Greater
Philadelphia, 1962 Edition, p. 46. Percentages calculated.

since 1954, and the three mayoralty elections since 1955 are shown in Table 5-2.

There is a very high Democratic registration among the Negro population of Philadelphia. It has increased from 170,491 in 1950 to 231,308 in 1962.[16] As is to be expected, there is a large concentration of the Democratic Negro registration in the seventeen Negro wards of the city. The Democratic registration in the seventeen Negro wards has increased from 132,848 in 1950 to 179,013 in 1962, but the percentage of registration has remained constant (see Table 5-3).

As the Democratic margin of victory decreases in city-wide elections, the Democratic majority of the seventeen Negro wards becomes a more significant factor in the Democratic victory. This is evident in the figures presented in Table 5-4. Thus, in the close election for city con-

William J. McKenna

TABLE 5-2

Democratic Party, Percentage of Total Vote, 17 So-Called Negro Wards of Philadelphia. Selected Elections, 1952-1963. Democratic Vote, Percentage of Total Vote.

WARDS	PRESIDENT			GOVERNOR			MAYOR		
	1952	1956	1960	1954	1958	1962	1955	1959	1963
4	59.4	61.7	72.8	51.4	56.0	57.1	57.0	57.9	76.8
13	44.8	74.5	81.1	46.0	74.1	78.0	57.4	76.0	81.3
14	60.7	71.2	80.3	54.8	73.6	76.1	62.8	77.4	78.5
20	67.8	73.7	83.3	59.2	76.2	77.9	61.6	77.5	79.6
24	71.2	71.1	79.9	63.2	75.8	73.4	73.8	79.2	76.0
28	73.6	73.8	83.6	68.4	78.0	69.4	70.2	79.4	80.3
29	68.3	68.3	79.6	67.3	73.4	74.2	69.2	77.4	77.1
30	74.3	69.0	79.7	65.9	71.5	70.8	70.6	72.9	76.9
32	81.3	78.7	83.1	75.8	79.1	72.9	76.7	78.2	79.7
36	76.8	71.3	83.2	75.4	78.2	74.2	74.4	78.8	74.1
37	58.7	61.2	73.5	58.8	71.1	71.5	63.1	76.4	76.4
38	59.3	57.4	71.8	60.7	63.1	57.0	60.5	66.9	57.8
44	74.8	68.7	80.0	67.6	74.2	70.3	71.4	75.8	78.0
46	55.7	58.7	70.7	59.1	65.8	62.9	61.0	72.1	71.0
47	76.7	74.0	84.0	68.8	76.5	76.6	72.4	78.6	81.6
52	72.1	72.2	76.5	70.1	75.1	70.8	72.9	77.2	72.6
60	–	–	–	–	–	67.8	–	–	73.7
All 17 Wards	68.3	68.0	78.0	65.2	72.6	69.4	67.9	75.2	73.8
City-Wide	58.5	57.6	68.1	57.7	61.7	56.7	59.3	65.6	54.6

Sources: Richard M. Scammon, America Votes, *Volumes I-IV (Governmental Affairs Institute, New York: Macmillan Company, 1956; Governmental Affairs Institute, Pittsburgh: University of Pittsburgh, 1958-1962). Percentages for mayoralty elections taken from data in City of Philadelphia election returns,* Annual Report of the Registration Commission for the City of Philadelphia, *1956-1962. Percentages for 1963 calculated from unofficial sources.*

TABLE 5-3

Negro Democratic Registration in Philadelphia, City-Wide and the 17 So-Called Negro Wards. Selected Years, 1950-1962

YEAR	CITY-WIDE	17 NEGRO WARDS	PERCENTAGE
1950	170,941	132,848	77.7
1952	178,365	138,196	77.4
1954	173,281	134,200	77.4
1956	195,469	152,278	77.9
1958	210,517	164,618	77.7
1960	219,232	170,569	77.7
1962	231,308	179,013	77.8

Source: Annual Report of the Registration Commission for the City of Phila-delphia, *1950-1962.*

TABLE 5-4

Democratic Majorities in Phailadelphia, City-Wide and 17 So-Called Negro Wards. Selected Elections, 1940-1963.

OFFICE	DEMOCRATIC MAJORITY		DEMOCRATIC MAJORITY OF 17 NEGRO WARDS AS PERCENT OF CITY-WIDE MAJORITY
	CITY-WIDE	17 NEGRO WARDS	
President			
1940	177,409	78,656	44.3
1944	149,987	78,983	52.6
1948	6,737	30,826	457.5
1952	160,867	101,694	63.2
1956	123,875	86,366	69.7
1960	331,544	130,233	39.2
U. S. Senator			
1950	63,995	35,018	54.7
1956	170,164	94,033	55.2
1958	133,413	80,809	60.5
1962	180,379	87,071	48.2
Governor			
1950	77,078	42,197	54.7
1954	118,273	63,471	53.6
1958	177,998	87,399	49.1
1962	106,738	73,316	68.7
Mayor			
1951	124,680	43,518	34.3
1955	132,706	68,866	51.9
1959	208,406	85,174	40.9
1963	69,310	85,214	123.0
City Controller			
1949	111,404	33,169	29.8
1957	77,523	50,544	65.2
1961	56,581	61,033	107.9

Source: Complied from data in Annual Report of the Registration Commission for the City of Philadelphia, *1954-1962; also Pennsylvania Manual, various years.*

troller in 1961, the 61,033 Democratic majority of the seventeen Negro wards accounted for 107.9% of the total Democratic city-wide majority. In the Gubernatorial election of 1962, a Democratic majority in the Negro wards was 68.7% of the city-wide Democratic majority. And in the mayoralty election of 1963 the 85,214 majority of the Negro wards was 123% of the total city-wide Democratic majority of 69,310.[17]

William J. McKenna

Factors Affecting the Negro Vote in Philadelphia

Many complicated factors influence the voting pattern of any bloc of voters. In Philadelphia there are several factors which seem to have influenced the Negro to vote and to remain Democratic. Among these factors are the following:

1. The identification of the Democratic party with the Roosevelt policies and philosophy. With the advent of the "New Deal" the Democratic party initiated many programs which have directly benefited the Negro. Social and economic legislation of the 1933-1940 period has laid the basis of much assistance to the Negro, because it was the group which was the most depressed. Although all administrations since Roosevelt have followed to some extent the social welfare policies of President Roosevelt, the Negro in Philadelphia seems to associate these policies with Roosevelt.[18]

2. Economic factors. The solidity of the Negro vote behind the Democratic party in Philadelphia is largely based upon economic factors. These include jobs, housing, and educational opportunities. The Negro in Philadelphia has in recent years been confronted with an unemployment rate of 10-20%. This is, of course, partly related to the lack of skilled occupations among the Negro group. But it is also affected by the slow rate of hiring of Negro workers by employers and the discrimination against qualified Negroes by certain unions.[19]

The Negro leadership of Philadelphia in the past two years has pursued a determined policy of lessening housing discrimination in Philadelphia. These leaders have felt that the local Democratic leadership has been more sympathetic to this goal than the Republicans.[20]

In order to increase the educational opportunities of the Negro population of Philadelphia there has been a concerted drive to transfer Negro pupils to predominantly white schools. This drive has taken the form of transferring Negro pupils to white schools by school buses. The policy has been opposed by the Republican leaders in Philadelphia as the wrong approach to the improvement of educational opportunities for the Negro.[21] At present there seems to be little likelihood that the Negro voter in Philadelphia will end his allegiance to the Democratic party until the Negro feels that the Republican party will offer at least an equal

79

opportunity for the Negro to improve his economic status.

3. Government jobs. The Democratic administration in Philadelphia has been especially active since 1951 in providing jobs for Negroes in the city government. No published figures are available, but it has been estimated that Negroes hold from 8,000 to 10,000 jobs in the Philadelphia city government.[22] In addition, the Democratic Governors of Pennsylvania from 1954 to 1962 have appointed Negroes to positions in the various state government agencies. Since 1960 a similar policy has been pursued by the Kennedy and Johnson administrations in Washington. The net effect of these policies has been to retain the loyalty of the Negro leaders and their following in Philadelphia.

4. Public housing. The Negro housing situation in Philadelphia is one of the blights of the city. Since improved public housing has been initiated under national Democratic administrations, there is a belief among Philadelphia Negroes that the Democratic party is more committed to a policy of improved public housing than is the Republican party. The advances in public housing under the Eisenhower administration did not materially change this attitude among Negroes in Philadelphia.

5. Civil rights. Rightly or wrongly, the Negroes in Philadelphia seem to feel that the Democratic party is the best hope for the improvement of civil rights. In recent years this issue has become a very emotional one in Philadelphia. The Negro leaders of Philadelphia are determined to secure full civil rights in housing, in schools, and in jobs. Until the Republican party in Philadelphia is able to convince the Negro voter on the issue of civil rights, there is little chance that the Republican party can make any headway among the Negro voters.

6. "Writing off the Negro vote." There was a definite feeling among the Negro leadership in the mayoralty campaign of 1963 that the Republican party had "written off the Negro vote."[23] This belief, whether it had a logical basis or not, tended to strengthen the Negro support behind the Democrats. The Republican candidate for mayor in 1963, James T. McDermott, vigorously denied the allegation that the Republican party had "written off the Negro vote."[24] He asserted that the issues in the campaign were political bossism and political corruption, and that local economic conditions were dominant in the campaign.

80

William J. McKenna

The Future

The issues of political bossism, political corruption, or inept municipal leadership have not been effective in winning the Negro voter to the Republican side in Philadelphia. Nor are they likely to do so in the immediate future unless these issues become far more explosive. The Negro in Philadelphia has a much greater identity with the local Democratic leaders. The Negro wards will, in my opinion, continue to stick with the Democratic party in Philadelphia until there is a material improvement in the economic position of the Negro; until the Negro feels that equal job opportunities are his; until housing is improved substantially; until educational opportunities and facilities are equal; in other words, until the Negro is convinced that he is guaranteed all his rights by both parties, not by word alone but by performance. Emotions may govern his political behavior, but he is convinced that the Democratic party offers him the realization of his hopes. This, in essence, is the challenge that confronts the Republican party in Philadelphia.

NOTES

1. In 1960 there were approximately 300,000 Jews and 530,000 Negroes in Philadelphia. There were also 700,000 Catholics out of a total population of 2,002,512.

2. The heavily Jewish wards (49th and 50th) have voted Democratic in all Presidential elections since 1936. They have also voted Democratic in almost all elections since the victory of Joseph S. Clark in the controller election of 1949. This has also been true of the Italian and Polish wards.

3. In 1928 the nomination of Alfred E. Smith as the Democratic candidate for President resulted in a total Democratic vote in Philadelphia of 276,000. In 1932 the total Democratic vote in Philadelphia decreased to 260,000. In 1960 Senator Kennedy received approximately 75% of the vote of the Catholic Italian wards.

4. The Jewish wards vote consistently for liberal Democratic candidates even though economically these wards are upper middle class.

5. This 554,400 estimate is that of the Philadelphia Chamber of Commerce (see the 1964 Edition of *Greater Philadelphia Facts,* Chamber of Commerce of Greater Philadelphia, December, 1963, p. 48). The 1950 Negro population of Philadelphia was 376,041. If the growth of the Negro population of Philadelphia continues, it may reach 40% of the city population by 1980. It is now 27.2%.

6. The areas surrounding the University of Pennsylvania and Temple University are areas of heavy Negro population concentration. The redevelopment of these areas is gradually encroaching upon the heavily populated Negro residential areas. These areas have been described as "slum areas" because of the large number of residential dwellings containing from four to six separate apartments.

7. In the mayoralty election of 1927 the total Democratic vote was approximately 10,000 and the Republican vote 296,551.

8. The Republicans won the United States Senate race in 1934 by only 3,012 votes and the 1938 election by 17,167 votes. The 1946 election for United States Senator went Republican by 108,853 votes. All such elections since 1946 have been won by the Democratic party by heavy margins.

9. The mayoralty Republican majorities were: 1935, 45,478; 1939, 30,006; 1943, 63,465; and 1947, 91,622.

10. In 1927 the Republican majority was 285,903 (96.4%) and in 1931 the majority was 336,523 (90.1%).

11. Joseph S. Clark won in 1951 by nearly 125,000, and Richardson Dilworth by 132,000 in 1955. He was reelected in 1959 by 208,000 votes. In 1963, James H. J. Tate was elected mayor by a 68,268-vote majority.

12. In the same year Dilworth was elected city treasurer. He also ran for Governor in 1950 and, although he carried Philadelphia by 77,000 votes, he was defeated in the state.

13. In 1953 the Republicans won the city controller election by the narrow margin of 15,579 votes in a very light election of 565,799 total votes.

14. The unusual percentage for 1948 reflects the 30,806 Democratic majority given by these seventeen Negro wards to President Truman in the face of a city-wide majority for Truman of 6,737.

15. See Table 5-4.

16. In the 1963 mayoralty election the total Negro registration in the city was estimated at 233,000.

17. James H. J. Tate, acting mayor of Philadelphia, was the Democratic candidate. He had become acting mayor as a result of the resignation of Mayor Richardson Dilworth, who resigned to run for Governor. The Philadelphia City Charter of 1951 provides that any elected official of the city government must resign from his office in the event he files for another elective office. Tate, as the president of the City Council, became acting mayor in February 1963.

18. Late in the mayoralty campaign of 1963 the Democratic leadership in Philadelphia had James Roosevelt make a campaign appearance in the Negro areas. This was in recognition of the lasting influence of President Roosevelt among the Negroes.

19. Under the leadership of 400 Negro ministers in Philadelphia there has been a successful drive to place Negroes in jobs in many Philadelphia industries. This result has been attained by a policy of general boycott and picketing of firms which allegedly practiced job discrimination. Cecil B. Moore, the leader of the Philadelphia Chapter of the NAACP, has also aggressively pursued a policy of ending job discrimination.

20. This drive for integrated housing has met with some opposition in the so-called "white wards," and they have tended to vote Republican in recent elections.

21. James T. McDermott, the Republican candidate for mayor in 1963, publicly opposed the policy of "busing" Negro pupils to white schools. He believed it was a sounder policy to improve the Negro schools and their facilities.

22. An attempt was made by certain Negro leaders to secure an actual census of Negro jobholders in the city government, but such a census was refused on the ground that color is not included in job applications.

23. This was one of the reasons given by Cecil B. Moore of the Philadelphia NAACP for his support of the Democratic candidate for mayor in 1963.

24. It is of interest that a Republican candidate for the state General Assembly from an almost 100% "white ward" in a conversation with me stated that: "When a voter asked him how he should vote, he replied, 'Vote white.'"

6

THE ELECTORAL POLITICS OF REFORM AND MACHINE: THE POLITICAL BEHAVIOR OF PHILADELPHIA'S "BLACK" WARDS, 1943-1969

CHARLES A. EKSTROM

Charles A. Ekstrom is a sociologist on the faculty of Temple University. In this article, expressly written for this volume, he explores patterns of electoral behavior in the predominantly Black wards of Philadelphia. His contribution is particularly useful because he draws on data covering a critical era in Philadelphia Black politics. Ekstrom's conclusions differ somewhat from those of Glantz and McKenna.

In many American cities, the vote of Black citizens is, or is becoming, the most important, if not the predominant, voice in the local electorate. At the same time, America's cities are said to be experiencing a "crisis," which is, in some of its most important aspects, largely a political crisis.[1] The capacity of cities to govern themselves effectively is affected by the simultaneous decline of cities' resource bases and their political machines, and by the milling efforts of disadvantaged persons and groups to use the city as a vehicle for the solution of their troubles. Hence, observers of the city urgently need objective information about the tendencies of such groups, especially as they relate to efforts to reform and reorganize cities as effective political units.

It is in this context that this study is presented. Philadelphia has a large and growing Black population, one which may become an electoral majority in the near future. At the same time, it has been asserted that this population has been ineffective politically, has largely accepted white leadership and agendas for action, and has been slavishly devoted to the Democratic party.[2] Yet, "white" leadership in a city is not always monolithic in nature, and the behavior of Blacks in relation to the appeal of a variety of white leaders and the issues which they have raised is a topic of considerable interest. This is particularly so insofar as past political tendencies give clues to likely behavior under the changed circumstances of the future. Also interesting is the political alignment of various white groups in relation to Black patterns, since this information may provide insight into possible alliances to come.

"Public- and Private-Regardingness"

It is said that, as a group, Blacks display unique characteristics in their participation in, and use of, politics in urban centers.[3] Wilson and Banfield have tentatively classified them as "private-regarding" in orientation; that is, they tend to approach public issues and the needs of the community as an entity from the point of view of personal-, family-, and particularly group-based criteria.[4] The opposite of "private-regarding" participants are the "public-regarding," who use criteria emphasizing the overall good of the community, and the enhancement of its capacity to approach its problems in an orderly and effective manner. Both a high level of service and rational coordination of political effort are goals sought by the "public-regarding."[5]

The two types of groups so identified are likely to differ in perception, definition, and evaluation of political events. The placement of a group as one of these types is a function of historical political patterns in cities as they affected different socioeconomic and ethnic strata. The birth, development, and decline of the political machine, as well as of parallel efforts to "reform" the structure and conduct of urban politics, are traced to the varying strength of groups committed to these two sets of criteria. The higher the socioeconomic status of community participants, the more "public-regarding" their behavior is predicted to be. Certain ethnic groups (including WASPs and Jews) are said to be especially "public-regarding" while others (such as Italians, Poles, and

Blacks) are said to be highly "private-regarding." It is, of course, understood that groups such as the latter will often be at odds with each other in the effort to advance their more private interests.

These patterns assume major importance in an analysis of support for candidates, parties, and their policies and even more in analyzing support for referenda and other proposals voted on directly by city electorates. It has been shown that public- and private-regarding types (specifically Blacks) may converge in supporting a high general level of municipal acitivty and service, yet diverge in *priorities* or the relative support given concrete measures.[6] Some private-regarding groups may strongly oppose measures perceived as primarily benefiting others.

More needs to be known about all forms of politics practiced by each group specified by these conceptions. Their entrance into and withdrawal from coalitions, party participation and rewards received, differential participation at various levels of government and decision-making structures, and many other topics deserve exploration. However, it is also necessary to study the behavior of specific groups in the electoral process. Evidence should be sought that groups' orientations have been correctly identified, and efforts should be made to specify the exact criteria evident in their behavior. One need is for longitudinal data which can show development and change in a group's voting patterns.

Black Patterns

PHILADELPHIA AND ELSEWHERE

Black behavior in urban politics, in Philadelphia and in general, is imperfectly understood but some things are known. For example, overwhelming Black support for the Democratic party is the norm, although it is not clear whether this pattern obtains as strongly for local politics as it does for state and national levels.[7] It is also the case that Blacks have been typically more closely tied to urban machines than to reform movements and politicians.[8] Here it is unclear whether Blacks exceed or trail other ethnic groups in this tendency. In some cases, Black votes have provided an important buffer, protecting machines from reformers and other opponents in close contests.

Black participation appears to be directed toward primarily limited and conventional goals, such as secure jobs, favors and protection by machines. Specifically racial and potentially radical objectives tend to be shunned. By and large, Blacks participate less than whites in all forms and levels of politics, including registration, voting, party involvement, and office-holding. The rewards received, in the form of representation, honor, employment, and policy output, seem disproportionately low, even considering low Black input. This seems to reflect discrimination and manipulation of the political system by whites.[9]

In the specific case of Philadelphia, Strange supports these general findings and adds others of interest: for example, there is no *Negro* political organization in Philadelphia now, or ever, and Negroes do not demand or propose legislation. With regard to voting, Philadelphia Negroes are said to vote Democratic, *not* to vote for candidates on the basis of race, and to be ineffective in ticket-splitting to support Negro candidates in multi-candidate elections.[10]

This study, using data drawn from three decades, yet including contemporary developments, seeks to examine some of these national and local generalizations for necessary specifications, qualifications, and limitations, if they are to fit the voting data for the city of Philadelphia for the years studied.

POLITICAL CONTEXT OF THE ELECTIONS STUDIED

Several salient aspects of Philadelphia's recent political history should be mentioned, since they provide the context for the electoral data to be examined.[11] First, Philadelphia's local machine was Republican. Groups which in many cities usually voted Democratic in elections at all levels often voted Republican in Philadelphia. After the New Deal, the city was largely Democratic in national and state elections, but continued Republican in local contests.

Second, "reform" efforts took place within the Republican party for the most part, with support from those groups identified as "public-regarding."[12] Low-ranked socioeconomic and ethnic groups provided a major bulwark of machine support within the party, especially in the so-called "river" wards and other "controlled" wards.

Third, despite some variations, the Democratic party was largely ineffectual locally until two leaders, Joseph S. Clark and Richardson Dilworth, were able to combine a reform appeal with increased Democratic strength to produce victory. Extra-party organizations, such as the Greater Philadelphia Movement and the Americans for Democratic Action, played some role in this development. Both Clark and Dilworth were members of traditionally high-ranked socioeconomic and ethnic groups, yet both were long-term Democrats and espoused "liberal" objectives and programs.

Fourth, Democrats took control by standing for governmental reorganization. Scandal played a major role in reform success, including the passage of a new city charter. Major fiscal malfeasance was indicated, and one official committed suicide. The machine had produced labyrinthine city and county governments in need of rationalization and consolidation. This issue appealed strongly to "public-regarding" groups. At the same time, changes in government (such as civil service rules) opened employment to groups, especially Blacks, which had not gained major rewards from the old system.

Fifth, Democratic party personnel were then able to fashion a new political organization through defection of Republican workers and the mobilization of new workers, increasingly recruited from Philadelphia's growing Black population. By 1960, under the leadership of Congressman William Green, the Democrats had built a powerful apparatus. By gaining control of state government in the 1950's, the party gained a major patronage base in the Philadelphia area.

Sixth, in part because of internal conflicts, some generated by friction between reformers and organization supporters, the Democratic juggernaut faltered at the height of its success. Chairman Green clashed with Dilworth on a number of occasions, notably over the latter's ambitions to be Governor. Dilworth resigned to run, unsuccessfully, for this office in 1962. Thus, the state patronage base was lost. He was succeeded by James H. J. Tate, a ward chairman and city council president who was Philadelphia's first Catholic mayor. In his race for reelection, his plurality dipped well below previous Democratic margins.

Seventh, the Republican party gained new life in subsequent years. Arlen Specter, a former Democrat and member of ADA, was elected district attorney in 1965, nearly defeated Tate in 1967 for the mayoralty, and was reelected in 1969 by approximately a three-to-two margin. In these achievements he drew support from many reform-oriented former supporters of Clark and Dilworth. After Chairman Green's death, the new Democratic chairman, Francis Smith, and some others, sought to oust Tate in the 1967 primary. Their candidate was Alexander Hemphill, city controller. Although not close to Clark and Dilworth, Hemphill was also an individual of upper socioeconomic and ethnic status and had been a long-term member of the reform administration. Mayor Tate was backed by many ward chairmen and by organized labor, while Hemphill was supported by ward chairmen following Smith and by some reform-oriented individuals hostile to Tate. Both candidates sought to gain the image of the "reformer" while branding the other as the tool of "bossism."

DESIGN OF THIS STUDY

As Democratic pluralities declined, dependence on Black votes became more and more important to the party. Blacks also became a potentially important force in internal struggles. While the more "public-regarding" may have led the way, all white groups showed some tendency to abandon the Democrats. This study is focused on this developing pattern and its antecedents in earlier trends. The years considered were turbulent, with shifting patterns observable for all groups involved. The main object of analysis is the interplay of electoral support for the old machine and the new, and for parties and political figures. The behavior of largely Black wards is examined, in comparison with largely white wards in general and with white wards classified by the hypothesized contiuum of "public-" and "private-regardingness." The time period is a relatively extended one: 1943-1969. Table 6-1 presents a chronology of major events in the years studied. The era can be subdivided into four units for closer analysis: (1) the end of Republican organization control, (2) the accession to power of a Democratic-reform coalition, (3) the consolidation of Democratic control, and (4) declining Democratic strength.

The largely Black wards selected for the study are identified in Table 6-2. Wards with Black population exceeding 50 percent of ward totals were selected for 1940, 1950, and 1960. In each decade, elections up

TABLE 6-1
Major Political Events: Philadelphia, 1943-1969

I. End of Republican organization control	1. 1943, mayor's election 2. 1947, mayor's election
II. Democratic reform era	1. 1949, "row office" election 2. 1951, passage of city charter 3. 1951, mayor's election 4. 1953, "row office" election
III. Consolidation of Democratic control	1. 1955, mayor's election 2. 1956, attempted charter revision 3. 1959, mayor's election

IV. Democratic decline	1. 1961, "row office" election
	2. 1963, mayor's election
	   a. primary
	   b. general
	3. 1965, "row office" election
	4. 1967 mayor's election
	   a. primary
	   b. general
	5. 1969, "row office" election
	6. 1969, school loan authorizations

to and including the midpoint year (1945, 1955, 1965) are analyzed using wards as grouped for the preceding census. For the first two decades, elections after the midpoint year are analyzed using wards as grouped for the following census; for the decade of the sixties only 1960 data are used for grouping.[13]

Wards were also classified by their socioeconomic status, using Shevsky and Bell's index of "social rank" for this purpose.[14] For largely white wards, the five highest in rank, the five nearest the midpoint, and

TABLE 6-2
Wards Classified as "Black," for Census Decades and after 1966

YEAR	WARD NUMBERS
1940	30, 47
1950	13, 14, 20, 24, 30, 32, 44, 47
1960	4, 13, 14, 20, 24, 28, 29, 30, 32, 36, 37, 38, 44, 46, 47, 52, 60
1966	3, 4, 6, 11, 14, 16, 20, 24, 28, 29, 30, 32, 36, 37, 38, 44, 46, 47, 52, 60

the five lowest were identified. Largely Black wards were grouped into highest, middle and lowest thirds on this dimension. For some purposes, largely white wards were also classified according to dominant ethnic group.[15]

The election data analyzed cover twelve general elections for mayor or major "row office," two special elections for adoption or revision of the charter, two recent primary elections and two recent school loan authorizations, one of which failed and one of which passed. Where appropriate, tabulations are given for shifts in support patterns from previous elections as well as for strength of support at given points in time.

Certain guiding questions should be kept in mind. As "white" politics have developed around the themes of "reform" and "machine" and the ebb and flow of party strength, how have largely Black wards responded? How full is their commitment to the Democratic party? How did these wards behave toward reform politicians and the issues of government reorganization and patronage? What role did they play in reform-machine struggles within the party? At what points do Black trends converge with those of "public-regarding" white status and ethnic groups, and at what points with the "private-regarding"? Are Black ward patterns homogeneous, or is there differentiation based on status? What do Black trends, in relation to the trends of other groups, portend for future developments in party politics and reform efforts?

Findings

THE END OF REPUBLICAN CONTROL

Table 6-3 presents data for this period. In the first contest examined, the 1943 victory of Republican mayor Bernard Samuel over Democrat William Bullitt, largely Black wards scarcely diverge from white in their pattern. This may obscure more than it shows, however, for the largely white wards have an interesting differentiation by status. Bullitt received least support in upper- and lower-status wards, where he ran 10.9 and 14.8 percentage points, respectively, behind his city-wide showing. Like the Black wards, *both* the presumably "private-regarding"

TABLE 6-3

Percentage Democratic, and Percentage Point Change Over
Previous Election for All Wards, and Wards Classified by
Socioeconomic Status, Race and Dominant Ethnic Group, 1943-1947

	PERCENTAGE DEMOCRAT OR CHANGE		
UNITS	MAYOR 1943	MAYOR 1947	CHANGE 1943-1947
All wards	45.1	43.7	−1.4
Largely Black wards	44.6	37.0	−7.6
Highest third, SES	a	36.7	a
Middle third, SES	a	39.5	a
Lowest third, SES	a	22.7	a
Largely white wards	45.0	47.0	+2.0
Highest five, SES[b]	34.2	37.1	+2.9
Middle five, SES[b]	48.6	46.5	−2.1
Lowest five, SES[b]	30.3	24.5	−5.8
"Italian" wards	40.2	34.6	−5.6
"Jewish" wards	44.3	46.9	+2.6

[a]*The small number of wards with Black populations over 50 percent in 1940 does not permit control for SES.*

[b]*Data for "white" wards, controlled by SES, is based on a sample of extreme cases for each third. Their average does not equal the overall "white" figure.*

Italian wards and the supposedly "public-regarding" Jewish wards voted slightly more Republican than the city as a whole, but less strongly so than either highest- or lowest-status white wards in general. The classic Republican machine pattern, yoking conventionally Republican upper-status voters with machine-dependent supporters from the lower class, is evident. It may be noted that the Black pattern, and the Italian and Jewish, more closely approximate that of middle-status whites in general than that of either status extreme. Such groups' interests may not have been so well served as those of the machine's disparate supporters.

By 1947, some shifts are evident. Richardson Dilworth raised a reform banner in a colorful street-corner campaign for the Democrats, stressing corruption and bossism. Yet the party lost ground slightly citywide. In largely Black wards, the loss was greater, as it was in Italian wards. Among white wards, the Democrats gained ground only among the five wards highest in socioeconomic status. Jewish wards also shifted toward the Democrats. While an aggressive, antimachine campaign made inroads into "public-regarding" wards, losses in others neutralized the advantage. Black wards shifted in the direction of machine support, and more strongly than middle- or low-status white wards. However, examining *relative* shift, considering the potential of a ward to shift in a given direction,[16] Black wards shifted only 1.7 units, less than low-status white wards (with 2.6 units) but more than middle-status white wards (with .4 units). Thus, Blacks supported the machine *less* than "private-regarding" status groups, but *more* than the "public-regarding." It may be that Blacks had less to lose than low status white wards, if the machine was giving greater benefit to the latter. In this election, Black wards gave more support to the machine than did white wards in general (63.0 percent vs. 53.0 percent).

The Democratic Reform Era

In 1949, Democrats, with both Clark and Dilworth running, captured two "row offices" after dramatic revelations of scandal which seemed to touch the entire Republican apparatus. In all wards, the shift to the Democrats was heavy, with a great deal of residual machine strength also shown. (See Table 6-4.)

Using Clark's race for controller for the analysis, the Democrats increased their city-wide vote by 13.1 percentage points. Largely Black wards produced exactly the same gain for the party, but registered a bare majority for them. In largely white wards, over 60 percent of the vote went to Clark. Thus, while Blacks shifted from machine support at the same rate as whites, Black wards gave the machine more votes (49.9 percent vs. 39.8 percent).

While all largely white wards moved toward the Democrats, an immense shift is found among the five highest in socioeconomic status; the least gain is found among the lowest. In *relative* terms, the highest five shifted 37.0 units, the middle five, 20.0, and the lowest, only 15.6. The polarization of wards grouped by socioeconomic status is very clear in this election. Middle- and upper-status wards voted approximately two

TABLE 6-4

*Percentage Democratic, Percentage Point Changes
from Previous Two Elections, and Percentage for
City Charter for All Wards and for Wards Classified by
Socioeconomic Status, Race and Dominant Ethnic Group, 1949-1953*

UNITS	PERCENTAGE DEMOCRAT, CHANGES, AND PERCENTAGE PROCHARTER				
	CON-TROL-LER 1949	CHANGE 1947-1949	CHANGE 1943-1949	CHARTER 1951	MAYOR 1951
All wards	56.8	+13.1	−11.7	65.0	58.0
Largely Black wards	50.1	+13.1	+5.5	50.6	54.2
Highest third, SES	52.7	+16.0	−	49.3	59.0
Middle third, SES	54.5	+15.0	−	53.0	61.0
Lowest third, SES	31.3	+8.6	−	28.7	35.3
Largely white wards	60.2	+13.2	+15.2	72.2	59.8
Highest five, SES	60.4	+23.3	+26.2	69.2	58.6
Middle five, SES	57.2	+10.7	+8.6	62.8	59.2
Lowest five, SES	36.3	+11.8	+6.0	34.0	42.7
"Italian" wards	51.7	+17.1	+11.5	40.6	53.6
"Jewish" wards	60.5	+13.6	+16.2	73.1	62.1

UNITS	CHANGE 1949-1951	CHANGE 1947-1951	CON-TROL-LER, 1953	CHANGE 1951-1953	CHANGE 1949-1953
All wards	+1.2	+14.3	48.7	−9.3	−8.1
Largely Black wards	+4.1	+17.2	50.7	−3.5	+0.6
Highest third, SES	+6.3	+22.3	51.2	−7.8	−1.5
Middle third, SES	+6.5	+21.5	55.8	−5.2	+1.3
Lowest third, SES	+4.0	+12.6	44.0	+8.7	+12.7
Largely white wards	−0.4	+12.8	47.7	−12.1	−12.5
Highest five, SES	−1.8	+21.5	47.1	−11.5	−13.3
Middle five, SES	+2.0	+12.7	51.2	−8.0	−6.0
Lowest five, SES	+6.4	+18.2	43.0	+0.3	+6.7
"Italian" wards	+1.9	+13.4	47.9	−5.7	−3.8
"Jewish" wards	+1.6	+17.8	49.8	−12.3	−10.7

to one for the Democrats, while lower-status wards gave nearly the same margin to the Republicans. The pattern of Black wards is more Democratic, and shifting more in that direction, than that of the lowest socioeconomic status white wards, but less Democratic, and less shifting, than the more "public-regarding" wards. Controlling for socioeconomic status among largely Black wards, it is among the lowest third that support for the Republicans remains high. Lowest-status Black wards showed even less tendency than lowest-status white wards to shift to the Democrats. On the whole, Black wards lagged somewhat behind white in their support of the Democrats and reform in 1949. Both Italian and Jewish wards swung to the Democrats, slightly more heavily than Black wards.

The Democratic-reform coalition won in the first instance as a result of massive defection of "public-regarding" upper-status white voters from the Republicans, and, while even the lowest-status wards shifted toward them, Democrats failed to win the latter. Republican strength collapsed at this point chiefly because of the reform-oriented behavior of upper-status wards, and considerable strength was retained in the organized wards. In largely Black wards, and other ethnic wards, on the other hand, the machine lost ground, somewhat less than in the highest socioeconomic status wards and somewhat more than in the lowest.

In 1951, a new city charter was passed, with a great deal of support from reform-oriented groups. The pattern of the special election held for this purpose is of major interest, for the "issues" of reform were here separated from personalities and party labels. Both the entrenched Republican organization and the emerging Democratic one stood to lose somewhat from proposed reorganization of city and county offices, although clearly the Republicans would lose most.

The charter received great approval city-wide. The same general pattern observed in 1949 obtained, with greatest support from the largely white wards high in socioeconomic status and least from the low. Largely Black wards barely approved the charter, and the lowest-status Black wards trailed all others in voting for it. The "private-regarding" Italian wards rejected the charter, while the "public-regarding" Jews favored it overwhelmingly. In a more or less "straight fight" on the issues of reform, largely Black wards occupied a position almost squarely in the middle between "public-" and "private-regarding" voting groups.

Democrats took control of city hall with Clark's election as mayor in the fall of 1951. While they improved their city-wide vote total, and gained among largely Black and low-status white wards, they slipped somewhat among the highest-status white wards, in spite of the patrician image of their candidate. Perhaps the cause of reform seemed well enough served by passing a charter and turning out minor officials, without placing the city fully in the stewardship of the Democratic party. Democratic gains were greatest among low-status largely white wards and middle-status Black wards. Both Italian and Jewish wards moved slightly toward the party. Some decay in machine strength is probably evident. Largely Black wards, on the whole, shifted toward the Democrats more strongly than white wards, with the exception of lowest-status wards.

In 1953, the Democrats suffered a setback by losing the "row office" contests. While they slipped by some 9 percentage points overall, they lost only 3.5 points among Blacks and 12.1 among whites. Among largely white wards, they maintained their 1951 strength with the low-est-status group, but lost in middle- and, particularly, in upper-status wards. While Italian and Jewish wards both switched to the Republicans, the decline was much greater in the Jewish wards. The Republican victory was produced, then, not by a reassertion of strength in former organization areas, but by a return to the fold of "public-regarding" supporters of reform. Largely Black wards again occupy an intermediate position, switching to the Republicans less than the "public-regarding" groups, but more than the former extreme machine supporters.

THE CONSOLIDATION OF DEMOCRATIC CONTROL

The returns for 1955 told a different story. (See Table 6-5.) Dilworth was elected mayor in a showing of increased Democratic strength among all groups, regaining most support lost among the "public-regarding" in 1953. In largely white wards, however, he did not match Clark's showing. Only in low socioeconomic wards did he make a substantial gain relative to Clark. Dilworth gained almost twice as much in largely Black wards as in the largely white, with the most substantial increase at the lowest socioeconomic status level. He gained less in Italian wards, and lost ground, relative to Clark, among Jewish wards. Dilworth's appeal was therefore unusual in that it rallied the "public-regarding" reform elements while simultaneously consolidating inroads into low socioeconomic status groups, formerly allied to the Republican machine. Largely

Charles A. Ekstrom

TABLE 6-5

*Percentage Democratic, Percentage Point Changes from Previous
Two Elections, and Percentage for Charter Revision for
All Wards and for Wards Classified by Socioeconomic
Status, Race, and Dominant Ethnic Group, 1955-1959*

	PERCENTAGE DEMOCRAT, CHANGES, AND PERCENTAGE FOR CHARTER REVISION					
UNITS	MAYOR 1955	CHANGE 1953-1955	CHANGE 1951-1955	CHAR-TER REVI-SION 1956	MAYOR 1959	CHANGE 1955-1959
All wards	59.3	+10.6	+1.3	37.6	65.6	+6.3
Largely Black wards	66.1	+15.4	+11.9	50.7	74.2	+8.1
Highest third, SES	64.8	+13.6	+5.8	51.0	71.6	+6.8
Middle third, SES	71.7	+15.9	+10.7	51.5	77.0	+5.3
Lowest third, SES	62.4	+18.4	+27.1	43.3	73.4	+11.0
Largely white wards	55.9	+8.2	−3.9	31.1	61.3	+5.4
Highest five, SES	57.5	+10.4	−1.1	31.2	68.4	+10.9
Middle five, SES	59.4	+8.2	+0.2	42.2	63.0	+3.6
Lowest five, SES	54.2	+11.2	+11.5	68.4	64.4	+10.2
"Italian" wards	59.7	+11.8	+6.1	62.0	64.4	+4.7
"Jewish" wards	59.6	+9.8	−2.5	37.2	67.1	+7.5

Black wards, for the first time, shifted heavily to the Democrats, becoming considerably more pro-Democratic than the predominantly white wards. The development paralleled, and even excelled, trends in white low-status wards. This may be evidence of the growth of Democratic party organization, including Blacks in reasonable proportions for the first time.

That this may be the case is supported, to some extent, by results of an effort to amend the city charter, voted on in April, 1956. Three amendments were backed by the Democratic party, and by Mayor Dilworth. The more consequential amendments, which dealt with removing some jobs from Civil Service for party patronage were ruled unlawful by the State Supreme Court shortly before the election. One amendment, permitting an office-holder to retain his post while running for another, remained on the ballot. All three, however, had been bitterly opposed by reform elements, who referred to them as "charter ripper" amendments. While the amendment received low support city-wide, it was approved by largely Black wards, by white wards lowest in socioeconomic status and by Italian wards. A clearer profile of groups said to be "private-regarding" might be difficult to find. It should be noted, however, that the largely Black wards were *less* strongly in favor of revision than the other two named. It is hard to assess whether this shows greater reform appeal to Blacks, less material reward offered by the machine at this point, or some combination. Objectively, however, Black wards once again occupied an intermediate point between reformers and machine supporters.

In 1959, Dilworth carried the city in a virtual landslide, gaining particularly in the largely Black wards, but also improving his showing among the largely white. He gained ground among the highest socioeconomic status white wards, but especially among the low-status white and Black wards. The election marked a zenith for Democratic candidates, and in the strength of the organization, which drew roughly the same high level of support from *all* socioeconomic and ethnic groups, reformers, and machine affiliates alike. Black wards, while a significant part of the Democratic majority, were not critical to it and simply followed a general trend, though more strongly than some other groups.

DEMOCRATIC DECLINE

In 1961, following two years in which internal Democratic dissension grew (including a semi-public abrasion between Dilworth and Controller Hemphill over a transit construction scandal), Democratic candidates slipped generally in their appeal at the polls. (See Table 6-6.) Hemphill, for example, was reelected by a margin down 7.9 points from Dilworth's. While the decline was general, it was greatest in the upper-socioeconomic largely white wards, and was negligible in both white and Black wards of low status. While the decline was less marked in Black wards in general, it was high in Black wards of highest socioeconomic status.

The 1961 election is significant for three reasons: (1) it was a significant dip from the Democrats' high-water mark two years earlier, (2) the socioeconomic profile of Democratic support began to resemble that of other big city Democratic parties, and (3) support for the party in largely white wards dropped near the break-even point, with the winning margin filled out in largely Black wards.

TABLE 6-6

Percentage Democratic, Percentage Point Changes from Previous Two Elections, Percentage for "Insurgent" Primary Candidates, Percentage Point Change in "Insurgent" Support, School Loan Authorizations, and Changes in School Loan Vote, 1961-1969

	PERCENTAGE DEMOCRAT, CHANGES, PERCENTAGE "INSURGENT," CHANGES IN "INSURGENT" SUPPORT, SCHOOL LOAN AUTHORIZATIONS, AND CHANGES IN SCHOOL LOAN VOTE					
UNITS	CONTROLLER, 1961	CHANGE 1959-1961	PRIMARY 1963	MAYOR 1963	CHANGE 1961-1963	CHANGE 1959-1963
All wards	57.7	−7.9	24.2	54.7	−3.0	−10.9
Largely Black wards	69.1	−5.1	14.7	73.5	+4.4	−0.7
Highest third, SES	63.2	−8.4	22.4	67.2	+4.0	−4.4
Middle third, SES	74.7	−2.3	15.0	78.7	+4.0	+1.7
Lowest third, SES	73.0	−0.4	7.0	73.6	+0.6	+0.2
Largely white wards	52.0	−9.3	28.9	45.3	−6.7	−16.0
Highest five, SES	52.2	−16.2	43.8	49.2	−3.0	−19.2
Middle five, SES	52.2	−10.8	19.6	51.4	−0.8	−11.6
Lowest five, SES	65.0	+0.6	5.4	54.8	−10.2	−9.6
"Italian" wards	55.2	−9.2	10.2	53.3	−1.9	−11.1
"Jewish" wards	59.0	−8.1	22.8	54.9	−4.1	−12.2

UNITS	DISTRICT ATTORNEY, 1965	CHANGE 1963-1965	CHANGE 1961-1965	PRIMARY 1967	CHANGE 1961-1965
All wards	47.0	−7.7	−10.7	34.4	+10.2
Largely Black wards	68.7	−4.8	−0.4	36.2	+21.5
Highest third, SES	60.2	−7.0	−3.0	38.2	+15.8
Middle third, SES	76.7	−2.0	+2.0	39.2	+24.2
Lowest third, SES	70.2	−3.4	−2.8	34.7	+27.7
Largely white wards	36.8	−8.5	−15.2	33.5	+4.6
Highest five, SES	34.8	−14.4	−17.4	34.0	−9.8
Middle five, SES	47.6	−3.8	−4.6	26.3	+6.7
Lowest five, SES	50.0	−4.8	−15.0	[a]	−
"Italian" wards	50.1	−3.2	−5.1	25.4	+15.2
"Jewish" wards	47.0	−7.9	−12.0	41.8	+19.0

TABLE 6-6 *(Continued)*

UNITS	MAYOR 1967	CHANGE 1965-1967	CHANGE 1963-1967	DISTRICT ATTORNEY, 1969	CHANGE 1967-1969	CHANGE 1965-1969
All wards	50.7	+3.7	−4.0	41.4	−9.3	−5.6
Largely Black wards	66.2	−2.5	−7.3	62.2	−4.0	−6.5
Highest third, SES	63.1	+2.9	−4.1	59.9	−3.2	−0.3
Middle third, SES	70.5	−6.2	−8.2	67.4	−3.1	−9.3
Lowest third, SES	72.3	+2.1	−1.3	67.0	−5.3	−3.2
Largely white wards	43.0	+6.2	−2.3	31.0	−12.0	−5.8
Highest five, SES	40.5	+5.7	−8.7	36.0	−4.5	+1.2
Middle five, SES	57.0	+9.4	+5.6	43.9	−13.1	−3.7
Lowest five, SES	−	−	−	−	−	−
"Italian" wards	54.7	+4.6	+1.4	44.1	−10.6	−6.0
"Jewish" wards	42.6	−4.4	−12.3	33.4	−9.2	−13.6

UNITS	SCHOOL LOAN MAY 1969	SCHOOL LOAN NOVEMBER 1969	CHANGE MAY-NOVEMBER
All wards	44.1	56.9	−12.8
Largely Black wards	76.1	86.8	+10.7
Highest third, SES	73.0	83.1	+10.1
Middle third, SES	79.5	90.2	+10.7
Lowest third, SES	76.3	87.3	+11.0
Largely white wards	29.6	43.3	+13.7
Highest five, SES	58.5	73.5	+15.0
Middle five, SES	30.1	49.6	+19.5
Lowest five, SES	−	−	−
"Italian" wards	36.6	54.1	+17.5
"Jewish" wards	48.4	62.0	+13.6

[a]*After the changes in wards of 1966, it becomes impossible to isolate the former 5 lowest in SES. They were combined with middle and upper status to form larger units.*

In 1963, a reform-machine battle took shape in the Democratic primary as Walter Phillips, supported by the ADA and other independent groups, challenged Mayor Tate. Phillips did not do well, though he received twice as much support from largely white wards as from largely Black. Support of his candidacy was almost entirely confined to the "public-regarding." It is worth noting that socioeconomic status is closely associated with the strength of Phillips' showing, for *Black* as well as white wards. He gained *least* support in the lowest-status white wards, where party control was evidently strongest.

In the general election of 1963, support for the Democrats dropped precipitously from their 1959 showing. Among largely Black wards this was not the case. Whatever tendency Blacks showed in the primary to resist the organization was dissipated in the general election. Largely white wards, on the other hand, edged away from the party, with wards high in socioeconomic status leading the way. Democrats lost the white vote in the city, and became dependent on Black pluralities for victory. Low-status white wards, which failed to support the reformer in the primary, expressed their dissatisfaction through a move to the Republicans in the fall. The commitment of Blacks to the Democratic party stood in direct contrast to Republican trends among upper socioeconomic status groups and, to a lesser extent, among lower-class wards. The "private-regarding" interests of the latter may have diverged from those of the largely Black wards in the early years of the racially explosive 1960's.

In 1965, Republican Arlen Specter was elected district attorney. Largely Black wards resisted the trend to some degree, giving Democrats some two-thirds of the vote, while largely white wards gave them approximately one-third. In *relative* terms, the Democratic decline in Black wards registered 6.4 units, in white wards, 19.0 units. The massive desertion of the Democrats, under Mayor Tate, by high-status wards continued. The Republicans, in their victory, had gathered the lion's share of the former reform vote. A decline in Black wards, at a much lower rate, was also evident, and the vote in these wards was no longer sufficient to prevent Republican victory. Blacks shifted, as a group, at about the same rate as low-status white wards and Italian wards.

In 1967, a serious challenge was mounted to Mayor Tate's leadership, drawing support from reform elements as well as from those in the organization who, like Chairman Smith, were dissatisfied with the mayor's performance and vote-getting ability. The Hemphill campaign was badly underfinanced and did poorly, although the candidate got about one-third of the vote. Largely Black wards supported him slightly more strongly than largely white wards. The Black pro-Hemphill vote appears to be a function of his support by organization workers allied to Smith. Evidence for this includes the fact that, for Blacks, there was little relationship between socioeconomic status and direction of vote. In Black wards, either Tate or Hemphill tended to carry a given ward by a pronounced margin. For example, Hemphill carried the Fourteenth Ward by 64 percent, while losing the adjacent Fifteenth with 24 percent, and the Forty-seventh Ward with 61 percent, while losing the adjacent Twenty-ninth with 29 percent. This pattern tends to indicate the influence of the particular ward leader, backed by his source of finances on election day. However, it is worth noting that, in this instance, largely Black wards did not line up monolithically as voters. It is unclear whether this phenomenon was a function of dissension within the machine, or a result of some independence by Black political leaders. Although Hemphill tended to gain support from "public-regarding" groups, his support was less marked than that given Phillips in 1963. On the other hand, Hemphill gained greater support than Phillips among "private-regarding" status and ethnic groups.

In the general election of 1967, Mayor Tate and the Democratic party barely survived. While some groups returned to the Democrats, relative to 1965, most groups drifted further away than in 1963. The slump was most pronounced among "public-regarding" status and ethnic groups and among *Black* voters. While whites, in general, swung back from 1965, Blacks retreated a little further. The trend data, however, should not obscure the fact that Black voters spelled the difference between defeat and victory for Mayor Tate and the Democrats. "Private-regarding" Italian wards moved slightly toward the Democrats, while "public-regarding" Jews moved strongly toward the Republicans. While largely Black wards did *not* follow "private-regarding" groups toward the organization, they provided it with the keystone of its victory.

The election of 1969 was a new low point for Democratic strength. All groups shifted away from them, especially the largely white wards. Their shift was partly the negation of the 1967 Democratic resurgence in these wards. The longer term 1965-1969 trend shows roughly the same degree of shift for wards classified by race. Largely Black wards continued to provide the party large pluralities, but the cumulative evidence of the last half of the decade indicates a steady backing away from their former overwhelming devotion. While largely white wards fled the party more conspicuously at some points, they also fluctuated and showed some tendency to return. Although Democrats remain in power in Philadelphia, the long-term prognosis appears bad among both racial categories. If Black trends away continue and whites rally no more strongly than in 1969, the party should experience a defeat in 1971. A change in style, either to reassert a reform appeal or to address the growing fear of the population for its safety, might alter the situation.

At least on some issues, there remains the possibility of racial polarization in politics. Evidence for this can be observed in the 1969 votes to authorize school loans. One measure was defeated in the May primary, although a much scaled-down proposal passed in November. Less than one-third of voters in largely white wards voted for the first loan, and only some 40 percent for the second. While all wards were more likely to vote for schools in November, the margin of improvement was nearly as great in largely Black wards which were already heavily committed in May.[17] In *relative* terms, the Black shift measured 44.8 units, more than twice as much as the white 19.5 units. The Black margin in November was nearly nine to one.

The school population of Philadelphia is made up disproportionately of Black children. High Black fertility and a median age well below that of whites contribute to this phenomenon, as do Philadelphia's well-developed parochial school system and many private schools. Some urban problems, especially connected to gangs, are most visible in the schools. Efforts to shore up the educational complex could be perceived as primarily for the benefit of Black children.

Among largely white wards, only those with highest socioeconomic status consistently supported the loans, and these with a rate well below Black support levels. The *relative* shift of upper-status whites toward the second measure was higher than that of middle-status whites (36.1 units versus 27.9). The "public-regarding" Jewish wards rejected the first loan, though shifting to the second. Italian wards also voted "no" first and then switched to "yes." In *relative* terms, the Italian shift was slightly greater (27.6 versus 26.4). Both sets of ethnic wards supported each loan more fully than did whites in general. Community dissent in supporting schools appears to have been more racial and socioeconomic than ethnic. Various community leaders and groups rallied to the school system for the second vote. Their effect appears to have been greatest on the "public-regarding" status groups and least on those low in socio-economic status. Although data are missing for the lowest-status white wards, it seems a reasonable inference that their general support, and their propensity to shift, were lowest of all.

As policy and fiscal issues voted on directly by the electorate, rela-tively divorced from other political considerations, the loans are of great interest. Several observations can be made about the response of groups to them. First, a general resistance to municipal effort and ex-penditure, heightened among low socioeconomic status to municipal effort and expenditure, heightened among low socioeconomic status whites, is evident. Second, this policy trend collides with the felt needs of the Black community and polarization, primarily racial but also socioeconomic, occurs. Third, with their children's interests at stake, the black electorate rallied strongly to defend the schools, especially after the threat of the first loss. The Black profile for the two elections differs markedly from any white group, especially in the overwhelming support given the second measure. Fourth, "public-regarding" groups also rallied, though much less emphatically than Blacks. A convergence of their support with Black strength was necessary to carry the day for the schools.

It is difficult to relate trends found in this direct election to trends complicated by party and personality. Yet certain conjunctions should be noted. Black voters acted purposively in their own interest in this election. They had help, to some extent, from those status groups which have been long-standing supporters of reform. They were opposed, chiefly, by low-status white groups which have supported machine poli-tics. Whether such events may accelerate a Black trend away from the machine and its supporters remains to be seen in future developments.

Conclusions and Interpretations

In the years examined, Philadelphia passed from support of an en-trenched Republican machine through a reform era to the establishment of a Democratic machine and beyond toward its decline and potential dissolution. Richardson Dilworth, especially, brought together a maximum voting coalition of reformers and organization Democrats, whites and Blacks. The Democratic party has been declining for a decade from this high point of organizational achievement, yet has retained control, recently by a narrow margin. Reformers have long since abandoned the party, and all groups have done so to some extent.

This study's primary interest has been in the response of largely Black wards to this situation, especially in relation to the response of other groups, including "public-" and "private-regarding" categories. The most salient conclusions follow:

1. Black wards have shown some commitment to both Republican and Democratic machines, and have lagged somewhat in following reform-oriented white wards away from them, but, across elections, Black wards have responded to antimachine appeals and do not appear as simple tools of a white organization *per se.*

2. While Black wards have saved Democrats recently from defeat, trend data show that their vote has become progressively less monolithically committed to the party. Like other groups, they have left the Democrats as they declined in support and effectiveness, although they have been somewhat more likely than whites to express disapproval in primaries, rather than general elections.

3. Black wards have *consistently* tended to take a position intermediate between "public-" and "private-regarding" white voting groups in most elections studied. This was true for issue elections, such as charter adoption and revision, as well as for candidate and party contests. That is, their behavior may be interpreted as partly influenced by the appeal of each extreme white tendency, and some degree of Black independence may be inferred.

4. Black wards cannot be counted on as passive supporters for the machine. In primaries, for example, they (a) provided more support than low-status white wards for the reformer in 1963, and (b) gave more support than white wards in general to the insurgent in 1965. While the latter pattern reflects confusion in the "white" organization as well as Black independence, both indicate some weakness in the system and in Black commitment to it.

105

5. Within the Black community, socioeconomic status has been associated with differential reform-machine appeal in much the same pattern evident among whites. This differentiation argues against assertions that Blacks respond to issues entirely as a bloc, or that middle-class Blacks lag behind middle-class whites in providing political initiatives for their community.

6. Earlier observations of Democratic hegemony over Black wards, and of a lack of Black independence and effectiveness, may need to be tempered. The present situation is fluid, and Blacks cannot be pigeonholed as permanent Democratic vassals. Black commitment to the party peaked in 1959, although Blacks appeared out on a limb with the collapse of white support in 1963. The Republican party has recently had greater appeal for "public-regarding" whites, but all groups, including Blacks and low-status whites, have drifted toward them. Blacks have not yet supported them in great numbers. Future alliances, however, may be open and negotiable. The vital question is posed by asking which of three groups—upper-status whites, lower-status whites, and Blacks—may join together in supporting a future winning party.

As their numbers increase, Blacks should become a more potent political force, articulating their own interests and shaping, instead of responding to, events in the city. Their needs will place a greater demand on the goods and resources available for consumption by the public. Creaking, underfinanced urban institutions will experience a crisis in public support. Some harbingers were evidenced in the school loan campaigns. Here Blacks' interest coalesced, to some extent, with those of the old supporters of reform and rational effort in city government. Low-status whites appeared to back away from the costs of a program needed for Black advancement. It may be that this configuration will continue, with low-status whites and Blacks polarized over the costs of urban programs.

The traditional concerns of "public-regarding" whites have provided the framework for efforts to reform and reorganize America's cities for some years. As Black populations become urban majorities, such concerns must recede before those felt by Blacks themselves. The relevance of the "public-private regarding" continuum may diminish as Black numbers and leadership gain the initiative and seek to use urban politics as the vehicle for redressing historic grievances and inequities. The distinctions between public and private goods and the rights and duties they imply for the citizen of the modern city may also decay in an era where welfare services become essential and public education becomes the indispensable key to the economic order.

"Public-regarding" whites may be forced to distinguish in their earlier attitudes those elements which supported the abstract public good from those which defended private interests from the machine and its low-status clients. The initial appeal of reform to the "public-regarding" white electorate stressed that *both* greater efficiency (with lower cost) and greater effectiveness were possible in local government. Alignments of the future may turn on which of these themes is more salient. Unless massive federal or state aid is forthcoming, the needs of urban populations will demand greater local organizational and financial commitment in the years to come. Whether the "public-regarding" will make this commitment to greater effectiveness, and greater cost, remains an open question.

NOTES

1. This point of view is expressed, for example, by Jeffrey K. Hadden *et al.*, in *Metropolis in Crisis* (Itasca, Ill.: F. E. Peacock Publishers, Inc., 1967).

2. See John Hadley Strange, "The Negro and Philadelphia Politics," in Edward Banfield, ed., *Urban Government* (Glencoe, Ill.: The Free Press of Glencoe, 1969), pp. 408-421.

3. *E.g.,* James Q. Wilson, *Negro Politics: The Search for Leadership* (Glencoe, Ill.: Free Press, 1960), and Edward C. Banfield and James Q. Wilson, *City Politics* (Cambridge: Harvard and M.I.T. Press, 1963).

4. Wilson and Banfield, "Public-Regardingness as a Value Premise in Voting Behavior," *American Political Science Review,* 58 (December, 1964), 876-886.

5. Compare "public-" and "private-regardingness" with the various "role of government" conceptions cited by Oliver P. Williams and Charles R. Adrian in *Four Cities: A Study in Comparative Decision-Making* (Philadelphia: University of Pennsylvania Press, 1963).

6. Charles A. Ekstrom, "Community Social Structure and Issue Differentiation: A Study in the Political Sociology of Welfare," *Sociological Focus,* 1 (Spring, 1968), 1-16.

7. Wilson, *Negro Politics,* and Banfield and Wilson, "Public-Regardingness . . . ."

8. *Ibid.*

9. Strange, "Negro and Philadelphia Politics."

10. *Ibid.*

11. Useful descriptions of the first part of the era covered include: James Reichley, *The Art of Government: Reform and Organization Politics in Philadelphia* (New York: Fund for the Republic, 1959), and Joe Alex Morris, *The Richardson Dilworth Story: Candidate for Greatness* (Philadelphia: Mercury Books, 1962).

12. The historical roots of this pattern are shown by Philip S. Benjamin in "Gentlemen Reformers in the Quaker City, 1870-1912," *Political Science Quarterly,* 85 (March, 1970), 61-79.

13. It should be recognized that the unit of analysis is the ward, not the individual voter. No "ecological fallacy" is involved; rather, it is assumed that aggregate ward characteristics produce organizational effects not predictable solely from a knowledge of residents' individual characteristics. See W. S. Robinson, "Ecological Correlations and the Behavior of Individuals," *American Sociological Review,* 15 (June, 1950), 351-357. See also Herbert Menzel, "Comment," *American Sociological Review,* 15 (October, 1950), 674.

As shown in Table 6-2, a different array of wards is used for the years after 1967. Radical changes in the city's ward structure were made in 1966, adding six wards and changing the number, size, and boundaries of most wards. New wards were matched with old by an overlay technique. For largely Black wards, a reasonable fit was achieved.

14. The index of "social rank" is based on occupational and educational data for a given population. It is a standardized index, using the proportion of a group holding "blue-collar" jobs and having less than an eighth grade education. Computational procedures may be found in Eshref Shevky and Wendell Bell, *Social Area Analysis* (Palo Alto: Stanford University Press, 1955), pp. 54-57.

15. All data, except election statistics, were obtained from the U.S. Bureau of the Census, *U.S. Census of Population and Housing: Census Tracts* (Washington, D.C.: U.S. Government Printing Office, 1940, 1950, 1960). Election statistics were obtained from *The Bulletin Almanac and Year Book* (Philadelphia: *The Evening Bulletin,* 1944-1970). In Philadelphia census tract boundaries are based on ward boundaries.

The dominant ethnic groups identified were "Italian" and "Jewish." The latter was found using percentages born in Russia as a surrogate, since religious data are not available.

16. This figure is obtained by dividing actual by potential percentage point shift in a given direction (if a group shifted to 100 percent support in a given election).

17. It is difficult to separate the roles of actual change of votes from differential turnout in producing these results.

7

BLACKS AND PHILADELPHIA POLITICS: 1963-1966

JOHN HADLEY STRANGE

John Hadley Strange, a member of the political science faculty at Livingston College of Rutgers University, explores the allocation of political resources to the Philadelphia Black community. He concludes that Blacks are underrepresented with regard to political benefits and he sees no significant change in the situation in the near future.

   This article, based on material in Strange's unpublished doctoral dissertation, "The Negro in Philadelphia Politics: 1963-1965" (Princeton University, 1966), was written expressly for this volume.

One of the most intriguing and important questions asked by students of politics is "Who Gets What, When, and How?" In this paper I consider this question as it specifically applies to the Black population of Philadelphia. What benefits, if any, do Blacks receive as a result of their participation in Philadelphia politics? To deal with this question several others must also be addressed: What is the nature and extent of political participation by Blacks in Philadelphia? What benefits do Blacks receive from the Philadelphia political system? Why do Blacks receive fewer political benefits than whites in Philadelphia? What are the opportunities that Blacks will receive increased benefits? I attempt to answer these questions by observing Black political participation in Philadelphia politics from 1963–1966.

How Blacks Participate in Philadelphia Politics

In examining the political activities of Blacks, it is useful to distinguish between two groups of participants: voters or "indirect participants,"

109

and others more active in politics, those who are "direct participants."
It is also useful to distinguish between *how* Blacks participate in politics
and the extent of their participation.

"DIRECT" PARTICIPATION BY BLACKS

Nine important descriptive statements can be made, on the basis of
the research reported here, describing the ways in which Blacks directly
participated in Philadelphia politics between 1963 and 1966.

First, *Blacks did not participate in politics through a Black political
machine in Philadelphia.* Only white-controlled Democratic and Republican organizations exist in Philadelphia; only the Democratic one is
important. Black politicians, successful and aspiring alike, publicly
acknowledge that the white-dominated city political organizations determine which Blacks are nominated and elected.

The Democratic City Organization has successfully defeated all
attempts to create a Black political organization. One of the most effective methods has been legislative apportionment. Both the Pennsylvania
General Assembly and the senate were reapportioned in 1963. In the
senate redistricting, the nonwhite percentage of the population was reduced in every Philadelphia senate district, despite an increase of over
forty percent in Philadelphia's Black population between 1950 and
1960. The only senate district with a Black majority in 1963 (represented by a white senator) was reduced from eighty-one percent to
sixty-nine percent nonwhite. The number of assembly districts in Philadelphia with a majority Black population was decreased from eleven,
electing thirteen assemblymen, to six, electing eight assemblymen. Before the reapportionment there were nine Blacks in the general assembly; afterward there were eight.

But the city Democratic organization has not been content with
keeping a close check on reapportionment. Moves to replace white ward
leaders with Blacks, on those rare occasions when they occur, meet with
strong resistance. Patronage is withdrawn, rules are ignored, and the
white political machine retains control. For example, in January, 1965
the Democratic City Committee successfully defeated a plan to elect a
Black, Edgar Campbell, to the vacant ward leadership in the Fifty-
second Ward, a ward that was approximately sixty-five percent Black.

Campbell was the expected (and some claim legal) successor since he was then serving as chairman of the ward committee. But through the open use of its patronage and other threats, the City Committee had Campbell defeated 50-9 even though forty-one out of the seventy-one committeemen eligible to vote for ward leader were Blacks. (Herbert Fineman, whose brother Irving Fineman had been ward leader, was elected. Later Campbell lost his job as assistant to City Council Democratic Majority Leader George X. Schwartz. Fred Handy, a Black committeeman from the Fifty-second Ward and one of Campbell's supporters, was also fired from his state job as the only Black inspector in the Bureau of Weights and Measures.)

When Blacks are appointed or elected to political office the decision to give an office to a Black is made by whites and the Blacks are selected by whites. There has been no Black political organization in Philadelphia. Blacks work for whites in Philadelphia politics.

Second, *Blacks have not participated in Philadelphia politics as a monolithic bloc.* Not only has there been no Black political organization in Philadelphia, but the multitude of Black groups and individuals interested in politics lustily competed among themselves for the relatively few opportunities for positions of power. This excessive competition internal to the Black community decidedly weakened their influence.

Four major, but not distinct, groups of Black activists existed between 1963 and 1966. First, there were the *politicians,* those who held elective and appointive office. Second, there were the *clergymen* seeking political gain, some of whom held a political office, aspired to hold a political office, desired to rent their churches to the city for school classrooms, or wanted to protect their churches from demolition under urban renewal. Third, there were the *civic leaders* who represented Black civic organizations in appeals before political bodies. Fourth, there were the *civil rights leaders* who attacked the political status quo with boycotts, picketings, and mass demonstrations.

There was great antagonism and competition between and within these four groups. They disagreed over goals, tactics, personalities, and patronage rights. They also waged bitter and vituperative attacks upon each other.

Third, *Blacks made no demands for legislation, nor did they propose*

111

legislation. The principal advocates and sponsors of legislation were church groups. Demands made by Blacks concerned five policy areas: education, housing, employment, police brutality, and political appointments. In each of these areas Blacks called for administrative action rather than legislation. The school board was called upon to institute *policies* leading to improved and integrated schools and faculties, employment of Blacks in supervisory positions, and an end to overcrowding. Demands were made that the Bureau of Licenses and Inspections enforce existing housing codes. Demonstrations were held to force the mayor to take *administrative action* against construction unions to bring about increased employment of Blacks. The enforcement of existing contract provisions prohibiting discrimination in city building projects was demanded, rather than new legislation. Economic boycotts were used to force alterations in hiring practices by private employers. Blacks in Philadelphia also called for administrative actions to end police brutality and to punish offending policemen. Political offices and appointments were also sought by Blacks, but not through legislation.

Fourth, *Blacks in Philadelphia did not advocate radical changes in Philadelphia's economic and political systems.* They desired to succeed on the same terms and in the same system as other Philadelphians, to end discrimination in its most overt forms, and to open new opportunities for advancement within the system. Robert Dahl considers this fact an important element in ethnic politics. He notes in his book, *Who Governs?*, that the early ethnic groups in New Haven did not consider the socioeconomic order illegitimate, but they did so consider discrimination. The evidence in the case of Blacks in Philadelphia, although limited, supports this conclusion.

The nature of the political system was not questioned by Black political activists in Philadelphia—only the distribution of rewards and benefits.

Fifth, *Blacks generally did not make election appeals based on race.* Rather they claimed to represent the Democratic party, "the working man," or "all Americans." One exception to this was the 1964 primary in which Cecil Moore, the caustic, militant former president of the city's National Association for the Advancement of Colored People, sponsored five candidates to run as Blacks. Four of these five opponents were

Negroes. They were dubbed "so-called Negroes" and "tools of the white power structure" by Moore and the Moore-backed candidates. Moore and his candidates were soundly defeated.

Although it was not customary to make racial appeals to Blacks, it was the practice in Philadelphia to demand positions for Blacks from the white political organizations. Demands were made that Blacks be slated for the state senate, that Blacks be appointed as judges and ward leaders, and that Blacks be given particular administrative jobs. This appeal for representation *because of race* was, however, infrequently made to the electorate, and when the electorate was appealed to on the basis of race, large numbers of Negroes cried out in opposition.

Sixth, *Blacks who held appointive and elective office did not engage in activities on behalf of their ethnic group.* Black officials acted as if their primary responsibility was to serve the political organization, or reform group, or civic faction that secured their job for them, rather than to pursue goals or interests of large numbers of Blacks. The holding of a political position was apparently a sufficient reward, or perhaps Blacks felt they would risk the jobs they held should they try to use their position to increase the rewards and benefits going to Blacks.

Seventh, *Blacks in Philadelphia did not contribute to the financing of political and civic organizations.* There were no major Black contributors to either the Democratic or Republican party. In fact, very few Blacks made even small contributions to political organizations. Blacks probably accepted more money from political organizations than they contributed since both Black Philadelphia newspapers benefited from large amounts of political advertising and between twenty and thirty percent of campaign funds expended by the parties was paid to Black campaign workers.

Eighth, *Blacks did not have organizations with permanent staffs continuously engaged in pursuing the interests of Blacks.* There were no groups to initiate proposals for governmental action or to lobby for certain goals. The NAACP, the major Negro organization in Philadelphia, operated without an executive director from 1963 to 1966 when it was divided into five chapters. (This action was taken by the national NAACP in order to reduce the influence of Cecil Moore.) Because the Urban League is financed largely through the United Fund, it avoided becoming involved in local politics. Moreover, the League elected its first Negro president only in 1964. The League has long been dominated by white business and professional men. CORE, a relative newcomer to Philadelphia, was often insolvent and thus ineffective. This absence of Black organizations was in contrast to the multitude of white organizations active in Philadelphia politics including the AFL-CIO, the Archdiocese of Pennsylvania, the Greater Philadelphia Movement, the Old Philadelphia Development Corporation, and many others.

Ninth, *Blacks engaged in direct protest activities against the city government and its officials.* Although demonstrations, boycotts, and picketing are not new tactics, having been used by labor and other groups for many years, the use of these tactics against local governments is new. Direct protest activities in Philadelphia took the form of picketing city officials' homes, "sit-ins" in public offices, and mass picketing of construction and other sites. The first use of these tactics was by the Congress of Racial Equality on April 13, 1963. Seven CORE members, led by CORE Regional Director Louis Smith, picketed Mayor Tate's home for two hours carrying placards protesting discrimination in unions involved in municipal construction projects.

Between April 1963 and June 1965, Black organizations conducted at least seventy-eight demonstrations, boycotts, and picketing campaigns. Some picketing lasted several days, the longest being the seven and one-half months of continuous picketing by the NAACP of all-white Girard College. Twenty-four of these protest activities were directed against local government officials and agencies; six against federal officials (including two general protests by CORE of conditions in Mississippi), and one against the Democratic City Committee. The remaining forty-six protests were directed against local business firms.

In addition to the seventy-eight demonstrations actually carried out, there were forty-two threats of boycotts and demonstrations. Nineteen of these threats were made by the 400 (Black) Ministers of Philadelphia. These ministers led a successful mass boycott of consumer goods manufactured or processed in the Philadelphia area in 1963 and 1964. The boycotts substantially reduced sales, and the representatives of the ministers were consequently listened to. Because of the reputation for success which the boycotts attained among Philadelphia businessmen, over half of the companies approached yielded when the threat was made, obviating the necessity for a boycott.

PARTICIPATION BY THE ELECTORATE

Four major descriptive statements (based on data covering elections from 1947 through 1964) can be made about the participation of the Black electorate in Philadelphia politics.

First, *Blacks in Philadelphia voted overwhelmingly for the candidates of the Democratic party.* In sixteen out of the sixty wards in Philadelphia in 1964, over half of those registered to vote were Blacks. Not a single one of these wards had a Democratic vote for president of less than seventy-five percent. Ten out of the sixteen returned Democratic margins of over ninety percent. Out of the 1,647 election districts in Philadelphia in 1964, there were 210 in which Blacks constituted at least ninety percent of those persons registered to vote. Johnson received at least ninety-five percent of the vote cast in seventy-four percent (155) of these Black election districts. Only seven had Democratic margins of less than ninety percent, the lowest being eighty-one percent.

However, 1964 could be considered an unrepresentative year. Yet, none of those wards in which Blacks constitute at least half of those registered has given a majority to the Republican head of the ticket since 1954. At least half of these wards have voted Democratic in every election since 1948. Sixty percent of the time since 1947 these wards have been at least seventy percent Democratic, and in only 12.3 percent of the cases in the last eighteen years has the Republican at the head of the ticket won in these wards. This is truly a phenomenal record of Democratic strength in these "Black wards."

Second, *not only have Blacks voted Democratic but they have registered as Democrats.* Until 1955 Black wards did not have predominately Democratic registration lists. Since 1958, however, there have been no Black majority wards with a majority of those registered calling themselves Republicans.

Third, *Blacks, unlike other ethnic groups, did not vote for candidates on the basis of their race.* Take for example the 1964 Democratic primary contest in the seventh Senatorial District between Charles R. Weiner, Democratic minority leader in the state senate, and Rev.

115

Marshall Lorenzo Shepard, Jr., son of one of the two Black city councilmen. Shepard, whose campaign was sponsored and supported by Cecil Moore, campaigned primarily on the theme that a Black senatorial district should elect a Black state senator. This was the first recent campaign in Philadelphia in which a Black candidate used race to appeal to the electorate. A campaign emphasizing race was possible in 1963, since sixty-four percent of the voters in the seventh district were Blacks. The racial appeal was, nevertheless, ineffective. Shepard received only 23.6 percent of the vote.

That race is not a primary consideration for Philadelphia Blacks when they vote is evidenced by data that follows in support of the fourth statement about the ways in which Negroes participated in Philadelphia elections. Fourth, *Black voters in Philadelphia did not effectively split the straight party ticket to support Black candidates in multi-candidate elections.* In Philadelphia all city magistrates, seven city councilmen at large, and three city commissioners are elected on ballots with more than one candidate competing. Voters may vote for, and each party can nominate, two-thirds the number of magistrates to be elected, five city councilmen, and two city commissioners. Consequently the minority party is guaranteed at least one-third of the magistrate offices, two city council seats-at-large, and one city commission post. This electoral system facilitates voting strategies in which one or two of the minority party candidates are supported at the expense of one or more majority party candidates. This is known as "cutting." This voting system also permits "bullet voting"; that is, a voter can cast a ballot for only one candidate thereby avoiding support of potential rivals, even in the same party, since all candidates run against each other. Blacks have been somewhat more successful in securing nominations in these multi-candidate contests, especially from the minority party, than in situations where either a Democrat or a Republican wins. In these elections Blacks can be nominated, thereby indicating recognition of the importance of Black voters, without too great a risk to the white political organization that a Black might be elected. Negroes come in last among the minority party candidates. They lose while the white minority party candidates win.

The 1963 race for city council is a good case to observe the effects of "cutting" and "bullet voting" on Black candidates since both the Democrats and the Republicans nominated a Black for city councilman-at-large. The Democrats nominated Rev. Marshall Shepard, Sr., an incumbent and long an active Democratic politician. The Republican Black candidate was funeral director Robert Evans, former football star for the University of Pennsylvania. Seven at-large council seats were being contested, but each political party was limited to five nominees. The Republicans had little hope of electing all five of their candidates in 1963; the real contest therefore was to see which two Republicans would win. A Republican voter who had one or two Republican favorites would, to maximize his candidate's chances for victory, cast a "bullet vote" for his Republican choices (not over two so as not to vote for the real opponents—the other Republicans) and throw away his other votes. A Democrat, if he wanted to determine which two of the Republicans would be elected, would vote for one or two Republicans and "cut" one or two Democrats—since the likelihood that all the Democrats would be elected anyway was high. Of course, the Democrat might cast a "bullet vote" also. If either of these activities were especially prevalent, then there should be a fairly large difference in the totals for the Republicans with the highest and lowest number of votes. The same would be true among the Democratic candidates. Out of the 120 "contests" (among the Republicans and Democrats in 60 wards) there were 44 instances in which the lowest candidate of a party got less than ninety-five percent of the number of votes of the leading candidate of his party. These situations can be arbitrarily designated "cutting contests." In 25 out of these 44 contests, or in 56.8 percent of the cases, it was the Black candidate who was "cut," trailing the other candidates of his party. In seven other instances the Black candidate was next to last. In the twelve remaining cases the Black candidate benefited from "cutting"; that is, he led his party. Republican candidate Evans led in eight "cutting contests," all of them being in wards in which a majority of those registered to vote were Blacks. Marshall Shepard, Sr. led in four "cutting contests," but none of these was in a Black ward.

In eight out of the fifteen Black wards Evans benefited from cutting. In one Negro ward, Ward Thirteen, Evans was the victim of cutting tactics, finishing fifth out of the five Republican candidates. Cutting tactics were used against Evans in fifteen out of forty-five white wards. In three of these wards Evans was cut more than ten percent. Although in a large percent of Black wards Evans profited from cutting, more white wards hurt Evans by "cutting" him.

In the Democratic contests only one Negro ward had a "cutting contest." Marshall Shepard, Sr., the Black Democratic candidate, was the victim of cutting tactics in this Black ward as well as in fifteen white wards.

According to this analysis, whites used cutting tactics against Blacks in minority party contests. In addition, Blacks used cutting tactics to aid Black candidates in these contests, but the cutting tactics employed by Blacks were not effective in electing Black candidates.* In majority party contests, Philadelphia Blacks apparently did not use cutting tactics to support Black candidates. Yet even in the majority party contests, whites did cut Blacks. The evidence indicates that whites are both more persistent and more proficient in cutting Blacks than Blacks are in cutting whites.

The Extent of Black Political Participation

It is not enough to look at the way in which Blacks, both activist and voter alike, participate in politics. The magnitude, or the extent, of that participation must also be investigated. Again, with no other intention than to distinguish voters from other, more active participants in political affairs, the following analysis separately examines the extent of political participation in Philadelphia by politically active Blacks and by the electorate between 1963 and 1966.

PARTICIPATION IN POLITICS OF POLITICALLY ACTIVE BLACKS

There are two ways of observing the extent of political participation by Black political activists without using sophisticated research tools such as survey analysis: the extent of office holding and the number of Black political organizations.

---

*This has been true for all recent elections in Philadelphia, not just the election analyzed.

118

Office Holding. Since one of the most effective positions from which to influence politics is a political office, the number of political offices held by a group of people is an important clue to the extent of their political participation. Of course, political decisions can be influenced by people not holding office, and often are. But public office is an important base for political power. In Philadelphia Blacks have held political offices, but they have not held offices in numbers proportionate to their representation in the electorate. The more important and powerful the political office, the less frequently do Blacks hold that position.

Of course, there has been no Black mayor of Philadelphia. Blacks have also been excluded from the Pennsylvania Senate, and no Black has held the post of City Commissioner. Blacks were elected to the city council as early as 1884, but in modern times Blacks have served as councilmen only since 1936.

State legislative posts were the first political offices opened to Blacks in Philadelphia in any numbers, and they have been the only political offices which the Blacks have held in numbers proportionate to their representation in the electorate. Since 1920, Blacks from Philadelphia have been members of every session of the Pennsylvania General Assembly.

The extent to which Blacks have participated in public office can be expressed in terms of an Index of Black Job Opportunity. This index is constructed by taking the percentage of the jobs which are held by Blacks and dividing this figure by the percentage of the electorate (registered voters) who are Blacks. Thus, if 10 percent of the job holders are Black and 10 percent of the registered voters are Black, the proportion of Blacks in both cases is the same and the Index of Black Job Opportunity is 100. Another way of putting this is that Blacks would have 100 percent of their quota of the jobs if the jobs were distributed in such a manner that Blacks had the same chance of holding a political (or other) job as they have of being registered to vote.

Participation by Blacks in the Pennsylvania General Assembly has been quite high. Since 1924 Blacks have held at least half as many seats in the general assembly as they could expect on the basis of their proportion of the electorate. Since 1936 Blacks have had an Index of Job Opportunity in the general assembly ranging from 74.8 to 107.2.

Blacks have not been as successful in capturing other elective positions in Philadelphia. City council posts, since the city charter revision in 1952, and the county court judgeships have been the local offices most available to Blacks. The Index of Black Job Opportunity for council-man seats reached a high of 63.2 in 1956 and ten years later was 45. The Index for County Court Judges has been over 56 since 1948 and was highest (76.5) in 1956.

The most political of all local elective positions are the magistrate court offices. This is the patronage post most coveted by party workers including ward leaders. Blacks have been especially underrepresented as magistrates since 1948. Their magistrate job opportunity index for that period ranged from a high of 43.8 to a low of 22.2. The hostility of the political organizations toward Black office holding is clearly demonstrated in these low indices.

In appointive positions, the story has been the same. Only a handful of Blacks have been appointed to significant city positions. Only since 1951 has a Black headed a city agency, the Department of Records. Most of the boards and commissions in Philadelphia, including the Zoning Board of Adjustment (very important politically), the Department of Public Health, the Department of Welfare, the City Planning Commission, the Recreation Department and the prestigious Fairmount Park Commission, have remained totally white.

Negroes have, however, been able to gain appointments to race relations groups such as the Philadelphia Commission on Human Relations, the Mayor's Advisory Committee on Civil Rights, and the city's anti-poverty agency. Two Blacks are among the nine members of the City School Board.

Turning from elective and appointive positions to positions in the city political organizations, we encounter still further limitations on Black office holding. Although figures are unavailable as to the number of Black district committeemen (there are 1,640 districts in Philadelphia, each with two Republican and two Democratic committeemen) it is quite likely that they hold this unimportant post in a number roughly proportionate to the size of the Black electorate. Blacks do not, however, find it easy to become ward leaders in Philadelphia. In fact, both the Democratic and Republican organizations take specific actions to limit the number of Black ward leaders, as the fight over the Democratic ward leadership in the Fifty-second Ward, discussed earlier, clearly demonstrates. Between 1937 and 1943, neither party had any Black ward leaders. Since 1944, both the Republican and Democratic parties have had at least one Black ward leader. By 1964, 11 or 9.2 percent of the 120 ward leaders in Philadelphia were Blacks. The index of Negro job opportunity for ward leaders was then a low 35.0.

Participation through Organizations. Black participation in politics through organizations, directly or indirectly active in politics, has been, like office holding, very minimal. Henry Klein in a study of Philadelphia's voluntary civic, educational, and social welfare organizations found 4,410 board positions occupied by 3,010 different people. Only five Blacks were among the 79 men who were members of five or more boards. There were at least three additional Blacks among the 81 persons serving on four or more boards.[1] Although these board memberships may not be a source of *political* power, the lack of Blacks among the most active board members is indicative, at least, of the lack of participation by Blacks in organizational activities. This is made even clearer when it is recognized that there are only a very few Black-dominated organizations active in political affairs in Philadelphia; yet the number of white-run organizations include such groups as the Greater Philadelphia Movement, AFL-CIO, Americans for Democratic Action, Archdiocese of Philadelphia, Philadelphia Fellowship Commission, Chamber of Commerce, University Science Center Corporation, Old Philadelphia Development Corporation, Bureau of Municipal Research, Pennsylvania Economy League, Citizens for a Modern Constitution, and a seemingly infinite number of others.

PARTICIPATION BY BLACK VOTERS

The above evidence demonstrates that there are proportionately fewer Blacks among the politically active citizens of Philadelphia than whites. Moreover, the Black political activists in Philadelphia do not hold the important political positions in Philadelphia. Is there a correspondingly low rate of participation by Blacks among those citizens whose major political act is voting? Although a complete answer is impossible without conducting a sample survey, *it is obvious from an analy-*

sis of rates of registration and rates of turnout that Blacks are less active than whites in performing these two political acts.

Let us examine registration rates first. Between 1950 and 1960 the difference between white and Black registration rates increased. In 1950 Blacks had higher registration rates than whites in eighteen wards and lower registration rates than whites in thirty-four wards. In 1960 Blacks had lower registration rates than whites in fifty-five out of fifty-nine wards. In 1950 the percentage of the white population registered to vote exceeded the percentage of the Black population registered to vote by at least ten percentage points in fourteen wards. The percentage of Blacks registered exceeded the percentage of whites registered by the same margin in nine wards. In 1960 whites led Blacks in registration by ten or more percentage points in thirty-seven wards, and had registration rates lower than Blacks by the same margin in only one ward.

The increasing difference between the registration rates of Blacks and whites is even clearer when we examine the city as a whole. Between 1950 and 1960 the percentage of the nonwhite population in Philadelphia registered to vote *declined* from 44.4 percent to 41 percent while the registration rate of whites *increased* from 52 percent to 54.5 percent. For the third straight decade the registration rate of Blacks declined, and for the fourth straight decade the margin of the white registration rate over the Black registration increased.

The increase in the white registration margin deserves closer examination. If we look at those wards in which at least half of those registered are whites we find that the white registration margin increased by 5.9 to 17.5 points. In Black wards the change in the white registration margin was very slight, declining by 2.5 to 5.3 points. Yet even in the Black wards a higher proportion of whites registered to vote than did Blacks, and the increase in white registration in the white wards, an average increase of over 11.5 points, can truly be called phenomenal.

Whites not only registered in greater proportions than Blacks, they also voted in greater proportions than Blacks. If we examine the percentage of those persons registered who actually vote, that is the turnout rate, in white wards and Black wards, we find that turnout rates are consistently higher in the white wards. This is true for every election for major office in Philadelphia since 1947.

The Benefits of Politics

The ways in which Blacks participate in Philadelphia as well as the extent of that participation have been described. An examination of the benefits Blacks receive, or do not receive, from the political system is now in order. There are several difficulties involved in an analysis of political outputs going to Blacks. First, it is hard to distinguish outputs of the system that are specifically for Blacks from outputs which benefit Blacks as well as other citizens. The second difficulty comes in attempting to identify the *source* of the particular output under consideration. Are particular benefits the result of actions in the political system, the economic system, or the social system? Indeed the question might be whether these systems are separable or not. Even if it can be shown that the output is one of the political system, the output nevertheless must be identified, in this study of Philadelphia, as a product of not just the political system but of the local rather than the federal or state political system. A third difficulty is in determining whether a particular output is a benefit or not. Are benefits outputs that meet certain goals or desires of the persons affected? Or are they outputs that meet certain material or other needs whether desired or not? A third possible type of outputs that could conceivably be called benefits are outputs that increase the material or physical standard of living but which are niether especially desired nor badly needed. One might call these luxuries instead of benefits.

DIRECT BENEFITS OF THE PHILADELPHIA POLITICAL SYSTEM

Despite these difficulties, it is possible to identify some outputs that can be accepted as being produced by the Philadelphia political system and which benefit Blacks. First, Blacks are employed by the city of Philadelphia. The number of jobs and the salaries of these jobs can be compared with the jobs held by whites to estimate the impartiality of the employment process. The jobs are an output of the local political system, are beneficial to and desired by Blacks. Therefore, data on public employment avoid the difficulties cited above.

A second area in which data are available and which avoids most of the difficulties discussed above is public education. Certainly the Philadelphia School Board, although affected by federal and state actions, does directly determine the relative advantages of Black and white schools, and has available to it at least some powers to allocate some rewards and benefits equally to Blacks and whites.

Public Employment. The scarcity of Blacks in elective and appointive positions, as was discussed earlier, is not duplicated in civil service and other city positions. In 1963, 39.2 percent of the approximate 28,000 city jobs were held by Blacks. The index of Black job opportunity for city posts (excluding employees of the Board of Education) was 147, or in other words there were approximately one and one half times as many Blacks holding city jobs in 1963 as one would expect if city job holders had the same racial composition as the city population. Over 99 percent of all city employees earning more than $7,000, however, were whites. The Job Opportunity Index for holding a city post paying over $7,000 was an infinitesimal 3.0 for Blacks. Even more startling is the fact that over half of all the Negroes employed in 1963 by the city of Philadelphia received salaries of *less* than $4,000 per year. Clearly Blacks received very few benefits in terms of jobs from the city of Philadelphia.

Public Schools. Negroes received no more benefits from the Philadelphia public school system. The School Board certainly has not operated a racially-integrated school system. In May 1963 only 42 or 17 percent of Philadelphia's public schools were integrated.

If we look at other benefits that the school system might provide, such as schools that are not overcrowded, do not have part-time classes, have small classes, adequately-trained teachers, and sufficient textbooks and educational supplies, we find once again that the Philadelphia school system provides significantly fewer of these benefits for Black children than for white children. For example, 31 percent of Black schools compared to 5 percent of white schools were overcrowded in 1963. Black schools had seventy-four double-session classes; white schools none. Over half of the teachers in white schools had at least twelve years experience; only 34 percent of teachers in Black schools were as experienced. Twenty-three percent of classes in Black schools and only 17 percent in white schools had over forty pupils. The Special Committee on Nondiscrimination of the Philadelphia Board of Educa-

124

tion, after examining these and other data, concluded that "[I]t is possible to avoid the conclusion that the (Negro) schools . . . were definitely inferior in all major categories to the (white) schools or in most instances to the integrated schools. . . [T] he effect on the quality of education afforded the children was undeniable . . ."[2]

Blacks also received fewer benefits than whites in terms of employment in the public school system. Although approximately 32 percent of all teachers in Philadelphia are Blacks, in September 1962 only 5.5 percent (20 out of 360) of the professional employees of the school board earning $10,000 or more per year were Blacks.

INDIRECT BENEFITS OF THE PHILADELPHIA POLITICAL SYSTEM

In addition to city jobs and school board policies, Blacks are affected by governmental action in a number of other ways. It is not possible, however, to speak of these outputs as specifically affecting Blacks nor to identify them as products of only the Philadelphia political system. Nevertheless, it seems altogether reasonable that the general employment level of Blacks in Philadelphia, the type and condition of Black housing, the income level of the Black population, and the education and general health conditions of Blacks in Philadelphia should be discussed here. Although private employment, for example, depends on education level, the general state of the economy and previous training and skills, it is also affected directly by city political action. In fact there is a separate agency of the Philadelphia city government, the Commission on Human Relations, charged with the specific responsibility of assuring fair employment and fair housing practices. The city also directly affects (to some extent) the general health and education levels of its citizens. No claim is made that the Philadelphia political system is totally responsible for the conditions of Blacks in these specific areas, nevertheless local politics certainly does influence the distribution of benefits and the conditions of citizens in these areas. A description of the conditions of Blacks *vis à vis* whites on these various factors will therefore give an indication of the equality of political treatment Blacks receive in Philadelphia.

In the areas of general employment, housing, income level, and health, as was the case in public employment and public education,

Blacks get a smaller fraction of the benefits than whites, although admittedly the condition of Blacks has improved since 1950 and in a few cases the improvement for the Black has been greater than that for the white.

General Employment. Let us examine employment first. The unemployment rate for Blacks in Philadelphia has been consistently about twice that of whites. In 1960 the Negro unemployment rate was 10.7 percent. The white unemployment rate was 5 percent. In 1950 the respective rates were 11.7 and 5.4 percent. In 1964 unemployment increased to over 14 percent for Blacks and to 8.4 percent for whites.

The relative disadvantage Blacks have in gaining occupational equality with whites can also be seen by examining data on occupational categories. In 1940 and also in 1960 a considerably greater portion of Blacks, both male and female, were operatives and service workers than were whites. Just the opposite is true in the white-collar occupations. The proportion of the whites holding these positions is much larger than the proportion of Blacks. For example, 42.5 percent of the white males employed in 1960 were in white-collar occupations while only 19.3 percent of the male Blacks were so employed. In the same year almost 62 percent of all white females employed were in white-collar jobs. Only 22.1 percent of nonwhite females were in this classification. Additionally, 22.5 percent of the white males were semiskilled laborers and 7.8 percent were service workers. Over 30 percent of employed Black males were semiskilled laborers and operatives and 17.2 percent were service workers. Almost half of the nonwhite females, 41.7 percent, were service workers (including household workers) in 1960. Only 10.9 percent of white females were so employed.

When we examine the improvement between 1940 and 1960 in the opportunity for Black males to hold certain classes of jobs, we find that the index of opportunity has increased for professional jobs from 28 to 32 and for managerial positions from 19 to 23. Increases in the index for Black females between 1940 and 1960 were more significant, rising from 26 to 68 for professional and technical positions and from 27 to 42 for managerial positions. Black males did make some gains in skilled positions, the index changing from 28.4 to 54.0. Especially significant gains were made in semiskilled jobs. By 1960 the index for semiskilled

126

positions had reached 98.8 a near "perfect" mark. Black women scored significant gains in clerical and sales positions (from 7.9 to 41.9) and in both skilled and unskilled jobs.

The conclusion is clear that Blacks have gotten better jobs in Philadelphia between 1940 and 1960, but it is also evident that this gain has been primarily in semiskilled occupations and that there has been no major breakthrough in skilled and white-collar occupations. Blacks in Philadelphia, by and large, failed to achieve an improvement in occupation status between 1940 and 1960 despite the existence since 1949 of a well-financed and legally powerful City Commission on Human Relations that has the responsibility of enforcing fair employment practices.

Blacks have made no greater gain in the field of housing than in employment. The picture is mixed, of course, as was the case for employment. More Black housing units are sound than ever before. Of course, this is also true for white housing units. Also, the gap between the percentage of Black housing units and white housing units that are sound has narrowed considerably since 1940. In 1940, 54.5 percent of all Black units were sound compared with 86.0 percent of all white units. The difference between these two figures was 31.5 percentage points. By 1950 the gap had narrowed to 27 percentage points and in 1960 it stood at 14.5. Seventy-nine percent of all Black units and 93.5 percent of all white units were sound in 1960. Nevertheless 31,002 Black housing units were unsound in 1960.

Overcrowding also remains a problem for Philadelphia Blacks. In 1960, 16 percent of all nonwhite families lived in crowded units (more than one person per room). Only 5 percent of whites were crowded in 1960. In 1950, 22 percent of the nonwhite families and 7 percent of the white families were crowded.

One factor which showed no improvement was housing integration. The number and percentage of Blacks in Philadelphia living in segregated areas is increasing. The percentage of city blocks with over 50 percent of the households headed by nonwhites jumped from 11 percent in 1940 to 21.6 percent in 1960. More striking evidence of the increasing segregation of Blacks in Philadelphia is found in an analysis of census-tract data. Over half (57.5 percent) of the Blacks in Philadelphia in 1960 lived in census tracts which were at least 80 percent nonwhite. Only 27 percent of the Blacks in Philadelphia in 1950 lived in census tracts with such a large proportion of Blacks. *Despite a Black population increase of 156,065, exactly 39,732 fewer Blacks lived in census tracts less than half nonwhite in 1960 than in 1950.* In fact, fewer Blacks (in numbers) lived in areas less than 80 percent Black in 1960 than in 1950.

Education. In the area of education, as reported in census bureau data, Blacks have made advancements in terms of the number of grades completed. The median school years completed for nonwhites has increased from 8.2 years in 1950 to 9.0 years in 1960. The percentage of Blacks that have completed at least high school rose from 8.0 in 1940 to 16.4 in 1950 and was 23.6 percent in 1960.

Health. Although data for 1950 were not available for comparison with 1960 information the Philadelphia Commission on Human Relations reported that Blacks suffered severe disadvantages in terms of health in 1960. The commission said, "Non-whites showed more health problems than whites, including more infants born immature (16 percent of non-white infants and 7 percent of white infants weighed 5 pounds 8 ounces or less at birth); higher infant mortality (the non-white rate of 47.6 deaths per 1,000 live births was double the white rate of 23.4); higher death rates for eight of the ten leading causes of death in Philadelphia (with population adjusted for age differences); a lower median age at death for nine of the causes."[3]

Income. If we examine Black and white differentials in income we find that the income gap between whites and Blacks narrowed slightly between 1950 and 1960. The nonwhite median income was 65 percent of the white median income in 1949 and 71 percent in 1959. When these percentages are calculated for the standard metropolitan statistical area this improvement practically disappears, nonwhite median income being 63.8 percent of the white median income in 1949 and 64.4 percent in 1959.

OTHER REWARDS OF PHILADELPHIA POLITICS

The preceding analysis has sought to identify benefits which Blacks in Philadelphia have received from the Philadelphia political system. In the course of the analysis two specific types of outputs were examined:

(1) outputs directly affected by the Philadelphia government—city jobs and public school hiring practices, facilities, and integration; (2) outputs not directly affected by Philadelphia government—the general employment, housing, education, income, and health status of Blacks *vis à vis* whites. In all cases fewer benefits are being directed to the Black population than to the white population. Does this mean then that Blacks do not receive *any* benefits from the Philadelphia political system? Are there no political rewards for Blacks in Philadelphia?

The answer to both these questions is no. The political system has rewarded Blacks in several ways, usually as a result of specific political activities undertaken by Blacks. First, the political system has provided Blacks with some low-level patronage positions. Second, several investigations of discrimination against Blacks in Philadelphia have been undertaken by city agencies and officials (after Blacks had expressed discontent with the situation). Blacks have also received some benefits from protest activities. The benefits in these cases have been limited and relatively unimportant. The nature of these benefits can perhaps be best understood by examining a few selected examples.

Patronage. Blacks have been given low-level patronage positions by the Philadelphia political system. For example, in 1964 in the Fifty-second Ward, Blacks held one elective position (City Councilman Shepard at $15,000 per year), four paid appointed positions (two over $14,000 per year, two under $5,000 per year) and two civil service jobs. A point made earlier, however, should be emphasized here. When the benefits Blacks receive are compared with the benefits distributed to whites, the evidence is overwhelming that Blacks do not get their proportionate share. In 1964 Blacks constituted 53 percent of the registered electorate in the Fifty-second Ward; nevertheless, Blacks held only five of the thirty patronage posts held by residents of this ward. White patronage jobholders included four elected officials (two with salaries over $10,000, two over $5,000) and twenty-one appointed officials (four with salaries exceeding $10,000, five more with salaries over $5,000 and twelve earning less than $4,000 from their patronage positions).

Studies and Investigations. The second kind of benefits for Blacks are "studies" and "investigations" of their problems. After several years of bringing complaints, issuing study documents, and finally after filing a civil court suit in order to end discrimination in the Philadelphia public school system, a thorough study of the conditions Black students faced in Philadelphia's schools was undertaken. The study was not carried out without difficulty, however. Some nine months after the committee began its work, four citizen members of the subcommittee on school sites, including two whites, resigned, stating, "We can only conclude that our committee at this time is being used to enable the board to claim that they are working on a plan when in fact they are not."[4]

Political Office. The third type of reward that participation in Philadelphia has gained for Blacks is political office. As has been seen, however, these political positions are normally limited to a very small number of Blacks.

Rewards from Protest Activities. Blacks have also received benefits from the political system as a result of their special activities outside regular politics. If we examine the results of the 119 protests, demonstrations and threats discussed above, we find the following benefits going to Blacks as a result:

DEMONSTRATIONS	OUTCOME
Eight days of mass picketing at school and city construction sites.	Investigation of labor union hiring practices; five Blacks employed as apprentices.
Twenty-eight threats and boycotts of consumer products.	Approximately four thousand jobs for Blacks.
Various threats to demonstrate.	Abolitions of "blackface" in Mummers' parade.
	Increased inspection of housing violations and increased fines assessed for violations.
Seven and one-half months of picketing Girard College.	Appointment of two lawyers (one Black) by the state of Pennsylvania to file a suit against the trustees of Girard College.
All other demonstrations.	Bussing of Black students from two schools.
	Abandonment of plans to build

130

DEMONSTRATIONS (cont'd.)	OUTCOME (cont'd.)
All other demonstrations. (cont'd.)	high school at Forty-sixth Street and Market.
	Ending of part-time classes in two churches.
	Ultimate closing of Philadelphia Council for Community Advancement.
	Three Blacks hired by the Greyhound Bus Co.
	Scott-Smith Cadillac Co. hired five Black salesmen and agreed to hire secretarial and other Black help.
	Traffic light installed at Eighth Street and Susquehanna.

Clearly, Blacks have received some specific benefits from political actions and from protest activities. But it is also evident that these achievements have been insignificant in altering the basic condition of life for Blacks in Philadelphia. This is contrary to the situation pictured by Robert Dahl in New Haven: "In comparison with whites . . . Negroes find no greater obstacles to achieving their goals through political action, but very much greater difficulties through activities in the private socioeconomic spheres."[5] In Philadelphia, the conclusion is obvious that Blacks do not benefit from the political system to any special extent, and have achieved no major changes in their political, economic, and social status as a result of the operations of the political system in Philadelphia.

Prospects for Urban Blacks

The central question of this study was identified earlier as follows: What benefits, if any, do Blacks in Philadelphia receive as a result of their participation in political activity? No direct answer to this question has been established. The findings of this study indicate that Blacks neither participate in nor reap the benefits of Philadelphia politics proportionate to the size of the Black electorate. This study also demonstrates that Blacks encounter greater obstacles than whites in achieving benefits through political action. But very little evidence has been offered to substantiate a *direct* link between participation and benefits. Investigations of "problems" have been undertaken, and some jobs, in both the public and private sectors, have gone to Blacks as a result of various forms of political activity. But for the most part the relationship between participation and benefits remains an assumption; and likewise, the corollary argument that an increase in participation would bring an increase in benefits remains unproved. Nevertheless, the discipline of political science assumes that political activity does make a difference in how the rewards of politics are distributed.

WHY BLACKS RECEIVE FEWER BENEFITS THAN WHITES

It is necessary, therefore, to explore this question of "linkage" more fully. Assuming that political activities are related to political benefits, one can raise the question of why Blacks receive fewer benefits than whites. There are at least four possible explanations: institutional arrangements preclude the distribution of benefits to Blacks regardless of their participation; whites ignore or do not recognize the problems facing Blacks and consequently take no action designed to bring about equality; whites engage in political actions explicitly designed to limit benefits distributed to Blacks; and finally, the nature of Black political participation is such that benefits do not result. It is apparent that all four of these factors are responsible in part for the fact that Blacks get fewer benefits than whites, not just in Philadelphia, but in practically every large urban area in the United States. Let us examine each of these explanations more closely.

Institutional Arrangements. First, it was suggested that Blacks receive fewer benefits from politics than whites because of institutional arrangements that make equal distribution of benefits difficult. In recent years, suburban governments, both the newly formed and the reinvigorated, have increased in size and number. The residents of these suburbs have been almost exclusively white. At the same time the central cities increasingly have become Black cities. Between 1950 and

132

1960 almost a million and a half whites left the central cities while the Black city population increased by over two million persons. During the same period the white suburban population increased by 10,667,000; the Black suburban population increased by only 343,000, a mere 3 percent of the total increase. By 1960 over half of all whites living in metropolitan areas in the United States lived in suburbs.

These suburban governments possess legal powers which enable them to control their racial and class composition. Blacks are effectively, and legally, barred from most suburbs. Zoning requirements as high as a five acre minimum lot, condemnation procedures, exceedingly rigid enforcement of building regulations, and, on occasion, violence are some of the favorite protective techniques used by suburbs for this purpose.

The institutional separation of the races into separate governmental units that results from the population growth patterns and the exclusion of Blacks from the suburbs limits the political benefits Blacks receive and will receive. One reason is that the tax structures of the cities are seriously affected by the white migration to the suburbs. In addition to the loss of their taxes, the cities are also losing revenues from the many retail establishments now operating in shopping centers, service businesses, and light industrial and research plants locating outside central cities. Not only are the cities' tax bases being affected, but the fact that the Black population is expanding increases the total expenditures necessary to provide equal benefits for Blacks and whites. Because segregated neighborhood governments are rapidly increasing in size and importance, the provision of equality for Blacks through politics is becoming more and more difficult.

White Inaction. The second reason why Blacks receive fewer political benefits is that whites ignore or do not recognize the problems of Blacks and consequently take no action designed to bring about equality. Action is not taken for several reasons. Some of the problems facing Blacks are invisible to whites, or unrecognized, and are therefore neglected.

Even when the problems are recognized, they are often not acknowledged. The Philadelphia Board of Education refused to acknowledge as late as 1963 that the Philadelphia School System was segregated despite the fact that in that year fifty-two percent of the children

133

attending public schools in Philadelphia attended segregated schools.

Another reason whites take no effective action is because many believe that the problems facing Blacks are being solved, that the Blacks are being assimilated into American life. Most of the proponents of this position point to the assimilation of other ethnic groups in American life, and eagerly predict the same thing will happen to Blacks. Others believe that the evidence of increasing incomes, educations, and of better housing clearly proves that problems of Blacks are fast disappearing. However, as has been shown, the *relative* progress of Blacks in Philadelphia has been slight.

Other whites make no effort to aid Blacks because they rationalize that problems of Blacks are being solved by recent legislation. Yet few positive improvements have been achieved as a result of existing legislation. For example, the Philadelphia Commission on Human Relations found legally-remediable discriminatory practices, as defined by law, in only 3.3 percent of the 121 complaints lodged with the commission in 1962 and in only 3.1 percent of the 98 complaints filed in 1963. Discrimination in housing and employment practices still abounds in Philadelphia.

Discriminatory Action by Whites. A third reason for the discrepancy between Black and white benefits is that whites have taken political actions designed explicitly to limit Black political participation and the benefits accruing from politics. In Philadelphia white politicians successfully used legislative gerrymandering to reduce the number of assembly districts in Philadelphia with a majority Black population and to lower the Black population in every senatorial district. In addition, the white political organization has made special efforts to prevent Blacks from becoming ward leaders in Black wards. The political organizations have also limited the positions for which Blacks can run under the party label, and they have not given patronage distribution rights to Blacks.

White political participation has effectively stifled the distribution of rewards to Blacks on an equal basis by preventing the election of Blacks and by controlling Blacks once elected.

Black Political Participation. Fourth, the nature of political participation by Blacks severely limits the benefits they can receive from the political system. In the first place Blacks in Philadelphia have greater

134

obstacles to overcome than whites in achieving benefits from the political system. Thus the level of efficiency of participation needed to receive payoffs is much higher for Blacks than for whites. But Blacks in Philadelphia do not register and vote to the extent that whites do, and they have not supported Black candidates if a Black is opposed by a white nominee of the Democratic party. Moreover, Blacks do not act as a monolithic bloc, but engage in vigorous and costly competition among themselves for leadership positions.

Even when Blacks have succeeded in being elected to public office in Philadelphia, they have been severely constrained in acting as agents for their race. Most Black officials depend upon jobs provided by the political organization to sustain them if they are defeated, or to supplement their incomes while serving in political office. Such controls encourage support of the organization's goals rather than the goals of Blacks as a racial group. Blacks have been either unable to gain political office, or if they have gained office, they have been unwilling or unable to represent forcefully the interests of their racial group.

OPPORTUNITIES FOR INCREASED BENEFITS FOR BLACKS

If these four factors—institutional segregation, white inaction, discriminatory actions by whites, and the nature of Black political participation—explain the difference between Black and white rewards from politics, then what are the possibilities that this gap in rewards will be narrowed in the future?

Benefits through Assimilation. Robert Dahl argued in 1960 that there is an excellent chance that this change will occur. Dahl suggested that Blacks will be assimilated into the society and will achieve a reasonable measure of political and social equality. He says that the Blacks in New Haven are already in the second stage of a three stage assimilation process.[6]

Could it be that Dahl's hypothesis is correct and that Blacks in Philadelphia are just in the first stage of the assimilation cycle? Although Dahl's description of New Haven does not completely correspond to the situation of Blacks in Philadelphia, it is entirely consistent with the evidence presented in this study. If there is an assimilation process, then we can perhaps look forward to an eventual accommodation of Blacks into

135

the political system. Other evidence supporting this optimistic outlook includes the relatively slow progress of other ethnic groups in Philadelphia. Only in 1963 was the first Catholic mayor elected. Perhaps Blacks in Philadelphia are in the first stage of the evolutionary process, a process somewhat more delayed than in New Haven.

On the other hand, Dahl may be completely wrong about the chances for Negro assimilation, at least as far as Philadelphia is concerned. Dahl's optimism is based on the assumption that the three step assimilation process applies in the same manner to Blacks as to previous ethnic groups. There are, however, several reasons to question this assumption.

First, and most important, is the existence of *color* prejudice which was not involved with the immigrants. Names could be changed, brogues lost, and the immigrant could easily escape identification. But not the Black American. His presence is obvious; he cannot assimilate unnoticed.

Second, assimilation is limited because of restraints on Blacks internal to the Black community. Assimilated Blacks are obvious to their fellows as well as to whites, and Blacks often raise as many questions about the assimilation of the members of their race as do whites, attacking those who assimilate as "race-traitors" or "so-called Negroes."

Third, many of the institutions which existed during the immigrants' assimilation and aided them in this process no longer exist. Small businesses which offered an avenue to economic independence are rarely realistic economic ventures today. Another agency of social mobility for the immigrants, the political machine, has been replaced by impersonal and impartial "welfare assistance," and civil service. Moreover, the political reform movement as well as overt discrimination has practically eliminated the underworld and the rackets as an avenue for ethnic advancement. Certainly Blacks have been successfully barred from high positions in the numbers and other illegitimate activities in Philadelphia.

Fourth, the immigrants arrived in the United States at a time of an insatiable demand for labor. Today Blacks, unskilled and semiskilled alike, are faced with a declining demand for physical labor.

Possible Changes in Benefit-limiting Factors. These four arguments seem sufficient to question Dahl's acculturation theory as it is applied to Blacks. Consequently, other explanations must be sought if the argu-

136

ment that Blacks will achieve political and economic parity with whites
is to be supported. If, as was suggested earlier, the low level of Black
political benefits can be explained by four factors—white inattention to
the problems of Blacks, the separation of whites and Blacks into separate governmental units, the determined efforts of whites to limit Black
political power and benefits, the nature of political participation by
Blacks—would not changes in these conditions possibly alter the distribution of political rewards? The question then becomes: what is the
possibility that one or more of these factors might be modified in such
a way as to distribute more outputs of the political system to Blacks?

One point, that whites ignore the problems of Blacks, may be modified. These problems are increasingly being identified, but identification
and acknowledgment of the problems will not necessarily result in
change. The magnitude and complexity of the problems facing Blacks
practically preclude this. Problems which are difficult to solve, or which
involve stupendous costs, are most often shunted aside or merely weakly
attacked. In fact, considerable evidence indicates the problems are getting worse instead of better.

The second factor contributing to the Black-white benefit gap—
segregation of the races under separate local governments—is not likely
to be stopped. White suburbs have the ability to limit Negro population
despite fair housing laws, and in many states even these laws are either
unenforceable or under attack. Certainly all available evidence indicates
a declining white and an increasing Black population in the cities, and a
rapidly increasing white and an increasing Black population in the suburbs. Reapportionment has also given white suburbanites even more
political power with which to protect their values and interests. White-
dominated and racially-segregated "neighborhood governments" will
undoubtedly continue to increase.

The third possible change, white political action specifically designed
to relinquish political power to Blacks, is no more likely to occur than
desegregation of our cities. White politicians can be expected to continue to attempt to avoid the loss of political power to Blacks. Yet
whites may not be able to avoid this situation. As the Black population
increases and as Blacks begin to make racial appeals for support, Blacks
are likely to be elected and appointed to public office more frequently.

They will also be less dependent on the white political organizations for support. This has begun to occur in Philadelphia. In December 1965, eleven additional Negroes were appointed ward leaders. Moreover, the number of Black professionals financially independent, to a certain extent, of the white political organization is increasing.

But the evidence presented so far argues that Blacks *do not* partici-pate in politics in a way that would lead to Black political control or increased benefits for Blacks. Even if institutional developments did not follow the course I predict, if whites did recognize the problem and if they either took action to aid the development of effective Black poli-ticians, or were unable to prevent their semi-emergence, the nature of Black political participation, as it exists today, does not indicate a basis for change in the distribution of political rewards. In fact, some indices used in this study indicate a decline in the use of politics by Blacks. Black turnout-rates are static and the registration rates are actually de-clining. Furthermore, other students of Black politics argue that the vote, even if used effectively by Blacks, will not result in significant change. William Keech says:

> With few exceptions the vote has failed . . . Negroes when they sought to change the law in order to eliminate existing discrimina-tion. . . . If social justice demands the eradication of the effects of past discriminations, the vote is even less useful.[7]

Moreover, Blacks are oriented toward only one party—the Demo-cratic party. As long as interparty competition is limited (competition which would necessitate concessions to Blacks in return for votes), as long as the Democratic party can take Black support for granted, the output for Blacks of political action is unlikely to be radically altered.

The conclusion cannot be escaped: Black political participation, as it exists in Philadelphia, gives no evidence of providing a base for rapid movement toward equality through politics.

What then is the possibility for Black political and economic equality as a result of actions of the local political system? We have rejected Dahl's contention that the Blacks are in the middle of an assimilation process which will produce equality. We have found little evidence to indicate that the four factors we tenuously linked to low Black benefits could be changed sufficiently to bring about equality. What other possibilities are there?

Benefits through Protest Action. Perhaps we might say that the real hope for Blacks lies in recent protest activities. There seems to be a growth of militancy among some Blacks. Blacks are not being satisfied by the few political benefits presently accorded them. If protests continue and dissatisfaction increases, a new awareness and activism on the part of Blacks may emerge with important implications for politics.

But not even protest activities seem sufficient to solve the problems of Blacks. Protest activities in Philadelphia have resulted in few changes. Those protests reviewed in this study resulted in the hiring of five journeymen, the installation of traffic lights, the opening of several hundred jobs to Blacks, and the investigation of discriminatory educational practices. But life is still much the same for Blacks in Philadelphia. The public schools are still segregated, Blacks are still employed in lower level occupations by industry, as well as by the city government. More than twice as many Blacks as whites are still unemployed. Blacks still receive harsher treatment by police than whites. All of these problems have been the objects of recent protest activities—yet little has changed; consequently, another possible source of optimism is closed.

THE NATURE OF THE POLITICAL SYSTEM MAKES CHANGE UNLIKELY

The above argument is only one of several which indicates that the gap between the rewards of the political system for Blacks and whites is not likely to be narrowed. The most compelling argument, however, has not been made: the type of change looked for is impossible because the nature of the political system in Philadelphia itself prohibits such a radical and thoroughgoing alteration.

Robert Dahl, Wallace Sayre, and Herbert Kaufman, in their studies of New Haven and New York, have described political systems much like that which exists in Philadelphia. New York's political system, Sayre and Kaufman write, is "vigorously and incessantly competitive." There is no ruling elite which dominates the political and governmental system of the city. There are a multiplicity of decision centers, and every decision of importance is the "product of mutual accommodation."[8] Philadelphia's system is quite similar.

The consequences of this type of system have been clearly deline-
ated by Sayre and Kaufman and also by Dahl. As Sayre and Kaufman
point out:

> Every proposal for change must run a gauntlet that is often fatal. The
> system is more favorable to defenders of the *status quo* than to inno-
> vators. It is inherently conservative.[9]

Dahl also points out the difficulties in making major alterations in
the operation of the system:

> A challenge to the existing norms is bound to be costly to the chal-
> lenger. As long as the professionals remain substantially legitimist in
> outlook the critic is likely to make little headway. Indeed, the
> chances are that anyone who advocates extensive changes in the pre-
> vailing democratic norms is likely to be treated by the professionals,
> and even by a fair share of the political stratum, as an outsider, pos-
> sibly even as a crackpot whose views need not be seriously debated.[10]

Philadelphia's political system has the same characteristics as New
York and New Haven. The changes in the system which would be necessary to redistribute the benefits of politics equally to Blacks and whites
are certainly substantial. If Dahl, Sayre, and Kaufman are correct, and
there is every reason to believe they are, it is indeed highly unlikely that
the Philadelphia political system will soon provide equal benefits for
Blacks and whites alike.

Conclusions

Starting with the query what benefits do Negroes receive from political
activity, this investigation found few rewards going to Blacks and limited political participation by them. An attempt was then made to determine why Blacks benefited less than whites (assuming politics did
affect the distribution of political rewards). After discussing four possible explanations, an evaluation of possibilities for equality for Blacks in
the future through political action was made. All the possibilities as-
sessed proved unlikely to bring about political and social parity. The
answer to the central question is obvious. Blacks receive few benefits

from political action; they are unlikely to achieve a significant measure of political and social equality, in Philadelphia at least, in the foreseeable future.

THE POLITICAL SYSTEM IS QUESTIONED

If, as has been argued, there is little prospect for political and social equality for Blacks in the immediate future as a result of the operation of the local political system, and if it is also true that this conclusion holds without regard to the nature of Black political activity because the *nature of the local political system precludes radical and sudden alterations of this type,* then one additional question must be raised. Is the existing local political system acceptable despite its failure to provide for, or offer hope to, urban Blacks, or should the nature of the political system be altered?

Although this question cannot be answered here, it must nevertheless be raised. It has already been raised in many Black ghettos. The riots in Los Angeles in 1965 and in Philadelphia, New York, Chicago, and elsewhere in 1964 stand as grim reminders that this question is important to Blacks. It is also important to political scientists, although few have recognized this. The *evaluation* of the local political system constitutes, in fact, the source of the real differences between the two schools of community-power scholars in the United States, the "pluralists" and the "elitists." It is true that the explicit arguments between these intellectual camps have been over methodology and about how power is distributed in the system. Nevertheless, the real disagreement between Dahl, Polsby, Sayre and Kaufman on the one hand and Hunter, C. Wright Mills and the Lynds on the other is over the answer to the normative question: does the local political system, as it exists, satisfactorily accomplish its purposes?

In 1961 Dahl identified the question of how one evaluates "the distribution and patterns of influence over political decisions in American life" as one which should not be neglected.[11] Hunter is equally clear as to what is crucial. "The real question . . . arises over who is to derive the most benefit from the composite of activity . . . The crucial question perhaps is 'How can policy be determined so that it takes into account the interests of the largest number of people?'"[12] How this question is

141

resolved divides the pluralists and power elitists more than methodologies or descriptions of the system. Dahl, although dissatisfied with the system, nevertheless accepts it:

> In our system of dispersed inequalities, almost every group, as said before, has access to some resources that it can exploit to gain influence. Consequently, any group that feels itself badly abused is likely to possess both the resources it needs to halt the abuse and the incentive to use these resources at a high enough level to bring about changes. Nearly every group has enough potential influence to mitigate harsh injustice to its members, though not necessarily enough influence to attain a full measure of justice. The system thus tends to be self-corrective, at least in a limited fashion. *If equality and justice are rarely attained, harsh and persistent oppression is almost always avoided.*[13]

Sayre and Kaufman echo Dahl's cheerful opinion:

> All the diverse elements in the city, in competition with each other, can and do partake of the stakes of politics; if none gets all it wants, neither is any excluded. Consequently, no group is helpless to defend itself, powerless to prevent others from riding roughshod over it, or unable to assert its claims and protect its rights.[14]

The so-called elitists answer the question differently. Hunter, also unhappy with the system, cannot accept it without change:

> The community structure is not adequate to express effectively the demands that are real enough but which reside with the silent members of the community. . . . Some modification of existing structure seems necessary if certain problems which arise chronically in this community are to be met. . . .
>
> If one is not completely compelled by pessimism, he may remember that government is still dedicated theoretically to both the bottom structure and the top structure of power. If this condition does not hold true in practice, then *one must, with others, find ways of realigning theory and practice. If the ideal of democracy is to endure and be strengthened, ways and means must be found to approach a solution to the problems raised here. The search must not be restricted by fear and pessimism . . . [although] [t]he task of social reconstruction may never be finished once and for all.*[15]

Although students of political science have failed to identify the question of the *evaluation of the system* as an important one, especially in the disputes over the distribution of power in local communities, it is certain that Blacks will not fail to pursue this task. And they will do it in an active rather than in an academic way. Even if the normal modifications in benefits which an accommodating system makes are not delayed or reduced, Blacks will not gain equality from the existing political system. This inequality, and the conservative, slowly-accommodating political system which inhibits rapid and fundamental changes cannot help being questioned by Blacks. The prospects in that event are perhaps most accurately predicted by Robert Dahl:

> If a substantial segment of the electorate begins to doubt the creed, professionals will quickly come forth to fan that doubt. The nature and course of an appeal to the populace will change. What today is a question of applying the fundamental norms of democracy will become tomorrow an inquiry into the validity of these norms. If a substantial number of citizens begin to deny not merely to *some* minorities but to minorities *as such* the rights and powers prescribed in the creed, an appeal to the populace is likely to end sooner or later in a call to arms.[16]

Are the riots in Harlem, the Watts section of Los Angeles, and the "Jungle" in North Philadelphia merely the first episodes in that call to arms? Whatever the answer, the need for a critical evaluation of the political system and its relation to Blacks is urgent. The time for equality is now.

NOTES

1. Henry Klein, "The Anatomy of Power: The Closed Circle," *Greater Philadelphia Magazine* (October 1963), p. 53.

2. Social Committee on Nondiscrimination of the Board of Public Education of Philadelphia, Pennsylvania, *Report* (July 23, 1964), mimeographed, Philadelphia, pp. 10, 11, 19, 22.

3. Commission on Human Relations, *Philadelphia's Non-White Population 1960: Report No. 3, Socioeconomic Data* (Philadelphia, December 1962), p. 2.

4. *The Evening Bulletin,* December 12, 1963.

5. Robert A. Dahl, *Who Governs?* (New Haven: Yale University Press, 1961), p. 294.

6. Dahl, *Who Governs?* p. 36.

7. William Keech, *The Impact of Negro Voting: The Role of the Vote in the Quest for Equality* (Chicago: Rand McNally, 1968), p. 107.

8. Wallace Sayre and Herbert Kaufman, *Governing New York City* (New York: Russell Sage Foundation, 1960), pp. 709, 712.

9. *Ibid.,* p. 716.

10.. Dahl, *Who Governs?* p. 320.

11. Robert A. Dahl, "Equality and Power in American Society," in William V. D'Antonio and Howard J. Ehrlich, eds., *Power and Democracy in America* (Notre Dame, Ind.: University of Notre Dame Press, 1961), pp. 79-80.

12. Floyd Hunter, *Community Power Structure* (Chapel Hill, N.C.: University of North Carolina Press, 1953), pp. 5, 242.

13. Dahl, "Equality and Power . . . ," p. 89. Italics added.

14. Sayre and Kaufman, *Governing New York City,* pp. 720-721.

15. Hunter, *Community Power Structure,* pp. 237-38, 242, 253. Italics added.

16. Dahl, *Who Governs?* p. 325.

8

CECIL MOORE AND THE PHILADELPHIA BRANCH OF THE NATIONAL ASSOCIATION FOR THE ADVANCEMENT OF COLORED PEOPLE: THE POLITICS OF NEGRO PRESSURE GROUP ORGANIZATION

PAUL LERMACK

Paul Lermack, a graduate student in political science at the University of Minnesota, analyzes Cecil Moore's rise to power in the Philadelphia branch of the National Association for the Advancement of Colored People. In this excerpt from his master's thesis, Lermack describes Moore's political style and some of the organizational problems he encountered. Moore remains a key Black political leader in Philadelphia by virtue of some of the activities Lermack analyzes.

Cecil Moore, the president of the Philadelphia Chapter of the National Association for the Advancement of Colored People, is unquestionably a "mass" leader. His effect on the NAACP has been to make it responsive to the "little person." To some extent, he has done this by building up a cult of personality around himself.

> Cecil Moore represented to that little person the hope that he never had before.
> Now that Cecil Moore has come, and he is a natural leader, selected by the people, the people feel they have a stake in the NAACP.[1]

It is difficult, in the above quotation, to separate Moore and the NAACP.

Moore, who was elected in October 1962, quickly made a grab for the reins of power. Because of his position, some have referred to him as the leader of the poor Negro community,[2] while others have called him the "first single spokesman the Philadelphia Negro community has ever had."[3] In actuality, while he claims both positions, he holds neither.

Moore does not come from ghetto stock. He was born in West Virginia to a family of college graduates. His father was a doctor and "community leader." In the late 1930's, he "took to the road," working for several years as a bartender and an insurance salesman. This was the beginning of a lifelong drive to make himself "one of the masses." In 1942, Moore joined the Marines. He fought well, and turned down a battlefield commission. Following the war, he remained in the Marines, at Fort Mifflin, until 1951.[4]

During this time, Moore began to go to Temple University Law School at night, ". . . on the GI Bill, or else I wouldn't have been able to go to Law School."[5] He was graduated in 1953. Today, he maintains "one of the largest criminal practices in the country," handling thirty or forty cases a week.[6] Although he does a large volume of business, the bulk of his practice involves the very poor. For this reason, Moore does not appear to be getting rich.

Moore's entire style of living is carefully calculated to appeal to the "lower classes." In essence, he talks the language of the poor. He lives (near Seventeenth and Jefferson Streets) in the heart of the poor neighborhood. And, as we shall see, he has concentrated attention on "field hand" problems.

Moore had always been very active in civil rights causes. "For years Cecil Moore had fought the taproom situation in North Philadelphia and had almost singlehandedly led the fight against bias in the Unions."[7] He has been a member of the NAACP for "over 30 years" and was, apparently, held down by the conservative nature of the local leadership. He had run for president before and had been soundly beaten. Power seems to have come to him rather suddenly. He was the leader of a dissident, militant faction partly within and partly without the NAACP.

146

Sudden optimism caused by the civil rights movement accounted for his election by a narrow margin.[8]

To a certain extent, the activism of Moore can be explained by his having personal ambitions. Certainly he has always been interested in politics. He was a ward leader in 1954 and a Republican delegate to the National Convention. He ran against Democratic incumbent Robert N. C. Nix in 1956 for the congressional seat from the fourth Philadelphia district. He seems to have been obsessed with the successful career of Manhattan Negro leader Adam Clayton Powell.

Moore has been denying future political ambitions for a long time.[10] Even when the membership of the NAACP was at its highest, it was reported:

> He [Moore] denies reports that he hopes to take advantage of their current voting strength and his newly won prestige by making another race against Representative Robert N. C. Nix, a democrat and a Negro, who defeated him handily. . . .[11]

Close observers suggest that Moore would *like* to be a congressman, but that he has, in fact, done nothing about becoming one. Even after he announced his candidacy in March 1966, a close associate denied that Moore had any sort of political organization or funds available for this campaign.[12]

Moore's aims may or may not be political. There is no doubt that he wants sincerely to build a strong unified Negro community that can be successful in bargaining with the whites. It is also true that he wants to be the leader of that community. For this reason, discipline, in addition to unity, becomes important:

> Before you can fight a war you've got to have an army, you've got to have a loyal, disciplined army with everybody interested in the same purpose and the same method.[13]

Much of the style of Moore's leadership is dictated by the need to maintain personal control over the Negro masses. In order to keep his following, the "mass" leader must denounce the whites. He must also denounce opposition Negro leaders as "Uncle Toms."[14] Moore has done this with a vengeance. One of his favorite greetings is "welcome back to the Negro race." It has been suggested that, in order to strengthen his position with the masses, Moore may welcome attacks on himself by conservative leadership.[15] Such attacks have been frequent.

Related to this is the need to insist on a populist approach to leadership. Moore has managed to spread the impression that he was "elected by the people," implying that other Black leaders aren't. Part of Moore's style is to make the "mass" Negro believe that for the first time, the decisions which affect his life may be influenced by leaders whom he has helped to pick. The result has been to emphasize the difference between the Negro and the white communities. A natural channel has been found for the impatience of the poor Black. Moore can blame everything on the white community, or on "sellout" Negro leaders. He thus uses hate to produce unity. Most of this hate is channelled against leaders. Some of it is directed against the white community as a whole:

> There is little difference between the Negro here and the Negro in Alabama. . . . There the Negro has no vote and no responsibility; here the Negro has the responsibility but does not reap the benefits.[16]

His style of leadership is the direct opposite of the late Reverend Martin Luther King's. Moore arouses the hatred of the Negro for the white. King aroused the love of the white for the Negro.[17]

Any movement involving strong emotion must have a goal. One of Moore's weak points is that he has not always been able to find an outlet for this race hatred, and has ended up taking it out on such politically unimportant people as night club singer Nancy Wilson. The closest he has come to a realistic goal is to forecast Negro dominance at the polls: "We're going to run the damn City."[18]

Moore's style of leadership, then, is to arouse strong emotions that prompt unity and show him as the uncorruptible unifier. Or, as he has expressed it, "You gotta use a little demagoguery, now and then."[19] The reactions to himself and to his leadership from both whites and Negroes have been mixed.

From supporters within the NAACP, reactions range from approval to hero worship. Moore has been surprisingly successful in presenting the idea that he represents a change from previous, established leadership. "Cecil Moore is the only leader we have ever had who was selected by the people. All the other leaders were picked for us."[20] His colleagues tend to excuse his faults. According to Paul Vance, for instance, Moore's "fanaticism" is not fanaticism at all, but merely the reflection of his dynamic energy.[21] Some of the civil rights workers in other groups have expressed favorable sentiments. For instance, Andrew G. Freeman, the executive director of Philadelphia's Urban League, says, "I think Cecil Moore is performing a service for Philadelphia."[22]

Many NAACP members consider Moore to be somewhat extreme in his views:

> Said one former NAACP colleague, who departed from the organization when Cecil Moore came to the top: 'Cecil Moore is as close to Malcolm X and the Black Muslims, without being an avowed follower, as anyone I know.'[23]

Moore's law colleagues see him in an entirely different light.

> I think he's capable, smart and competent, but I don't think he pays much attention to the law itself. He's a real maneuverer. He depends on wit rather than competency. And he's glib.[24]

Official Philadelphia has, for the most part, underreacted. The mayor has not taken sides for or against Moore. However, Moore has made some powerful enemies. Philadelphia magistrate John P. Walsh, referring both to Moore's civil rights activities and his casual treatment of his law practice, wearily observed to him, "You've been getting away with murder."[25] By far Moore's most outspoken critic has been Philadelphia City Council President Paul D'Ortona, who has several times blasted Moore's "irresponsible" leadership.[26]

Most of the journalists have been favorable. About the worst criticism was that of Joseph Alsop: "[he is] . . . vivid, violent, intensely dramatic, almost too highly colored in everything he wears and says and does."[27] A remark of Frank Ford's is, perhaps, more typical:

> He is not concerned very much with what people think; he is very much concerned with what people do. . . . I think there is little question that he is a champion of a people who need a champion.[28]

The reaction to what Moore *is* is mixed. What has he *done*? The answer is that in one sense, he has done a great deal, while in another sense, he has done very little.

In terms of *activity*, Moore has been keeping busy. Moore has been known to threaten pickets or court action as a result of a single complaint.[29] Several large campaigns are particularly associated with him. The first, beginning soon after he took office, was a massive effort to call attention to segregation in the trade unions. He first received press attention with an extensive campaign of picketing at the construction site of the new Municipal Services Building to call attention to the discriminatory hiring practices of the building unions. This campaign began on May 11, 1963, and lasted several weeks.[30] Moore used this activity to rally support for his militancy. This was followed almost immediately by a campaign of picketing at a school construction site at Thirty-second and Dauphin Streets in North Central Philadelphia. The objective was the same. During the picketing, which lasted through most of June and July, there were several instances of violence.[31] The final large campaign was mounted in December 1963. It involved the picketing of the Trailways Bus Terminal in Philadelphia to protest the exclusive hiring practices that company was alleged to be following. On December 15, thirty members of the NAACP were arrested because of their participation in this activity.[32]

It is important to note that each of these campaigns eclipsed some activity of another civil rights group. The Municipal Services Building picketing stole the thunder of the Congress of Racial Equality which had been picketing the same site since April 13th.[33] The Trailways campaign deflected attention from the activities of the Camden branch of the NAACP which picketed apartment buildings in Cherry Hill, New Jersey, alleging discrimination.[34]

Moore did not get very satisfactory results from these efforts. "The building trades still discriminate."[35] Only a few Negroes were hired as a result of the Municipal Services Building picketing.[36] The only documented result of the school site picketing was that the construction unions hired five Negroes.[37] The Trailways bus dispute was settled when Moore got the company to hire sixteen Negro drivers.[38] However, the required number was never hired.[39] The most colossal failure was the

150

failure of Negroes to turn out for the mass work stoppage Moore called on May 24, 1963, as a memorial to Medgar Evers. The turnout was small.[40]

Moore's successes have come in quieter enterprises. He takes credit for the increase in the number of Negroes employed as clerks in small businesses.[41] He also brought to light and had corrected discriminatory hiring practices in the Philadelphia Post Office and in the Pennsylvania Railroad.[42] During a voter registration drive, Moore claims to have registered nearly 70,000 voters in nine weeks.[43]

The large campaigns, then, were practical failures but symbolic successes. They were much more important in this regard than anyone will admit. For Moore, riding on the hatred of the masses, is to a great extent their slave. He can remain the leader of the lower-class Blacks only so long as he can call forth the hatred of the whites and "Uncle Toms" that give them unity. He must, therefore, keep his leadership to the front. He must continuously hammer away, call names and run demonstrations. He must blow his own horn.[44]

In the spring of 1965 Moore was required to increase his efforts in this respect. He had not had a mass campaign of his own since 1963. His image was such that he could not delay activism much longer. Several cracks were appearing in his organization. The animosity between him and his first vice-president, Georgie Woods, had come to the public's attention, and he feared the defection of followers. He needed an action to keep the lower-class Negroes clustered around his banner.

A rival source of power, in the form of the Philadelphia Antipoverty Action Committee, was about to get under way. If this project became successful, rival leaders might be created. The energy of the masses, diverted to economic betterment, might become difficult to control. If Moore decided to work against the Committee, he needed some way of winning the masses to his side. If he decided to work through the Committee, a united army behind him would give him more bargaining power. Either way, he had to heal the dissidence within his ranks, and he had to get in his bid for leadership before the committee was completely off the ground.

Moore also hoped to silence another group of leaders. He has always envied the power of the Philadelphia Negro ministers. They can communicate with an estimated 100,000 Negro churchgoers.[45] They have used this power, exercised through the calling of selective boycotts, to have Negroes hired at all of the large industrial plants in the Philadelphia area.[46] Moore had at one time hoped to carry out programs similar to those of the ministers and, to this end, had tried to build up the size of the NAACP.[47] However, he has not been able to develop that kind of a communications network. His relations with the ministers were cat-and-mouse: "The Negro ministers watch him carefully, supporting him when they find him constructive, quietly opposing him when he becomes too violent or too obviously racist."[48] The proper campaign would get the ministers to support Moore and, with them behind him, he would be strengthened in his dealings with the antipoverty committee and with the dissidents in his own ranks.

Moore was also faced with a now-or-never situation in his own political ambitions. If he were going to run for Congress or for other political office, it would have to be within the next few years. The success, or even the optimistic activity, of the antipoverty program was bound to cut into his following. Also, he cannot make Blacks hate forever without bringing about either a letdown or a riot. The poverty program had already begun to call forward new community leaders. Moore was, in short, in a do-or-die position. He had one strength. He had just been reelected as President of the NAACP by a five to one margin. However, even this strength was an impulse to action. The NAACP had reelected him so that he would *do* something. He needed more than a campaign. He needed one with a hope of victory.

Cecil Moore, in the spring of 1965, was trapped by his position. He was a leader of the poor Negroes. If he wanted to retain his leadership, for whatever reason, he was going to have to commit his reputation to some drastic activity.

In 1965, the NAACP was suffering from a bad press and a worse public image. The national NAACP was "the largest, best organized and most efficiently run of the Negro leadership organizations."[49] In 1962, it had 1,494 branches (in forty-eight states) and 471,060 members.[50] However, despite its mass membership, the Reverend Wyatt Tee Walker, a national civil rights leader, could say "the N.A.A.C.P. has become bureaucratic [and] it has lost contact with the grass roots people."[51]

152

The leadership of the NAACP has been accused of being "conservative."[52] This term is perhaps best paralleled by the Communists' term "revisionist" in its connotation of good intentions but wrong politics. Also, the Negroes, especially the lower classes, began to associate the NAACP with the slow legal process.[53] Following the Birmingham, Alabama riots and the noncompliance with the Supreme Court school desegregation decisions, the opinion widespread among Negroes was that legalism would get them nothing but more subtle means of segregation.

To a great extent, the NAACP was a captive of its past. It was created as an "upper-class" Negro institution, and its first objective was to insure the acceptance into the white community of those Negroes who, by hard work, thrift, and morality, had proved themselves qualified.[54] Its membership has always been "heavily populated by middle-income professionals."[55] Traditionally, it has relied heavily on the Negro clergy and especially on those clergymen with standards of middle-class reference.[56] Given the separation between the two Negro communities, it is doubtful whether the NAACP was ever a "mass" organization at all. More likely, it was an organization controlled by middle-class Negroes with a token membership among poor Blacks and whites.

The national organization is set up in such a way that it is easy to maintain control at the top. The rank-and-file membership can suggest policies at conventions, but cannot compel their acceptance. Only the executive board which is made up of leaders with "time" (i.e., is made up of middle-class Negro and white leaders who have lesiure to devote to the organization) can do that. The national executive board may discipline or suspend any member, chapter, or chapter officer. It is not surprising, then, that the executive committee has always managed to carry the organization for middle-class concerns, and that the lower-class Negroes have lost the little faith they had in the organization. Louis Lomax stated the problem clearly: "I am convinced that the NAACP has failed to launch a program whose visible goals capture the imagination of the Negro masses."[57]

The Philadelphia chapter of the NAACP has suffered from the bad image described above. In part, this bad image is simply a reflection of that of the national organization. In part, it is due to the past history of the Philadelphia branch, for, as Lomax says, "N.A.A.C.P. leadership tends to be conservative both at the top and bottom."[58] The NAACP was organized in Philadelphia in 1912. Through the years, it has successfully integrated hotels, restaurants, and railroads. It has always worked quietly through the courts and through the threat of economic pressure.[59] It had always conceived of its function as that of making things easier for the middle-class Negro, and of encouraging Negroes to become middle class. It desegregated restaurants, for instance, so that Negroes who had earned the money could eat in them. Indirectly, it hoped to encourage other Negroes to earn money by holding out to them the reward of being able to eat in the restaurants.

Before Cecil Moore, middle-class Negroes held all the offices in the Philadelphia branch, which had 6,000 members.[60] This elite determined policy. The problems they undertook to solve were those of the middle class. They integrated the restaurants and they undertook to provide education for the children of a small number of Black families.

The perception of the lower-class Negroes of all this was, as can be expected, dismal. "[Before Moore] I think the organization never belonged to the masses. . . . we didn't take the organization to the people or to the streets."[61] The masses were effectively excluded because, "You couldn't come to the meetings unless you were dressed and you couldn't talk [on the floor] unless you could use good grammar."[62] And, finally, the methods used were quiet ones:

> We had people that frowned on direct action, picketing or any type of personal involvement in what they considered extreme methods of getting the rights . . . and because of this, there were those who frowned on the new element, the new Negro or the "young Turks."[63]

Small wonder, then, that *The Philadelphia Independent* made the charge that before Cecil Moore the NAACP was a "private" organization.[64]

A drastic change came about in the organization with Moore's administration. The organization became militant, as evidenced by the picketing campaigns described in previous sections. The Philadelphia chapter became a "people's organization." For the first time, as the programs of the NAACP began to reflect the needs of the poor Blacks, the mass of Negroes began to take an interest in the organization and to participate in it.[65]

This new involvement was reflected in an immediate increase in membership. Moore took office in January 1963. By June the membership had increased to 19,000,[66] and Moore claimed he would speak for 50,000 Negroes by the end of that month.[67] The membership reached a peak of 23,400 in October, and began to decline. By the time of Moore's second election, it numbered 12,400.[68] At the same time, the membership of the youth group increased to "over 750."[69]

Most of the middle class remained within the organization. As old leaders, they had a difficult time adjusting themselves to the loss of power they had suffered. Also, as the organization swung toward objectives of occupational and housing concerns to satisfy the newly-recruited mass membership, the middle class began to find their traditional concerns of homeownership and education slighted. They responded in three ways. They tried to recapture leadership by supporting the Reverend Henry J. Nichols for the presidency in 1965. They sought to have Moore discredited before the national organization. Finally, some broke away to found rival groups or to support established rival groups.

The "old guard," which disagreed with Moore, seized the candidacy of Nichols as an opportunity to eject Moore. Nichols made no bones about his campaign issue. He charged Moore with running a "one man show."[70] This line of attack immediately reallied all the dissatisfied around him. He amplified his charge, and appealed to the legalistic middle class by complaining that Moore ran roughshod over many of the organization's rules and bylaws.[71]

In addition to the issues, controversy was raised over the location of the polling places. Nichols, counting on the strength of the middle class, wanted a single center-city location. Moore wanted several locations so that the "common man" could vote. It is instructive to look at the breakdown of residences of the members submitted by Moore: 2,100 lived in Germantown, 5,600 in West Philadelphia, 3,900 in the North Philadelphia ghetto, and 1,400 in the South Philadelphia ghetto. The middle class, in numbers, was still strong in the organization.[72]

Shortly before the election, Nichols charged that it was "fixed" and that Moore and the national office were conspiring against him.[73] These charges gained wide circulation in the days before the election.

Moore was eventually reelected 2,215-474, a margin of about five to one.[74] The great size of his victory would seem to indicate that he had won a number of the middle-class Negroes to his side, and that his support was deep and genuine. However, Nichols' vehement charges left a legacy of division and suspicion within the organization. Moore's victory cry, ". . . I'm still the goddamn boss,"[75] did nothing to help the situation.

The second revolt of the "old guard" took place during the campaign. In January 1965 several "dissidents" charged Moore with "fiscal irresponsibility."[76] He was given three hearings, the last of which took place on January 8. This hearing became a sounding board for anti-Moore sympathies. Financial charges took up most of the meeting. One member testified that it was common practice to advance funds without the treasurer's approval.[78] Moore was eventually cleared of all charges. However, the disclosures of "fiscal irresponsibility" doubtless isolated Nichols' followers even more from the bulk of the membership. The attempt to drag their leader through the mud aroused hostility on the part of Moore's followers. Like the election, the hearings produced division.

During this time, the middle class was pursuing its third course of revolt. Large numbers were defecting. Moore's opponents had been disgruntled with him from the very beginning, but most remained in the organization to avoid the spectacle of an open split.[78] The first publicized defections occurred with the resignation of four members in early 1963 to protest Moore's firing of former executive secretary Tom Burgess.[79] From then on, the exodus grew larger.[80]

The most serious defection took place in April 1965. A group of old leaders, led by Regina Black, broke away to form the new "Philadelphia Association for Negro Achievement." Their parting blast was, "Moore criticizes Negroes just because they happen to live in middle-class Germantown."[81] These defections robbed the NAACP of a source of educated members and money, both of which it badly needed.

In the spring of 1965, the NAACP was a divided organization. The "unity." that Moore called for in his inaugural address[82] was sorely needed. For, at that time, the NAACP was facing a series of problems which required unity. One of the charges that Nichols made against Moore was that his actions were closing the channels of communication between the NAACP and the other civil rights groups active in the city.[83] The most serious falling out occurred with CORE. CORE is a much smaller group than the NAACP. In September 1963, when the membership of the NAACP was still over twenty thousand, the membership of CORE was about nine hundred.[84] The difficulty actually began with the preempting by the NAACP of the Municipal Services Building and school site picketing. These were projects which CORE had started. Both Moore and CORE attempted to take credit for the hiring of sixteen Negro drivers by Trailways. Again, CORE had begun the activity before the NAACP moved in. A feud ensued,[85] culminating in CORE's blast against Moore's "deals."[86] This split seriously weakened the Philadelphia civil rights movement.

A similar difficulty was the threat of the late Reverend Martin Luther King to begin activity in Philadelphia. His well-united movement was able to steal prominence from the badly divided NAACP at the very time when the NAACP needed all of its prestige to gain a bargaining position in the new city antipoverty action committee. Some experts felt that the entire campaign to integrate Girard College, a local private school for male, white orphans, was a tactic to steal King's thunder. They noted:

> Some observers believed it more than coincidental that Moore's demonstration was scheduled on the first appearance of Dr. King in Philadelphia since he said he would bring his own movement here. The latter was attending an all-day Law Day program at the University of Pennsylvania on Saturday [May 1, when the Girard campaign began] and ignored the picketing.[87]

The second large rally at Girard College, on May 11, was also timed to coincide with a speech of King's.[88]

At the same time, the NAACP was having financial difficulties. "Fiscal irresponsibility" is very real in this organization and the treasurer's report shows a paper deficit of $6,147.52;[89] this was at the end of a long campaign to keep the organization's head above water. An index of the trouble can be found in the revelation that the chapter's contribution to the legal defense fund, which was $9,000 in 1963 and was supposed to be $5,000 in 1965, was $50 as of October 1965.[90]

157

The membership of the organization was dropping drastically. The reported membership in 1963 was over 20,000. As of October 15, 1965, it was 3,855. In 1964, 10,877 members had been lost and apparently 7,649 in 1965.[91] Some of these can be accounted for by the defection of the middle class. However, the magnitude of the number indicates that the lower-class Blacks are also leaving. The year 1964 had been slow, and action-oriented members sank back into apathy.

The Philadelphia chapter, then, was a disunited, poorly-organized group. Cecil Moore had succeeded in first building up and then destroying a large part of the organization's membership. His flamboyant leadership of the NAACP was a significant part of the 1960's era in Philadelphia Black politics, but it is difficult to see many long-term benefits from his tenure as the chapter's president.

NOTES

1. Interview with Mrs. Gertrude Barnes, second vice president of the Philadelphia Chapter of the NAACP, October 14, 1965.

2. "Goddamn Boss", *Time* LXXXIV (September 11, 1964), p. 24.

3. Gaeton J. Fonzi, "Cecil Storms In", *Greater Philadelphia Magazine* LIV (July, 1963), p. 21.

4. *Ibid.*, p. 48

5. Interview with Cecil Moore on the *Frank Ford Show*, March 27, 1966 (author's transcript). Cited below as "Frank Ford interview".

6. Fonzi, "Cecil", pp. 49-50.

7. Frank Ford interview.

8. Interview with Gertrude Barnes.

9. Fonzi, "Cecil", pp. 48, 50.

10. *Ibid*; also see *The Pennsylvania Guardian,* June 7, 1963, p. 10.

11. *The New York Times*, August 15, 1963, p. 1.

12. Interview with Mr. Walter Rosenbaum, former member of the executive committee of the Philadelphia Chapter of the NAACP, October 2, 1965.

13. Fonzi, "Cecil", p. 52.

14. Theodore White, *The Making of the President* (New York: Atheneum House, 1960), p. 283.

15. *The Pennsylvania Guardian,* June 7, 1963, p. 3.

16. *The Philadelphia Independent,* March 6, 1965, p. 24.

17. *The Philadelphia Independent,* August 12, 1965, p. 1.

18. *The New York Times,* August 15, 1963, p. 1.

19. *Ibid.*

Paul Lermack

20. Interview with Gertrude Barnes.

21. Interview with Paul Vance, adviser to the youth council of the Philadelphia Chapter of the NAACP, October 16, 1965.

22. Fonzi, "Cecil", p. 48.

23. *The Pennsylvania Guardian,* June 7, 1963, p. 3.

24. Fonzi, "Cecil", p. 48.

25. *The Crisis* LXXI (February, 1964), p. 106.

26. *The Philadelphia Inquirer,* May 10, 1965, p. 31. D'Ortona observed, somewhat wishfully, "Thank God that the rank and file of the colored people do not believe in him."

27. *The New York Times,* August 15, 1963, p. 1.

28. Frank Ford interview.

29. *The Pennsylvania Guardian,* June 7, 1963, p. 3.

30. *The Philadelphia Inquirer,* May 12, 1963, p. 8.

31. Fonzi, "Cecil", pp. 22-23.

32. *The Crisis* LXXI (February, 1964), p. 106.

33. *The Philadelphia Inquirer,* April 14, 1963, p. 24.

34. *The Crisis* LXXI (April, 1964), p. 220.

35. Interview with Gertrude Barnes.

36. Hanna Lees, "Philadelphia, Pa.: A Process of Fragmentation", *Reporter* XXIX (July 4, 1963), p. 20.

37. *The Pennsylvania Guardian,* June 7, 1963, p. 3.

38. *The Crisis* LXXI (February, 1964), p. 105.

39. *The Philadelphia Independent,* January 16, 1965, p. 7.

40. *The New York Times,* August 15, 1963, p. 1.

41. Frank Ford interview.

42. Interview with George Sellers, third vice-president of the Philadelphia Chapter of the NAACP, October 2, 1965.

43. *The Crisis* LXXI (October, 1964), p. 534.

44. His sound truck at Girard College bore a large sign reading "Go with Moore," the *Philadelphia Inquirer,* May 2, 1965, p. 1.

45. *The Pennsylvania Guardian,* June 7, 1963, p. 3.

46. See Hanna Lees, "The not-Buying Power of Philadelphia Negroes," *Reporter* XXIV (May 11, 1961) 33-35.

47. *The Pennsylvania Guardian,* June 7, 1963, p. 3.

48. Lees, "Fragmentation," p. 19.

49. *Ibid.*

50. Louis E. Lomax, *The Negro Revolt* (New York: Harper and Row, 1962), p. 111.

51. Robert Penn Warren, *Who Speaks for the Negro?* (New York: Random House, 1965), p. 229.

52. Lomax, p. 105.

53. William Brink and Louis Harris, *The Negro Revolt in America* (New York: Simon and Schuster, 1964), p. 41.

54. Lomax, p. 105.

55. Brink and Harris, p. 113.

56. *Ibid.*, pp. 107-108.

57. Lomax, p. 115.

58. *Ibid.*, p. 105.

59. Fonzi, "Cecil", p. 47.

60. Interview with Gertrude Barnes; interview with Samuel Branham, community organizer, Germantown Settlement House, March 29, 1966.

61. Interview with Gertrude Barnes.

62. *Ibid.*

63. *Ibid.*

64. *The Philadelphia Independent,* February 6, 1965, p. 1.

65. *The Wall Street Journal,* June 21, 1963, p. 1.

66. *Ibid.*

67. *The Pennsylvania Guardian,* June 7, 1963, p. 3.

68. *The Wall Street Journal,* January 14, 1965, p. 14.

69. Interview with Paul Vance.

70. *The Philadelphia Tribune,* January 19, 1965, p. 1.

71. *Ibid.*, January 9, 1965, p. 1.

72. *Ibid.*, January 16, 1965, p. 5.

73. *The Philadelphia Independent,* February 6, 1965, p. 20.

74. *Ibid.*, February 13, 1965, p. 20.

75. *Ibid.*

76. *The Philadelphia Tribune,*January 9, 1965, p. 3.

77. *The Philadelphia Independent,* January 9, 1965, p. 19.

78. Fonzi, "Cecil", pp. 45-46.

79. *Ibid.*

80. Interview with Samuel Branham.

81. *The Philadelphia Independent*, April 24, 1965, p. 3.

82. *Ibid.*, March 6, 1965, p. 24.

83. *The Philadelphia Tribune,* January 19, 1965, p. 2.

84. "C.O.R.E. Goes Slumming," *Great Philadelphia Magazine* LIV (September, 1963, p. 89.)

85. *The Philadelphia Independent*, January 2, 1965, p. 1, January 16, 1965.

86. *The Philadelphia Tribune*, January 12, 1965, p. 1.

87. *The Philadelphia Inquirer*, May 2, 1965, section II, p. 1.

88. *Ibid.*, May 12, 1965, p. 5.

89. Report of the treasurer of the NAACP, September, 1965.

90. *The Philadelphia Evening Bulletin,* October 24, 1965, p. 3.

91. *Ibid.*

PART THREE

THE POLITICS
OF BLACK
PARTICIPATION IN
COMMUNITY-
CONTROLLED
ANTIPOVERTY
PROGRAMS

Introduction

Studies of political participation[1] throughout the United States all show the same result: the rich, the educated, the Caucasian are politically involved and reap the benefits that politics can bestow, while the poor, the uneducated, the nonwhite are only minimally involved and receive few, if any, of the significant rewards that the government has to offer.[2] Some theorists have argued that this low level of political participation is good for our democratic system, for it indicates a great amount of satisfaction with the society.[3] Others, sensing that a lack of self-confidence and political know-how may be the primary cause of low participation, have suggested that nonparticipation or apathy on the part of the urban masses is a symptom of illness, not of health, in the body politic.[4] It was out of these latter sentiments that early New Left organizers first went into the ghettos in 1963.[5] Similar feelings among governmental advisors led to the development of community action programs as a part of the broader Economic Opportunities Act of 1964.

As John Donovan has observed, Title II of this Act, ". . . when read casually, sounds pedestrian enough":[6]

Section 202 (a)
    The term "community action program" means a program—(1) which mobilizes and utilizes resources, public or private, of any urban or rural, or combined urban and rural geographical area (referred to in this part as a "community"), including but not limited to a State, metropolitan area, county, city, town, multi-city

163

unit, or multi-county unit in an attack on poverty;

(2) which provides services, assistance, and other activities of sufficient scope and size to give promise of progress toward elimination of poverty or a cause or causes of poverty through developing employment opportunities, improving human performance, motivation, and productivity, or bettering the conditions under which people live, learn and work;

(3) which is developed, conducted, and administered with the maximum feasible participation of residents of the areas and members of the groups served; . . .

The key phrase appears in Section 202 (a) (3): "maximum feasible participation." Although the drafters of the bill never came to grips with the full implications of such an experiment in political engineering, the intent of these words was to bring the poor into positions of power in the administration of programs affecting their own livelihood, and thus to train them for broader involvement in politics and to convince them that effective political participation can bring direct and worthwhile benefits. Community action was a bold new concept, offering to the poor—and particularly the poor Black—an opportunity to overthrow the old-fashioned ethnic politics that had ruled their lives for upwards of a century and to create a new style of urban politics based on the active participation and political power of the American Negro. Needless to say, the program met serious opposition from the "establishment" in many cities.[7]

In Philadelphia, city hall's response was both positive and quick. By February, 1965, Mayor Tate had created a citizen task force to draw up plans for Philadelphia's war on poverty, submitted a thirteen million dollar grant proposal to the federal government, and reconstituted his citizen's group to make it more representative of the city's poor. The program began in earnest in late May 1965, when elections were held in the so-called "target" areas for seats on the local community action councils—Philadelphia's answer to the "maximum feasible participation" requirement of the Economic Opportunities Act. Funds began flowing into the city from Washington shortly thereafter. Professor Harry A. Bailey, Jr. has described the early development of the Philadelphia program, its organization, and its mission in Chapter 9.

164

Shortly after the poverty program began in Philadelphia, the city held "antipoverty elections" (1965) to choose 144 representatives to local community action councils. While initial observations led to the conclusion that the program had been a success in stimulating participation among the poor, more serious and detached commentaries were less sanguine. Professor Elliott White, in Chapter 10, concludes that the election and subsequent antipoverty activities really produced a minimum—not a "maximum"—level of participation among the city's poor and did little to educate or to encourage the poor for increased political involvement.

Kenneth Clark and Jeanette Hopkins in their book, *A Relevant War Against Poverty*, reached much the same conclusion from a different perspective.[9]

> One observes in the Philadelphia story the high degree of suspicion and alienation with which the poor greeted the antipoverty program, . . . and the emphasis of the elected councils, despite a frequent verbal militance, on patterning themselves, or being patterned after, the social services opportunity orientation of the settlement house-political club facility of the past. One may speculate on the extent to which the representatives of the poor are inadvertently being used by the majority culture to sell its concept of self-help to the poor and even to tamp down the expectations and aspirations of the poor. To the extent that this *is* the consequence, such programs fail to lead to effective social change and indeed may serve as a positive impediment to change.
>
> There is a real question . . . whether the elected poor have been able to be effective in representation of the poor in Philadelphia or elsewhere.

By 1967 the flow of monies from the national government to local poverty programs across the country had been seriously curtailed. By this time, too, the Philadelphia antipoverty organization was teetering on the verge of chaos. Although the two articles printed here do not examine the problems that eventually overwhelmed the Philadelphia Antipoverty Action Committee in Philadelphia, the sources of these problems are already evident: awkward relations with city hall, low levels of grassroots participation, and the development and manipulation

165

of an elite structure among the poor themselves. In effect, all of these reflect the historic condition of the poor—and especially the poor Negro—in Philadelphia politics. Clearly, the old order quickly adapts to new conditions and new structures. What these authors demonstrate is that the level and style of political participation necessary to make the Negro a viable force in Philadelphia politics cannot be engineered through artificial means imposed from outside the city.

This leads us back to those early efforts by members of the SDS and to more indigenous movements such as the Muslims and Black Panthers. Since the publication of *Black Power* by Carmichael and Hamilton and their call for Blacks ". . . to think of the black community as a base of organization to control institutions in that community . . . ,"[10] local control over neighborhood social and governmental bodies has been a major theme in the urban political conflict. Perhaps the extreme militancy of the two forenamed organizations is dysfunctional in the long run to the political needs of todays ghetto residents, but indigenous community control is not the same as armed rebellion. As Alan Altshuler has argued community control is both consistent with the traditional, decentralized character of our federal system and may be the only mechanism which can hope to effectively increase political competence throughout the Black community.[11] Altshuler points out:

> There is substantial reason as well to hope for more specific benefits [from community control]. A great many black problems are due to pathologies of the ghetto spirit—or rather, more accurately, to behavior patterns that are adaptive to the ghetto as it is, but which constitute severe obstacles to improving it. These problems are the products of black self-hatred, despair, fatalism, and alienation from authority much more than of poverty itself. . . . These characteristics have been fostered primarily by oppression, but also by paternalism. The active oppression is decreasing rapidly, but the legacy of the past will be spinning out its consequences for a long while to come.
>
> There is almost surely a greater potential for improving the ghettos by transforming their spirit than by inundating them with paternalistic programs. This is not to deny that resources are essential. Quite obviously, rapid change will be impossible without massive infusions of outside aid. But it is to maintain that resources are

166

not enough. . . . Self-determination might not produce any better results. But a great many people, including just about all the nation's black leaders, believe that it would. It would certainly seem to merit serious trial.

NOTES

1. By "participation" we mean, at the minimum, regular voting.

2. See, for example, Robert E. Lane, *Political Life* (Glencoe, Ill.: The Free Press, 1959), 4, 5, 6, 17, and 18 and Lester W. Milbrath, *Political Participation* (Chicago: Rand McNally, 1965), 5.

3. Bernard R. Berelson, *et al.*, *Voting* (Chicago: University of Chicago, 1954), 14. See also the writings of the Pluralistic school of democratic theorists.

4. On the importance of self-efficacy for political participation, see Milbrath, ch. 3.

5. Massimo Teodori, *The New Left* (Indianapolis: Bobbs-Merrill, 1969), pp. 128-149.

6. John C. Donovan, *The Politics of Poverty* (New York: Pegasus Books, 1967), pp. 39-40.

7. For a general description of the community action programs and the nation's response, see Donovan, 3-5.

8. There were twelve local councils, each with twelve elected members.

9. Kenneth Clark and Jeannette Hopkins, *A Relevant War Against Poverty*, (New York: Harper Torchbooks, 1970), p. 118.

10. Stokley Carmichael and Charles V. Hamilton, *Black Power* (New York: Vintage Books, 1967), p. 166.

11. Alan A. Altshuler, *Community Control* (New York: Pegasus Books, 1970), pp. 210-211.

9

POVERTY, POLITICS, AND ADMINISTRATION: THE PHILADELPHIA EXPERIENCE

HARRY A. BAILEY, JR.

Harry A. Bailey, Jr., Chairman of the Department of Political Science at Temple University, analyzes the organization and activity of the Philadelphia Antipoverty Action Committee in this study published here for the first time. A number of PAAC's administrative and public relations problems are described as well as the over-all impact of the agency on Philadelphia's poor Blacks. This analysis was written expressly for this volume.

This study focuses on the origin and development of Philadelphia's antipoverty program, the nature and extent of poverty in the city, and organizational arrangements in Philadelphia's antipoverty agency. Throughout the paper an assessment is made of the administrative and political issues within the agency as it was evolved and is developing. In all, the purpose is to provide a broad perspective of Philadelphia's war on poverty.

I

Officially, the war on poverty in Philadelphia began on February 22, 1965.[1] For purposes of record, however, its gestation dates from the action of Mayor James H. J. Tate in May 1964 establishing an organization entitled "The Mayor's Program for the Elimination of Poverty" (PEP). The agency's staff was instructed to begin work on the develop-

168

ment of a comprehensive program for the city's war on poverty.[2]

PEP failed to gain either federal or local acceptance. The failure to gain support was due largely to the lack of any representation of the lower economic groups at the highest decision-making level in the organization. The agency itself consisted entirely of members or former members of the mayor's administration. City Records Commissioner Clarence Dockens, the only Negro appointed to PEP, was there simply to provide token representation for Philadelphia's large Negro community.[3]

At the urging of the Office of Economic Opportunity (OEO), the mayor turned to the Philadelphia Council for Community Advancement (PCCA), a local nonprofit group financed by the Ford Foundation to deal with poverty problems in North Philadelphia, to develop an anti-poverty program within the PEP framework.[4] The mayor's willingness to utilize a group outside the city administration was enhanced by his realization that the city lacked the money to finance the local share of the program. The mayor hoped PCCA would provide this money.[5]

This effort came to naught. Earlier PCCA had itself been sharply criticized for its failure to obtain grass-roots support in its efforts in North Philadelphia. As a consequence, the mayor's selection of PCCA to develop an antipoverty program came under heavy criticism from the Philadelphia branches of the Americans for Democratic Action (ADA), the Congress of Racial Equality (CORE), and the National Association for the Advancement of Colored People (NAACP).[6]

The mayor subsequently dropped the PEP proposal and set up a new agency called the Mayor's Antipoverty Program (MAPP). The PCCA, however, continued to participate in the antipoverty program. The essential difference between PEP and MAPP was that the latter included a Human Services Committee (HSC) composed of almost every conceivable type of local religious, business, civic, and ethnic group. The mayor's city aides, however, continued to outnumber the other members appointed to this organization. Further, the mayor made no provision for representation of the poor.

The Human Services Committee of MAPP gathered ideas for a war on poverty from various civic and welfare agencies. These ideas were put together as a program proposal and forwarded to OEO. However, the OEO staff rejected all the proposals in October 1965.[7] Its rejection

169

of the proposals was attributed to the lack of representation of the poor, the preponderance of city officials in the HSC, and evidence of a considerable amount of local opposition to the proposals. In November 1965 PCCA withdrew from participation in MAPP for many of the same reasons which had caused the federal government to reject the program proposals.

The next step in the city's efforts to develop an acceptable antipoverty program came when the mayor replaced his city aides on the Human Services Committee with a racially and religiously balanced group of Negroes, Jews, Catholics, and white Anglo-Saxon Protestants. It was this new group under the chairmanship of Robert Hilkert, president of the Health and Welfare Council and vice-president of Philadelphia's Federal Reserve Bank, which developed an acceptable organizational structure for a community antipoverty agency, including ample representation of the poor.

The structure developed by the Hilkert committee which became the Philadelphia Antipoverty Action Committee (PAAC), was put into effect by executive order of the mayor in February 1965.[8] Thus PAAC became the city's official advisory agency to carry out those phases of the antipoverty war provided for in Title II, Part A, of the Economic Opportunity Act.

PAAC was organized under the powers granted to the mayor in section 3-100 (h) of the Philadelphia Home Rule Charter which authorizes him to appoint committees to act in advisory capacities. It was the creation of PAAC as an advisory agency which was later to cause problems for the city and the antipoverty program.

II

Before PAAC could develop a feasible program to combat poverty, it was essential that the socioeconomic characteristics of the poor be established and their location in the community determined. City officials and civic leaders knew that poverty existed in the community but the creation of the antipoverty program forced investigation and evaluation of the precise location, nature, and extent of poverty. While there is still uncertainty about the exact dimensions of poverty in

170

Philadelphia, there is no doubt that poverty in the material, spiritual, and psychic aspects prevails which does not recognize the color curtain.

Two reports were issued by which PAAC determined where the poor were located in the city and under what kinds of conditions they lived. The reports issued in December 1964—*Incidence of Poverty in Philadelphia*, prepared by the Community Renewal Program of the city government, and *Fact Book on Poverty*, prepared by the Philadelphia Health and Welfare Council—provided factual information. Later these two reports were updated by a third study, *Guidelines for the Mobilization of Services*, prepared for PAAC by the Philadelphia Health and Welfare Council. It was issued in January 1966.

The most commonly used measure of poverty is the annual income of families or individuals. The President's Council of Economic Advisers, using 1962 prices, decided in 1964 that $3,000 per family per year before taxes was the minimum income needed to purchase a liveable market basket of goods.[9] Using this definition, it was estimated that in Philadelphia in 1960 there were about 340,000 impoverished persons out of a population of slightly over two million. This figure represents 17 percent of all Philadelphia families.[10] Of the 381,584 white families in the city, 48,989 were in the poor category and a total of 36,690 of the city's 118,931 nonwhite families were poor.[11] Even though 57 percent of the families living in poverty were white, a greater proportion of nonwhite families fell into this category.

Poverty pockets were defined in terms of the number of persons with low income, low educational attainment and number of unemployed. Census tracts falling in the lowest quarter on at least one of these characteristics and the lower half on the other two, were considered the sections of the city with substantial amounts of poverty.[12]

Pockets of poverty were mapped out initially in such a way that about the same number of poverty households were located in each area in order that each population group would have equal representation in the PAAC. However, as finally constituted, some poverty pockets were made larger than others in order that those sections of the city with large numbers of poor families would be included in the area in which the antipoverty war would be concentrated. The total poverty population was divided into twelve parts designated A through L. The

171

range in population between areas is from 50,000 to about 200,000. Thus representation of the poor on the antipoverty governing board follows the upper house rather than the lower house plan of the federal government and many state legislatures. Smaller pockets of poverty not included within the poverty designations do exist in other places throughout the city. Persons in these areas are also entitled to the services of the PAAC program.

Income. According to the 1960 census, 64 percent of all Philadelphia families lived in the designated poverty areas. These families made up 82.3 percent of all families in the city with an annual income of less than $3,000 and 75 percent of all families having between $3,000 and $5,000 incomes. Using Leon Keyserling's measure of $6,000 for a "modest but adequate budget," and his argument that families with incomes below $5,000 are living in deprivation, it can readily be seen that a considerably large number of families who do not qualify as being legally poor or in the antipoverty program, under the President's Council of Economic Advisors measure, are without incomes needed for a decent standard of living.

A slightly different indication of low income in the poverty areas can be seen in the records of the Philadelphia County Board of Assistance. In April 1962, 96.6 percent of all welfare recipients in the city lived in such areas as well as 79.6 percent of all recipients of the blind pensions program. A total of 88.3 percent of all families receiving food under the federal government's surplus food distribution program in March 1965 were in these areas.

Education. Educational attainment is counted by the Bureau of the Census for adults 25 years of age and over. In 1960 such persons with less than an eighth grade education numbered over 550,000 in Philadelphia; 72.2 percent of this number lived in the poverty areas. Of those adults in the city classifying as "functionally illiterate," that is, having less than five full years of education, fully 80 percent lived in the poverty areas.

Unemployment. In 1960, the average rate of unemployment among the city's work force was 6.5 percent. In the poverty areas about 7.9 percent were unemployed. In some poverty areas, unemployment rates reached 13.4 percent.

172

Housing. The quality of housing is extremely bad in the areas of highest poverty concentration in the city. About 93 percent of all dilapidated housing in Philadelphia is located in such areas and about 88 percent of all overcrowded units are located there.

Births. Although the poverty areas contained only about two-thirds of the city's population, 70 percent of all live births occurred in these areas. In addition, about 95 percent of all illegitimate births in the city occurred to poverty-area women. Finally, the number of premature births in the poverty areas were much greater than in the city as a whole.

School Enrollment. Enrollment figures for poverty areas do not reveal the real numbers of inadequately trained people in these areas. Ninety percent of the population aged 14 to 17 years were enrolled in school in the poverty areas as against 93 percent in the city as a whole.

Juvenile Delinquency. In 1963, slightly over 70 percent of the estimated population aged 7 to 17 years lived in the poverty pockets. In the same year, however, police department statistics show that 82.6 percent of juvenile delinquency incidents resulting in police contacts occurred in these areas. Moreover, 87.8 percent of these contacts resulted in arrests.

Color of Poverty Population. In 1960, the nonwhite population of the city numbered over 500,000, 96.2 percent of whom lived in the poverty areas. But, as indicated earlier, poverty does not recognize the color curtain. The nonwhite population constituted only 38.7 percent of all persons living in high poverty locales. White persons made up 61.3 percent of all persons living in such areas. The number of nonwhite living in poverty areas, however, varies considerably from one area to another. The variations range from 2.1 percent in poverty area A to 99.5 percent in poverty area F.

It is clear that in Philadelphia at the inception of the poverty program the needs of the poor were not being fully met despite the many welfare programs in operation. PAAC promised the possibility of a more comprehensive and coordinated approach to the resolution of poverty in Philadelphia. To accomplish this goal, PAAC arranged for elective representation of the poor in compliance with the "maximum feasible participation" requirement of the Economic Opportunity Act.[13] The

173

three elections conducted in the poverty areas in 1965, 1966, and 1967 are discussed in the next section.

III

Philadelphia was the first major city in America to allow the poor to select their own representative to the local antipoverty governing board and thus to implement, in theory at least, the "civilian perspective" in the war on poverty. The "civilian perspective" is the counter approach of the "military perspective." Under the latter perspective, ideas and decisions "trickle down" to the poor. This perspective relies, primarily, on the energies and resources of the incumbent political administration and the major existing educational and civic institutions. In short, the poor are told what their needs are and the established organizations and their personnel formulate and carry on programs commensurate with these assumed needs.

The civilian perspective assumes providing the poor with effective power bases of their own from which they can criticize, dissent, and, where necessary, seek to compel responsiveness to their needs. Ideas and suggested decisions "percolate up" from the poor under the civilian perspective. The "maximum feasible participation" requirement of the Economic Opportunity Act was designed to make possible a significant measure of civilian perspective understandings. That the Philadelphia antipoverty program has not completely met these expectations will be discussed later. At this juncture it suffices to say that, in spite of the program providing for elected representatives of the poor, it has more of the image of maximum feasible participation than it has the substance.

The 1965 Election. In the latter part of March 1965 the subcommittee on community action councils of the PAAC developed the details of a plan to elect representatives of the poor to the antipoverty governing board. The representatives, 144 in all (12 representatives in each of the 12 councils), would, in turn, each elect one of their own to serve as a member of the 31-member PAAC board. Town meetings were planned for each of the council areas for the purpose of informing the poor of the impending election and the

174

procedures involved for participating in the election.

In mid-April 1965 the mayor appointed an executive director and several other persons to head up the temporary staff of PAAC. The new executive director planned and implemented a publicity campaign to inform the poverty community of the town meetings. Thousands of leaflets and posters were prepared and distributed throughout the designated poverty areas. Sound trucks of the Philadelphia Department of Public Property were used to announce the town meetings daily along with the local press, radio, and television. This publicity resulted in an attendance of over 8,000 persons at the town meetings.[15] The meetings were conducted in each of the poverty areas at locations provided by the board of education and local churches.

Election procedures were explained at the meetings. Persons desiring a post on the 12-person councils were each required to solicit 50 signatures (a nomination petition) endorsing his candidacy from persons in his geographical area. The boundaries of each council area were described. Candidates were permitted to have an annual income of $3,000 for a husband and wife and an additional $500 for each dependent up to a maximum of $6,000. Furthermore, to preclude undue influence from the established leadership and local politicians, the clergy and active members of political organizations were excluded from running for office.

Voting qualifications and procedures were also explained at the town meetings. Persons 21 years of age and over living in a designated poverty area were eligible to vote. Each poverty area was divided into quadrants with persons being expected to vote in their respective quadrant. A driver's license sufficed for voter identification.

A total of 354 persons filed proper nomination petitions and their names were included on the municipal voting machine.[16] Additional town meetings were held. Approximately 2,000 persons attended to meet the candidates and to learn more about the poverty program. Perhaps the major criticism of the town meetings was that not enough information was disseminated about the poverty program itself. PAAC, however, argued that this was not the purpose of the town meetings. Since, theoretically, the poor themselves would determine the shape of the poverty proposals, discussions about what the program would do would come later at meetings of the community action councils.

On May 26, 1965 approximately 13,500 or 2.6 percent of an estimated eligible population of 500,000 turned out to vote for members of the council governing boards in the respective areas.[17] Voter turnout, to say the least, was disappointing. The apparent low interest of the poor in "their own problems" cast a pall over the antipoverty program that has been with it ever since.

On June 7, the 12 elected representatives in each of the councils met in their respective areas to elect one of their own as representative to PAAC. At the same time, they elected officers—a chairman, vice-chairman, and a secretary—for their own councils.

The 1966 Election. The Office of Economic Opportunity was reluctant to fund the 1966 election because of the small turnout in the 1965 election.[18] Just how OEO intended the PAAC to fulfill the maximum feasible participation requirement of the Economic Opportunity Act is not known. What does seem certain is that the low voter participation and complaints of big city mayors to Washington about undue pressures from the poor, combined to cause OEO to back away from elections as the best way to select poverty representatives.[19] In any case, PAAC pressed the issue. It appeared to be keenly aware that elections modified the structures of hierarchical subordination and enhanced its own position in the political power structure. The political establishment could hardly argue with votes. In brief, PAAC gained a measure of autonomy which it perhaps could not have otherwise by deriving its legitimacy from below. After a great deal of discussion and delay, OEO approved an election grant on a 50 percent federal, 50 percent local basis rather than on a 90 percent federal, 10 percent local basis as was the case in the 1965 election.

Many of the same procedures were utilized in the 1966 election as in the 1965 election. Over 100 meetings were held in the poverty areas to have citizens meet the candidates for office. The noticeable differences in procedure in 1966 were a great amount of discussion of the poverty program and a decided increase in the amount of publicity given the election. Discussions of the antipoverty programs in operation consumed a great deal of the time at the meetings; election parades and talent shows were held in each of the poverty areas in addition to the publicity provided by the local media.

To the disappointment of some critics of the program PAAC decided that only 72 of the 144 council seats would be open for election. At the outset of the program, all 144 council members were to serve for a period of one year and all council posts were to be up for election annually. The PAAC group said this action was taken in the interest of council and program continuity. Some critics of the program said it was a move to guarantee business-as-usual. Co-opting 72 persons, it was said, is easier than co-opting 144. In any event, the federal upper house method of rotation in office—staggered terms—has prevailed in the antipoverty program as well as the upper house principle of representation—representation of geographic areas rather than people.[20]

The antipoverty election turnout of 1966 was decidedly greater than that of 1965. The increase of more than 100 percent in the voting turnout was lauded by both federal and local officials. Nevertheless, the 28,792 voting figure or 5.4 percent of the eligible population was far below the expectations of either.

The 1967 Election. If the 1965 and 1966 elections were disappointing, the 1967 election was even more so. The 1967 turnout of 17,546 persons or 3.5 percent of the eligible population was considerably lower than the 1966 turnout and only slightly above the 1965 election. The lower voter turnout in 1967 has been attributed primarily to two factors. First, there was the tremendous amount of uncertainty as to the future of the program. Since the beginning of 1967 PAAC had been under consideration for conversion to a nonprofit agency on the grounds that its present structure was illegal and that the poor were not able to participate and get the best programs under the organization as it was presently constituted. Second, the poverty election initially scheduled for July and then delayed until September resulted in an apparent lack of general interest for the antipoverty program.

The election device, notwithstanding low voter turnouts, has been the means by which persons are chosen to serve on the community action councils and to represent the poor. In the next section is described those councils and the roles they play in the antipoverty program.

IV

Each community action council is, in essence, a miniature of PAAC for the neighborhood which it represents and in which it operates. The councils are to be representative of their neighborhoods in the same way that PAAC is to be representative of the entire poverty community. The difference, of course, is that the councils do not include representatives of the city, labor, business, religious, and civil rights organizations, per se. All the representatives to the councils are elected without regard for such considerations from the areas they serve.

The councils' functions are to select officers to direct the activities of the council; to initiate, recommend, and review community action programs for their respective pockets of poverty; to participate in the selection of paid staff for their offices, including professional employees; to help in the development of lists of eligibles to be used by the delegate agencies;[21] to recruit children and adults for the various component programs; and to refer persons in need of services to appropriate social agencies.

The councils are theoretically the governing bodies for their respective areas. Each council's area is to be guided by its own staff and to receive only professional assistance and guidance from the PAAC staff. However, the working role of the council representative to PAAC has become an issue in the community action councils. Elected representatives to PAAC have been greatly influenced by the PAAC staff since it controls jobs which may go to the relatives of representatives. And although elected representatives of the poor are ineligible for paid jobs in the agency, the PAAC staff has been able to get some elected members of the councils jobs in other city agencies.[22] Under such circumstances it is highly unlikely that the council representatives will serve the needs of their constituencies rather than the demands of the antipoverty governing body. In conclusion, it is important to question whether the values of the "civilian perspective" or the "military perspective" are really being served.

Another major question concerning the councils is their role in political power struggles. Their relative independence from the established political structure and then susceptibility to influence from the PAAC staff places them in a position of considerable political importance to PAAC's leaders. PAAC's leaders, for example, have already used its staff and the councils in a political way on at least two occasions.[23] In November 1966 both the staff members and the councils were pressured to work for the passage of a city bond issue, and in the spring of 1967, they were directed to work in the primary campaign for the mayor's renomination to office. Once again, much of the effort to keep the councils as elective bodies can be viewed as a tactic to retain grass-roots support for partisan political activity.

V

In this section, the organization and operation of the Philadelphia Antipoverty Action Committee will be discussed. This discussion illustrates the multifaceted nature of the agency and some of the problems which have resulted.

When the formal war on poverty in America began with the passage of the Economic Opportunity Act in August 1964 and by the creation of the Office of Economic Opportunity, pressures to plan a program for Philadelphia, to get congressional appropriations allocated as early as possible in the fiscal year, and to spend money were tremendous.[24] Under such circumstances, reflection on what was done and on its administrative and political significance came after rather than before the creation of the Philadelphia Antipoverty Action Committee.

The executive order which authorized the local poverty committee was a simple document which became effective February 22, 1965. It merely established a committee to be known as PAAC consisting of members to be appointed by the mayor and it contained provision for nonmayoral appointees in accordance with the general language contained in the federal legislation.[25] In a brief section, the executive order also said the "committee will establish policies necessary to guide the city's antipoverty campaign under the Economic Opportunity Act, and which committee will exercise supervision over the total program."

In many respects PAAC is similar to an "independent" commission such as the city's human relations commission. As such, the mayor ostensibly gave PAAC a free hand in establishing policy and in supervising the entire poverty effort. Independence was assured to some extent by the provision of the Economic Opportunity Act allocating 90 percent of the cost of the local program to the federal government.

Secondly, PAAC can be viewed as a legislative body making policy and putting its stamp of approval on projects for which federal funding is sought. This view is possible because most of the PAAC's component program are operated by voluntary or public agencies which have contracted with PAAC to carry out one or more programs for the poor.

Finally, PAAC can be viewed as an administrative agency since it supervises the entire antipoverty effort in Philadelphia funded under Title II of the Economic Opportunity Act. Among other administrative functions it establishes personnel policies for members of its own staff and the councils; employs a staff of about 286 persons (86 office, 200 field staff), handles the distribution of grants for component programs, and oversees the work of the councils. Thus PAAC is eminently something more than an advisory agency.

Because PAAC is more than simply an advisory committee, the Philadelphia Citizens' Charter Committee has questioned the legality of its construction.[26] The charter committee is a legal nonprofit, nonpartisan organization which serves as a watchdog for violations of the Philadelphia Home Rule Charter. In February 1967 this committee in a letter to the mayor charged that PAAC, created nominally as an advisory agency, was in fact operating as an administrative agency, and thus, was in violation of Section 2-305 of the Philadelphia Home Rule Charter.[27] The citizens' charter committee urged the mayor to either include PAAC within the authorized administrative framework of the city by municipal order as provided by the charter, or re-create PAAC as a nonprofit corporation entirely outside the city government.

After receiving the charter committee's letter the mayor appointed a special citizen's committee to study the PAAC structure and to make recommendations for its improvement.[28] The special committee was given until June 30, 1967 to make its recommendations. A series of public hearings were set up by this committee. At these hearings, PAAC mustered its own supporters in favor of the present organizational arrangements.[29] Some individuals and local community organizations,

180

such as the Chamber of Commerce and the Americans for Democratic Action, argued for the re-creation of PAAC as a nonprofit corporation.[30] The results of the hearings were inconclusive and at this writing no recommendations have been announced by the committee.

The long-range role that PAAC will play in the community, given the controversy over the makeup of the organization and the pressures placed upon it, is still undecided. In any event, the thirty-one member governing board of PAAC is presently charged with the responsibility of (1) formulating policies and programs necessary to carry out its objectives, (2) reviewing and approving projects and proposals submitted to it by subcommittees, and (3) assuring maximum involvement and participation of the poor. In addition, PAAC is required to (1) meet at least once each month, (2) have four subcommittees made up of members of the full committee, and (3) give its consent to the membership of the subcommittees as appointed by the PAAC chairman.

The PAAC governing board conducts much of its work through its subcommittees. The four most important of these are (1) community action councils, (2) agenda planning, (3) program review, and (4) funded programs. Subcommittees of lesser importance are (1) public assistance, (2) personnel, and (3) by-laws. The subcommittee on community action councils has proved to be the most powerful of the committees since it is responsible for formulating policy guidelines for the implementation of programs by the councils. Moreover, it provides oversight and guidance for the councils. In practice, it is this committee that determines which proposals and programs emanating from the councils will reach the antipoverty governing board for full and, perhaps, favorable consideration.

VI

Operating below the Philadelphia Antipoverty Action Committee governing board is the PAAC staff. It is the latter part of the agency which is preeminently an administrative organization. This section examines the organizational arrangements of the PAAC staff.

The administrative organization and process of PAAC developed in accordance with parameters established by the Office of Economic Opportunity. At the same time programs as they were initiated created conditions, needs, and problems which are reflected in the makeup of the organization. The PAAC staff is charged with carrying out the operating functions of the antipoverty governing board. Members of the staff are in the employ of PAAC and are said to have no obligations to other organizations or individuals. However, the executive director though in theory responsible to PAAC after he has been appointed by the mayor, has remained responsible to the latter. The general counsel and the job training director owe their initial appointments to the mayor, but have remained responsible to the executive director.

The executive director had made all other appointments to the PAAC staff. With few exceptions none of the professional and clerical positions has been made a part of the city's civil service,[3] thus leaving the PAAC staff open for patronage appointments. Members of the PAAC staff are, however, subject to the federal Hatch Act provisions in Section IV, which suggests that there may have been some violations of the spirit if not the letter of the law. In the following subsections the administrative staff of PAAC is described and some of the problems they have encountered are discussed.

The Office of Executive Director. The executive director administers the community action program. He oversees the practices and procedures of the PAAC staff. He recommends to the governing body the approval and adoption of proposed projects. He confers with officials of federal, state, and local governmental agencies and nonprofit organizations in developing programs. He oversees the public relations efforts of his agency.

As stated earlier, the executive director is appointed by the mayor. After appointment he owes his tenure to the PAAC board, but the chain of responsibility continues to be characterized by a great deal of uncertainty. It is not clear whether the executive director is to receive his instructions from the chairman of PAAC or the PAAC governing board as a whole. Beyond the formal report which he makes at each monthly meeting of PAAC and the question and answer period that follows, the executive director operates independently or at the direction of the mayor.

The Office of Deputy Director. The deputy director directs and coordinates the activities of the four line divisions of the PAAC staff. He coordinates service for all activities of the subcommittees of the PAAC board. He acts as liaison officer for all delegate agencies and provides oversight and guidance for all component programs. He represents the executive director in his absence.

The Office of General Counsel. The general counsel reviews all proposals coming to the antipoverty governing body for conformity to local, state, and federal law. He advises on the legality of all proposed administrative actions with special emphasis on the legality of those that might subject and expose the City of Philadelphia or PAAC to liability. He develops programs setting out the legal rights of the poor in problems which confront them regularly. He acts as liaison between PAAC and the Philadelphia Bar Association and is responsible for the maximum utilization and involvement of the bar association.

The office of general counsel has been the source of some controversy since its inception. It was created by the mayor to satisfy Cecil Moore, head of the local chapter of the NAACP. Isaiah Crippens was Moore's choice for the executive directorship; Charles Bowser was the political ministerial alliance's choice for the post.[33] The political ministerial alliance won out; the NAACP received the runner-up prize.

Since the creation of the office, the question of whether PAAC needs a full-time general counsel has consistently been raised. An OEO evaluation team has said that PAAC does not need a full-time general counsel, and, since January 1967, OEO has agreed to pay only up to $8,000 a year for part-time legal counsel rather than the $15,000 which was initially agreed to. The city is currently paying the additional $7,000 for a total salary of $15,000 to the general counsel.

The Division of Operations. This division directs the activities of the community organization and social services program and shares with the councils the responsibility of implementing programs at the council level. Controversy about the work of this division has centered around the relationship of the councils to the information and referral offices who work under the chief of social services. Some members of the councils feel that these officers should be placed under the supervision of the councils thereby giving the PAAC staff less control over their activities.

The Division of Planning and Delegate Contract Supervision. This division develops the program ideas submitted by the subcommittee on program review. It provides technical assistance in proposal writing for community agencies desiring to submit proposals to PAAC. The staff of this division observes and assesses component programs operated by delegate agencies and reports through appropriate channels to the subcommittee on funded programs. The biggest problem for this division has been the retention of able planners. A number of planners have resigned, alleging undue interference from the top in the preparation of proposals for PAAC approval.[34]

The Division of Job Training. This division plans and implements the community manpower training program component of PAAC. It includes community action programs for vocational training, the Neighborhood Youth Corps, and the Job Corps. The division also initiates programs under the provisions of the Manpower Development Training Act through appropriate agencies. In addition, it integrates all job training with union apprenticeship. Controversy about this division, thus far, has to do with the mayor's action in 1965 assigning the city's job training program directly to PAAC and indirectly to this division. Because the division is responsible for the administration of job training contracts between the city and the United States Department of Labor, the mayor is seen as having too direct a hand in PAAC staff operations.

The Division of Fiscal and Administrative Operations. This division, perhaps the least controversial to date, carries on the accounting, auditing, budgeting, and office management functions of the PAAC staff.

VII

Politics is very much a part of the city's war on poverty. The mayor has used the antipoverty program to gain political support in his fight with the city's Democratic party chairman. Antipoverty workers were pressured to work for the mayor's reelection to office. In addition, Samuel Evans, one of the mayor's appointees to PAAC, has sought to gain control of the councils in order to exercise influence over the antipoverty governing board and the PAAC staff and, perhaps, to create a political force of his own. Evans has, however, been attacked several times in the press because of his inordinate influence over PAAC affairs and his future role in PAAC appears uncertain.

Administrative problems continue to plague PAAC. The present framework of the organization calls for the antipoverty governing board to make policy, the PAAC staff to carry it out. However, policy has been made by the PAAC chairman as well as by the PAAC board. Finally, policy has often been made by the mayor's appointees to PAAC who, in turn, communicate these policies to the executive director.

The community action councils are unhappy over the role they play in the decision-making process. They do not feel that their views count. Many members of the councils feel that their representatives have been co-opted by the PAAC board and staff because of the favors which the latter can give.

The component programs of PAAC, though not discussed in this study, have been relatively successful and have been well received by the community. In most cases of disillusionment and unhappiness in the community it has been a question of too little of what programs there are and a demand for additional types of antipoverty programs.

The future of the antipoverty program as it is presently constructed seems uncertain. Efforts to make PAAC a nonprofit corporation are unresolved and continue unabated. Those who support this effort argue that a nonprofit corporation status would free the program of political influence and give the poor a larger voice in the decision-making process. On the other hand, there are those who favor bringing the antipoverty program into the regular city administration. This plan also has the virtue of freeing the antipoverty program of partisan politics since to incorporate PAAC into the city's regular administrative structure would place poverty workers under the city charter and the city's civil service. This plan, however, is not seen as giving the poor a larger voice in poverty matters. Indeed, it is usually preferred by those who continue to favor the old welfare approach over the new community action approach and the military perspective over the civilian perspective.

Whatever the outcome of pleas to reorganize PAAC and despite the political mire into which the program has floundered, it represents at least the best attainable program to date. Yet it is only a grudging rejection of the old top-down approach to poverty problems. The need is still to support a strong commitment to a coordinated community action approach in dealing with the plight of the poor.

NOTES

1. City of Philadelphia, *Executive Order* 1-65, Mayor James H. J. Tate, February 22, 1965.

2. *The Evening Bulletin*, May 6, 1964.

3. Kalman H. Cohen, *Philadelphia's Community Action Program under the Economic Act of 1964* (M.A. thesis, the Wharton School, University of Pennsylvania, 1966), p. 38.

4. S. H. Kristal, "The Great Poverty Snafu," *Greater Philadelphia Magazine,* 56 (September 1965), 80.

5. The Economic Opportunity Act required the local share to be 10 percent of the cost of the program; the federal share 90 percent.

6. William H. Haddad, "Mr. Shriver and the Savage Politics of the War on Poverty," *Harper's Magazine,* 231 (December 1965), 44.

7. Kristal, "Poverty Snafu," p. 81.

8. City of Philadelphia, *Executive Order.*

9. Council of Economic Advisers, *Annual Report 1964* (Washington, D.C.: Government Printing Office, 1964), pp. 55-84.

10. Health and Welfare Council of Philadelphia, *Fact Book on Poverty* (Philadelphia: Health and Welfare Council, November 1964), p. 21.

11. *Ibid.*

12. Health and Welfare Council of Philadelphia, *Guidelines for the Mobilization of Services* (Philadelphia: Health and Welfare Council, January 1966), pp. 1-15.

13. Public Law 88-452, Sec. 202(a), 88th Congress (August 20, 1964). After March 1, 1967, the poor were to comprise at least one-third of the membership of a board which administers, conducts, or coordinates a community action program. See *Economic Opportunity Amendments of 1966*, Sec. 203, 80 *Stat*. 1457. The PAAC has from its inception fulfilled this requirement.

14. Edgar S. and Jean C. Cahn, "The War on Poverty: A Civilian Perspective," *The Yale Law Journal*, 73 (July 1964), 1317-52.

15. See Arthur B. Shostak, "Promoting Participation of the Poor: Philadelphia's Antipoverty Program," *Social Work*, 11 (January 1966), 66. The PAAC's figures are more liberal; their records indicate that approximately 10,000 persons attended the town meetings. See Philadelphia Antipoverty Action Committee, *Progress Report 1967* (Philadelphia: Philadelphia Antipoverty Action Committee, 1967), p. 28. Hereafter cited as *Progress Report 1967.*

16. *Progress Report 1967.*

17. An excellent analysis of the characteristics of the population which turned out to vote was done by Arthur B. Shostak, "Promoting Participation," pp. 67-68.

18. See *The Evening Bulletin*, March 10, 1966.

19. For an extended discussion of mayoral reaction in several cities see John C. Donovan, *The Politics of Poverty* (New York: Pegasus, 1967), pp. 43-48, 54-57.

20. In another context the federal government explicitly approved this arrangement. See Sec. 203, *Economic Opportunity Amendments of 1966*, 80 *Stat.* 1557. This section reads: "The Director shall not approve, or continue to fund after March 1, 1967, a community action program which is conducted, administered, or coordinated by a board which contains *representatives of various geographical areas* in the community unless such representatives are required to live in the area they represent." (Emphasis mine.)

21. A delegate agency is a voluntary or public agency which enters into a contract with PAAC to operate a given program for the poor. One of the delegate agencies of PAAC, for example, is the Philadelphia Board of Education. It operates Project Headstart, a program designed to prepare preschool children for regular schooling.

22. See *New York Times*, July 17, 1966, p. 50.

23. *The Evening Bulletin*, October 28, 1966: January 16, 1967.

24. For a detailed account of Philadelphia's behavior in this regard, see Kristal, "Poverty Snafu," pp. 80-84.

25. Pursuant to the mayor's executive order PAAC consists of 31 members— 5 citizens appointed directly by the mayor, the president of City Council, the President Judge of the County Court of the City and County of Philadelphia, a representative from each of the 12 elected councils, and a representative from each of 12 community organizations designated as having an interest in poverty matters.

26. *Letter to Mayor James H. J. Tate from the Philadelphia Citizen's Charter Committee*, February 8, 1967, with enclosure entitled "A Memorandum to the Mayor of Philadelphia Concerning an Erosion in the Philadelphia Home Rule Charter."

27. For a running account of the charter committee's criticisms and the questions it raised, see *The Evening Bulletin*, February-June 1967.

28. *Ibid.*, May 19, 1967, p. 1.

29. *Ibid.*, June 29, 1967, p. 1.

30. *Ibid.*, July 1, 1967, p. 8G and July 6, 1967, p. 3G.

31. *The Evening Bulletin*, January 25, 1966.

32. *Economic Opportunity Amendments of 1966*, Sec. 604, 80 *Stat.* 1469. See also *New York Times*, April 29, 1966, p. 42.

33. Cecil Moore and the NAACP are said to represent Philadelphia's black masses; the political ministerial alliance is said to represent the Black group as headed by City Councilman Thomas McIntosh and Rev. (Dr.) William H. Gray, pastor of the Hope Baptist Church and a member of the city's civil service commission.

34. *The Evening Bulletin*, January 4, 1966, January 6, 1966.

10

ARTICULATENESS, POLITICAL MOBILITY, AND CONSERVATISM: AN ANALYSIS OF THE PHILADELPHIA ANTIPOVERTY ELECTION

ELLIOTT WHITE

Elliott White, a political scientist on the faculty of Temple University, discusses a unique aspect of the antipoverty program—the election of poor people to positions of responsibility by other poor people. This leads him to an analysis of the degree to which the Philadelphia Antipoverty Action Committee was clientele-oriented. This study was written expressly for this volume.

Suppose an election were held in which only the poor could run as candidates. Such was the case in the 1965 Philadelphia antipoverty election. The city had been divided into twelve antipoverty areas. Each area was to elect twelve (unpaid) representatives to its Community Action Council (CAC). Each CAC in turn elected four of its members as officers, including a chairman and a representative to the Philadelphia Antipoverty Action Committee (PAAC), then the city-wide governing agency for the Community Action Antipoverty program. PAAC thus had twelve elected poor among its thirty-one members, the others of whom were either appointed by the mayor or chosen as representatives by designated civic, business, and religious groups, such as the Urban League, the Chamber of Commerce, and the archdiocese of Philadelphia.

In order to vote in the election, one had to be twenty-one years of age and to live within one of the twelve antipoverty areas. In order to run, however, one also could earn no more than $3,000 per year, with $500 per year for each dependent up to a maximum of $6,000.

Since only 144 of the 353 candidates who in fact ran during the 1965 election could win, the question arises: were there important characteristics and attitudes that set the winners apart from the losers? Similarly, were the elected representatives who were in turn chosen to become CAC officers significantly different from those who remained only winners? Finally, if significant differences do emerge, what were their implications for the Community Action Program? All of these questions assume special interest because the factor of socioeconomic background had, in effect, been controlled.

The Study

In order to answer these questions, most of the 353 candidates were interviewed during the last half of 1965 and the first half of 1966. A preliminary analysis of this data by John Giansello (1966), involving ninety respondents, forms the statistical basis for this paper. A more comprehensive study involving 220 candidates will be available shortly. Finally, partially for comparative purposes, a sample of voters and nonvoters was studied by John Pecoul[1] in the four antipoverty areas indicated to be the most impoverished on the basis of United States Census tract data (e.g., with respect to unemployment, substandard housing, etc.). Both samples—that of the voters and nonvoters and that of the candidates—were asked many of the same questions.

In the case of the candidates, the interview comprised four parts. The first involved demographic and socioeconomic background information; the second focused on political background questions, including measures of political efficacy and knowledge ability; the third centered upon the campaign experience of the candidate; and the fourth part explored the candidates' attitudes toward poverty and the antipoverty program.

The Results

We shall first briefly list those factors which turned out *not* to be associated with a candidate's winning or losing. In the first place, the fact that social class was controlled as a variable by the election requirements appears to be borne out by the findings. There are no significant differences between losers, winners (but non-CAC officers), and officers on the basis of income, formal education, or occupation. There were also no significant differences in the number of organizational memberships, which were well above what one might have expected for a lower-class sample. (See Table 10-1 for findings referred to in the text.)

Although 70 percent of the sample were women (roughly true for both Black and white candidates), sex was not a factor in whether a candidate won or lost. Marital status and size of family also lacked significance.

Turning to those factors which did make a difference, we find the following:

Position on the Ballot. In eleven of the twelve antipoverty areas, half or more of the first twelve candidates listed on the ballot were elected, while twenty-four or more names were entered in eight of the areas. (A voter could select a total of twelve names.)

There can be little doubt that many voters simply selected the first twelve names. Yet this simple interpretation must be tempered by the fact that a candidate's position on the ballot was determined by the time his nominating petition was filed. In other words, it is conceivable that the early entrants were more energetic and ambitious. The author interviewed one of the first to file a petition for any area, and his description of the dispatch and sense of purpose that went into his assembling the required fifty signatures corroborates this judgment. In those few areas, moreover, in which slates of candidates were organized, placement on the ballot became relatively less crucial.

Age. While there were no basic age differences between winners and losers in general, there were differences between officers as against both winners and losers. Fully 80 percent of the officers were forty years of age or under, compared to 33 percent of the winners and 46 percent of the losers.

190

Elliott White

This relative youth of the officers was probably responsible for the fact that they were much less likely to own their own homes than the winners: 24 percent of the officers reported owning their own homes, as against 68 percent of the winners.

Race. Over three-quarters of the sample were nonwhite; yet there was still a visible white minority of 23 percent. Interestingly, of this minority, fully 95 percent were winners. This phenomenon is currently being researched by Petkov.[2]

TABLE 10-1
Miscellaneous Data on Candidates

	TOTAL FAMILY INCOME PER YEAR				
	$0-1,000	$1,001-2,000	$2,001-3,000	$3,001-4,000	OVER $4,000
Losers (N = 35)	9%	29%	26%	14%	11%
Winners (N = 30)	10	20	30	17	23
Officers (N = 25)	4	28	24	36	8

	YEARS OF SCHOOL		
	UP TO 8	9-12	SOME COLLEGE
Losers	14%	69%	17%
Winners	23	62	13
Officers	0	72	28

	OCCUPATION						
	RETIRED	HOUSE-WIVES	UNEM-PLOYED	UN-SKILLED	SKILLED	CLERI-CAL	PROFES-SIONAL OR SEMI-PROFES-SIONAL
Losers	3%	31%	14%	14%	0%	31%	3%
Winners	7	23	20	13	10	13	13
Officers	8	12	12	8	12	24	16

TABLE 10-1 *(Continued)*
Organizational Memberships of Candidates

| | NUMBER OF ORGANIZATIONS | | | | |
	0	SOME IN PAST BUT NONE NOW	1-2	3-4	MORE THAN 4
Losers	14%	6%	37%	23%	9%
Winners	0	10	37	43	7
Officers	12	8	36	24	12

| | BIRTHPLACE | | | | |
	PHILA-DELPHIA	PHILA. AND METRO-POLITAN AREA	NORTH OF MARY-LAND	MARY-LAND OR SOUTH	ELSE-WHERE
Losers	34%	3%	10%	54%	0%
Winners	40	7	10	40	3
Officers	36	8	28	20	8

| | FATHERS' OCCUPATIONS | | | | |
	UNSKILLED	SKILLED	CLERICAL	PROFES-SIONAL OR SEMI-PROFES-SIONAL	UNKNOWN
Losers	83%	6%	6%	3%	3%
Winners	37	40	7	10	7
Officers	48	12	16	24	4

Family background. There was a tendency for the winners, especially the officers, to have been born in the North and for their fathers' occupations to have been a notch higher than that of unskilled labor.

ARTICULATENESS

By far the most striking finding emerged with respect to the interviewers' rating of the respondents' articulateness. Each candidate was rated on a four point scale, ranging from "not very" articulate, through "somewhat" articulate, "articulate," to "very" articulate. Each interviewer judged the respondents' articulateness as he would any individ-

Elliott White

ual; that is, the same common understanding that would normally apply would apply here as well: there was to be no separate standard. With this in mind, we can now turn to the results reported in Figure 10-1, which also reports the ratings given the sample of voters and nonvoters.

FIGURE 10-1
Rating of Respondents' Articulateness

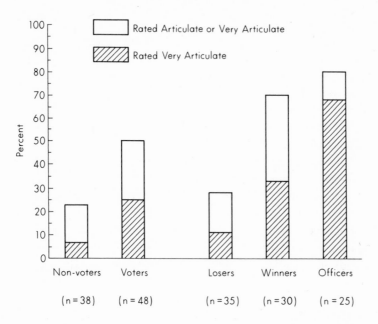

We can observe, first of all, that the voters were rated significantly higher in articulateness than the nonvoters; and, secondly, that among the candidates, the more successful were rated as being more articulate. Specifically, the losers were usually judged to be only "not very" or "somewhat" articulate; the winners were most frequently judged "articulate"; and fully two-thirds of the officers were seen as "very" articulate.

Before my further analysis, possible objections to this rating of articulateness should be considered. These objections might be listed as follows:

193

1. Such a rating on the part of the interviewer is subjective and arbitrary. Since about a hundred of the interviews were recorded on tape (the last two parts of each entire interview), it was possible to test this objection. During the spring of 1967, the author was a member of a panel, including representatives from anthropology, sociology, and history, teaching a course in urban affairs to twenty-seven public school teachers. The latter all taught junior high school in the inner-city areas throughout the Delaware Valley, mostly in Philadelphia itself, and they were mostly Black.

Both the class and the panel listened to excerpts of taped interviews which the writer had evaluated previously. The close correspondence of the preponderance of their replies (both of the class and panel) and the writer's ratings was manifest, despite some background noise and sound distortion in the tape. There was a basic, if tacit, consensus about who is and who is not articulate, so that subjective impressions tend to be clothed with a rough objectivity.

2. The interviewers' middle-class position resulted in a corresponding bias. Certainly the interviewers, mostly graduate and a few undergraduate students, might be identified as middle class, and may have made their evaluations accordingly. It is interesting, however, that the voters tended to select, whether consciously or not, the more "articulate" candidates, and that these more "articulate" winners then proceeded to choose the most "articulate" among themselves as officers. The writer recalls talking with one voter—in a different context, since we both happened to be on the staff of an Upward Bound antipoverty program— who explicitly mentioned the speaking ability of a candidate as one reason for voting for him.

Articulateness is simply not confined to, or understood by, middle-class standards. C. Eric Lincoln referred to Malcolm X when he was still a member of the Black Muslims, as "its most articulate spokesman."[3] And Malcolm X himself, who hardly had a middle-class background, consciously attempted to become "articulate" while in his early twenties and serving a term in prison:

> I became increasingly frustrated at not being able to express what I wanted to convey in letters that I wrote. . . . In the street, I had been the most articulate hustler out there. . . . But now, trying to write

194

simple English, I not only wasn't articulate, I wasn't even functional. How would I sound writing in slang, the way I would say it, something such as, "Look daddy, let me pull your coat about a cat, Elijah Muhammad. . . ."

Many who today hear me somewhere in person, or on television, or those who read something I've said, will think I went to school far beyond the eighth grade. This impression is due entirely to my prison studies.[4]

Few in the middle class, black or white, have emulated Malcolm X in verbal ability.

3. The white interviewers (more than half of all interviewers) may have misevaluated because of racial and, hence, cultural differences, including specifically the manner of speech. The example of Malcolm X cited above, as well as other Black leaders, indicates, however, that articulateness transcends racial lines. Furthermore, the interviewers of the voters and nonvoters were virtually all Black, but their basic pattern of evaluation conforms to the pattern revealed for the sample of candidates.

4. The respondents were consciously, even self-consciously, articulate in their interviews, but not necessarily in their everyday speech. The first half of that statement may no doubt be true, as it might also have appeared to be true to an observer of the candidates' speaking efforts during the various town meetings that were held during the election campaign. But in political life, the role of public speaker is not an artificial one. The further point is, of course, that efforts to be articulate do not necessarily succeed.

As for everyday speech, there was no way to gauge this in a "scientific" fashion, but it is of interest that one of the most "articulate" and successful candidates remarked that he also deliberately talked the language of the street while canvassing for votes in the street. He, like Malcolm X and Stokely Carmichael, was simply articulate in more than one sense; but it may be that both forms are related, at least in that they require a common skill. All users of street language and all hustlers are not equally articulate.

ARTICULATENESS AND POLITICAL MOBILITY

The articulate candidates, then, were the most politically mobile, that is, they moved up the political ladder formed by both the direct

195

and the indirect elections. Inasmuch as one of the ground rules of the election forbade candidates from holding any political office or appointed governmental position, it was a considerable jump from being a poor resident in an antipoverty area to becoming a city-wide representative of the agency governing the antipoverty program.

The connection between articulateness and political success has long been noted. Aristotle, for example, recognized the link between the power of speech and of persuasion and the power of politics in *The Rhetoric*. Carlyle wrote that, "No British man can attain to be a statesman or chief of workers till he has first proved himself a chief of talkers."[5] Michels observed of Continental European politicians and labor leaders prior to World War I that they were invariably "able speakers."[6] Merriam in his survey of American party leaders saw as one of six "common attributes of the political leader," a "facility in dramatic expression of the sentiment or interest of large groups of voters, usually with voice or pen."[7] Salter has commented that, "Politicians are avid and often good talkers."[8]

Finally, Stogdill, in his survey of early twentieth-century leadership studies, reported that "verbal fluency" is consistently associated with positions of leadership.[9] Articulateness and political mobility, therefore, appear to be closely related; and this is the conclusion of Sorokin, who in discussing politics as an "avenue of climbing" and the specific occupational skills that accompany such climbing, remarks, "In its essence, all this is the 'ability of speech-making,' whether in the form of writing or oratory. Hence, as I have mentioned, such jumpers are, as a rule, good orators and prolific writers (quantitatively)."[10]

Now to be articulate is not necessarily to be eloquent (or charismatic), but I believe that the converse relationship holds. To be articulate is also not necessarily to be political, but again, I believe that the converse tends to hold, at least for the highest political levels. When top political leaders are faulted for a lack of verbal grace or agility—Romney, Ike, and L. B. J., for example—it is only because they are being measured against the highest standards of public speaking, those imposed by the Churchills and the Roosevelts.

It is of note that when one of the most articulate candidates, who subsequently became a PAAC representative, entered (though later withdrew from) a 1967 race for city councilman, the lead paragraph of the story carried in *The Evening Bulletin* on March 8, 1967 read: "Mrs. Kathleen Hackett, a sandy-haired and articulate woman from the heart of a North Philadelphia slum, late yesterday entered the race for city councilman from the 7th district." It is also of interest that Mrs. Hackett informed her newspaper interviewer that during regular PAAC meetings, "she was constantly beset upon by many of the other representatives to ask questions during the meetings which they wanted to ask but did not because they felt they could not express themselves properly. She said that someone was always passing a handwritten note to her to ask a question for them." It is possible that self-assurance was also at issue here, although articulateness and self-assurance are usually related.

If speech and mobility are in fact associated (and the "How to Improve Your Vocabulary" books, etc. imply a relationship beyond the political realm), then the English have no monopoly on the emphasis upon speech as an index of social position. Perhaps the major difference is that American political Pygmalians can be and are more openly mobile.

Finally, we must briefly refer to two necessary attributes which presuppose articulateness.

First, cognitive ability is essential. Murphy, Murphy & Newcombe point out that "the ability to verbalize in itself, although undoubtedly having its environmental aspects, is certainly closely related to general intelligence level."[11] Goldstein, in a chapter entitled "The Abstract Attitude and Speech," shows this close relationship;[12] and the abstract attitude—the ability to transcend one's immediate situation in time and space by vicarious thought—should be a precise requisite for upward mobility, political or otherwise.

Secondly, articulateness, especially when associated with a lower-class background, denotes a motivation to attain, and an identification with, a higher social position. This was true even for Malcolm X with regard to his seeming desire to appear formally educated. Indeed, he took pride in his appearence before the Harvard Law School Forum (1962),[13] a pride which a McCarthyist (the 1950's variety) might have been reluctant to show. In the case of the officers in particular, the slightly higher occupational level of their fathers and their own somewhat more northern background no doubt contributed to a higher level of motivation and aspiration. But to make a difference, motivation must also be matched by ability.

ARTICULATENESS, POLITICAL MOBILITY, AND CONSERVATISM

If the articulate in the lower classes are also the aspiring, this relationship should be reflected in the attitudes of the respondents, especially the articulate officers. These attitudes should reveal an identification with the values and goals of a relatively higher social-class position, and therefore embody the conservatism which one would associate with a subjective feeling of upward mobility.

It is of course true that, for the officers in particular, an objective mobility was already in existence; and although during the first year (when this survey was in progress), this mobility remained mostly political and without tangible material benefit, it certainly may already have influenced attitudes. Yet one incident is revealing in this respect. Soon after the election when our questionnaire was being devised, assistance was sought from several candidates we had come to know. One young, articulate, newly chosen officer, speaking informally, described his motivation for running in terms of self-interest, as a means of getting "doors open" for him, an expectation later to be fulfilled. Some months afterward, however, during his formal interview, he described his motivations in notably less personal terms and a suitably altruistic sentiment crept in as well.

Ungar studied the candidates' responses to "the poor" in their area and discovered, particularly among the more successful, a deliberate effort to avoid an identity with them; "we," the candidate, was carefully distinguished from "them," the poor.[14]

Politically, the more conservative outlook of the successful candidate is shown in Table 10-2, which presents the partisan affiliation of the respondents.

The officers in particular are relatively more Republican and independent. This finding, incidentally, applied to voters in contrast to nonvoters in the election.

These findings, taken during the first year of the community action program, somewhat qualify Michels' thesis concerning the "psychologi-

198

TABLE 10-2
Candidates' Partisan Affiliation

	STRONG DEMOCRAT	NOT VERY STRONG DEMOCRAT	NOT VERY STRONG REPUBLICAN	STRONG REPUBLICAN
Losers	37%	31%	14%	6%
Winners	37	30	10	10
Officers	12	36	20	16

cal metamorphosis" which political leaders undergo after assuming power. Perhaps reflecting the less rigidly ideological nature of the American political climate, even for the lower classes, these candidates, if later objectively successful, were probably subjectively receptive to that success from the start (although Michels himself noted bourgeois aspirations on the part of the working class).[15] The officers were young, but not young militants. If later they became "co-opted," they were willing partners.

POLITICAL AND ECONOMIC MOBILITY

Although technically not in the province of our study, we shall refer to some relevant developments. Reported attitudes are best confirmed by subsequently reported behavior. Snyder[16] studied one community action council during the second year of the program and detected a split between the officers and the winners. The top officers were receiving jobs and remuneration, creating support on their part for PAAC and its policies on the one hand, and alienation on the part of the remaining CAC members on the other.

This alienation diminished somewhat as remuneration increased in its coverage. Through PAAC, in particular through mayoral appointee Samuel Evans, chairman of the subcommittee on community action councils, jobs became available to elected candidates—such as by the hiring of 200 persons to explain Medicare to the elderly. By the end of 1966, 118 of the 144 elected representatives of the poor, including virtually all who sat on PAAC, were reported as holding paying jobs in the antipoverty program (*The Evening Bulletin*, August 14, 1966).

The poor, like anyone else, are hardly immune to the lure of material gain. After all, they have more excuse for being co-opted than the many

199

in the middle class who have only their aspirations to blame for any personal betrayal on their part. As one CAC member told Snyder, "You don't send hungry dogs to guard your meat," referring "to the fact that the members of CAC are poor, and are being asked to dispense relief-giving measures to their poor friends and neighbors, without any formal remuneration."[17]

The poor were thus in no position to refuse the jobs that came their way, and the politically mobile therefore became economically mobile as well. Indeed, one of the results of the election was that a number of the representatives of the poor became ineligible for reelection (*The Evening Bulletin*, August 27, 1963).

This economic mobility also had the following additional results:

1. The elected poor, especially the PAAC representatives and the other officers, supported PAAC policies, as embodied in the job-dispensing person of Sam Evans. In a talk given February 11, 1968, Alvin Elchols, executive director of North City Congress, an alliance of neighborhood and civic groups in North Philadelphia, related how his organization worked to "control" the outcome of the election in five of the twelve poverty areas, only to lose that "control" to the co-opting influence of Evans and the PAAC administration.

The PAAC representatives in particular, with the interesting exception of Mrs. Hackett,[18] invariably supported Evans' policies. After Mrs. Hackett's departure, the twelve city-wide representatives were unanimous in their support of PAAC; for example, on February 10, 1967, they called a press conference to urge that the structure of PAAC remain intact and to defend it against critics (*The Evening Bulletin*, February 11, 1967). The latter included the Office of Economic Opportunity, which objected, among other things, to the elected poor being given jobs (a situation which might have been avoided had a moderate remuneration been made from the start, contrary to existing OEO policy).

The attitudes of these PAAC representatives may well have been exemplified by a former PAAC representative who, by July 1966, the date of a talk given by him and reported here, had already resigned his elected position because he had become a paid consultant to the program. He referred to his election to PAAC as an honor, including the privilege of sitting with "big wigs," and concluded that "maybe I'm middle class, but . . . ," ending the sentence with a defense of the by-then controversial Sam Evans.

We see, then, that the power of patronage and political organization is not yet dead. When the first executive director of PAAC, Charles Bowser, resigned, he became an assistant to Mayor James Tate, serving actively during the mayor's reelection campaign, which perhaps owed its success to the mayor's showing in most of the poverty areas. When Evans was under attack in April, 1967 for his alleged high-handed methods, he said of his relation to the mayor, who had not yet faced the voters: "He's probably grabbing for my coat tail more than I am for his." Also, in April, 1967 the OEO investigated reports that PAAC staff members working with the twelve neighborhood community action councils were involved in political activity on behalf of the mayor (*The Evening Bulletin*, April 3, 1967). It is of note that when the controversial PAAC structure was reconstituted in Commission form following the mayor's reelection in March, 1968, the changes seemed more semantic than real, and, if anything, strengthened the mayor's hand.

2. The support of PAAC by the elected poor, especially the officers, meant not only that an originally-expected split on PAAC between the poor and the other members did not materialize, but also that the divisions which did occur saw the poor voting with an established majority against a virtually powerless minority. The "other members" included CORE, the local NAACP, and, ironically, representatives of the established welfare agencies. In December, 1966, for example, Mrs. Anderson Page, representing the Delaware Valley Settlement Alliance, resigned as chairman of the PAAC subcommittee on program review as a protest against the "usurping" policies of Sam Evans (*The Evening Bulletin*, December 19, 1966).

3. The locally-organized movement against PAAC took the form of the Maximum Participation Movement (MPM), whose title, with its democratic participatory ideology, suggests its liberal-academic and ADA-type origins. Given the profile presented here of the elected poor, the title and the ideology of the movement were hardly calculated to win wide support among the elected poor. And they did not—just as such an appeal might fall on deaf ears on many a college campus and in many a middle-class suburb.

201

4. By the second election in July, 1966, black militant groups were calling for its boycott on the grounds that the mayor was running the poverty program and would continue to do so regardless of the election results.

A CITIZEN'S CONCLUSIONS

Only 2.7 percent or about 13,500 adults out of all those eligible in the poverty areas voted in the 1965 election. These figures were roughly doubled for the subsequent elections in 1966 and 1967, in which only half or seventy-two of the CAC positions were thrown open for election. And of the 144 elected poor, only several dozen became officers. We are therefore talking about a handful of people who became both politically and economically mobile as a result of the poverty program.

What of the others in the poverty areas? According to a United States Department of Labor survey, the unemployment rate in the nation's urban ghettos, including Philadelphia's 11 percent, was three times the national average (*The New York Times*, March 16, 1967). Obviously, opportunity made available for a few did not extend to all. When Potter, writing in the early 1950's, described the American national character as characterized by individual opportunity for upward mobility and the attainment of economic success, he saw Black America as a "conspicuous exception" to this generalization.[19] Our more recent findings suggest that diversity and degrees of mobility differentiate the poor, both Black and white, so that neither Black America nor the lower class are a monolith (nor, for that matter, are they one and the same), and therefore neither constitutes a sweeping exception to Potter's generalization.

Yet for many, poverty remains a subjective as well as objective reality. A riot commission study[20] indicates that the economic levels separating rioters and nonrioters were not significant, but that subjectively, the rioters (a category including whites in Detroit) were more dissatisfied with their job situation. The "counterrioter," on the other hand, was "considerably better educated and more affluent than either the rioter or the noninvolved."[21]

Interestingly, there is a certain rough parallel with Lane's categories[22] of politically "divorced," "alienated," and "allegiant" among his fifteen all-white working- and lower middle-class sample. The alienated are estranged from politics and government; more than disinterest, there is a feeling of rejection. The divorced, on the other hand, are so subjectively removed from political life that they fail to make any connection with it; thus there is no alienation, simply unknowing acquiescence to the status quo. The allegiant are supporters of the political order and optimistic regarding its effects. Lane proceeds to relate these attitudes to his respondent's objective and subjective socioeconomic position. Thus Flynn, one of the more intelligent, economically well-off, and subjectively satisfied with his job, holds allegiant views; Ferrara, who finds "its a tough life" and would like to escape its burdens, is politically alienated; while Dempsey, presumably because of a limited background and capacity, is simply divorced from the political world.

These concepts and categories are mentioned because I believe that they adhere roughly together to form a framework in which our sample of candidates might be related. This framework is outlined in Table 10-3.

TABLE 10-3
Riot Behavior and Subjective Attitudes

FACTOR	CATEGORY		
	(1)	(2)	(3)
Economic (Subjective)	Mobility Not Perceived nor Expected	Mobility Expected but Not Perceived	Mobility Expected and Perceived
Political	Divorced	Alienated	Allegiant
Probable behavior in riot situation	Nonrioter	Rioter	Counterrioter

It is clear that the voters and especially the successful candidates fall into category 3 (needless to say, PAAC policy is implicitly antiriot). Their individual qualities of skill and articulateness have found suitable opportunities, which have been lacking for most in category 2. The articulate Malcolm X found no doors opening for him as a young man—but rather the closing of a prison gate.

In category 1, finally, are the inarticulate, who perhaps need security more than opportunity, a suggestion unfortunately alien to mainstream America (as well as to most contemporary radical thought).

The fact that the elected poor fall into category 3 gives an interesting twist to Bowen and Masotti's observation[23] that an antipoverty election in which only the poor can run marks a complete policy reversal from the suffrage requirements that the Republic originally imposed. But the real irony lies in the Hamiltonian character of the election outcome. For the more articulate and conservative among the electorate selected the more articulate and conservative among the candidates to represent them; and the latter in turn chose the more articulate and conservative among themselves as their officers. Thus the outcome conformed to the effect Hamilton would have desired, while confounding the fears he would have expressed. It is instructive that only 15 percent of the successful candidates (and 29 percent of the losers) failed to name at least one of the two senators from Pennsylvania. The comparable figure for a national sample surveyed in 1965 was 41 percent.[24]

The Hamiltonian character of the election results of course displeased those of an ideologically more radical bent. But it does little good to moralize about the "rat race" and its conservative effects on the poor excluded from it and especially on those numerous poor already striving strenuously to get their toes on the treadmill. The real failing in the antipoverty program is not that a few became economically better off, but that they remained so few. Indeed, the elected poor should have been salaried from the start, thus helping them to attain a position of both economic and political independence, even if this meant breaking the rule that one must remain poor if involved in the antipoverty program—unless one is co-opted, already a part of the middle class, or a private contractor.

NOTES

1. John Pecoul, "Black Impotence in North Philadelphia" (M.A. thesis, Temple University, 1967).

2. S. Petkov, "Ethnic Politics" (Ph.D. diss. in progress, University of Pennsylvania).

3. C. Eric Lincoln, *The Black Muslims in America* (Boston: Beacon Press, 1961), p. 195.

4. Malcolm X, *Autobiography* (New York: Grove Press, 1966), p. 171.

5. R. Michels, *Political Parties* (New York: The Free Press, 1966), p. 98.

6. *Ibid,* ch. 5.

7. C. Merriam, *Four American Party Leaders* (New York: Macmillan Co., 1926), p. xii.

8. J. T. Salter, *Boss Rule* (New York: Whittlesey House, 1935), p. 9.

9. R. Stogdill, "Personal Failures Associated with Leadership," *Journal of Psychology* 25 (1948), 35-71.

10. P. Sorokin, *Social and Cultural Mobility* (Glencoe, Ill.: The Free Press, 1959), p. 488.

11. G. Murphy, L. Murphy, and T. Newcomb, *Experimental Social Psychology* (New York: Harper Brothers, 1937).

12. K. Goldstein, *Human Nature in the Light of Psychopathology* (New York: Schocken Books, 1966), ch. 3.

13. Malcolm X, *Autobiography*, p. 41.

14. E. Ungar, "Values of the Candidates for the Philadelphia Antipoverty Councils: A Content Analysis" (paper, 1967).

15. Michels, *Political Parties*, p. 271.

16. W. Snyder, "Co-optation in Philadelphia's Community Action Councils" (paper, 1966).

17. *Loc. cit.*

18. Petkov, "Ethnic Politics."

19. S. Potter, *People of Plenty* (Chicago: Phoenix Books, 1962), p. 96.

20. *Report of the National Advisory Commission on Civil Disorders* (New York: Bantam Books, 1968).

21. *Ibid*, p. 128.

22. R. Lane, *Political Ideology* (Glencoe, Ill.: The Free Press, 1967), ch. 10.

23. D. Bowen and L. Masatti, "Spokesman for the Poor" (paper, 1967).

24. A. Westin, ed., *The National Citizenship Test* (New York: Bantam Books, 1965).

ADDITIONAL SOURCES

Aristotle, *The Rhetoric and the Poetics* (New York: The Modern Library, 1954).

H. Bailey, "Poverty, Politics, and Administration: The Philadelphia Experience" (1968).

J. Giansello, "The Politicization of a Poverty Community" (paper, 1966).

A. Shostak, "Promoting Participation of the Poor: Philadelphia's Anti-Poverty Program," *Social Work* 11 (Jan. 1966), 64-72.

B. Tatem, ."Impact of the Antipoverty Program on Urban Government" (paper, 1967).

PART FOUR

EPILOGUE

Introduction

This final chapter of W. E. B. Du Bois' brilliant early study, *The Philadelphia Negro*, is a fitting epilogue for this collection of analytic essays. In reading this selection, it is important to keep in mind that Du Bois wrote it between 1896 and 1898 when he was an assistant instructor of sociology at the University of Pennsylvania.

11

A FINAL WORD

W. E. BURGHARDT DU BOIS

The Meaning of All This

Two sorts of answers are usually returned to the bewildered American who asks seriously: What is the Negro problem? The one is straightforward and clear: it is simply this, or simply that, and one simple remedy long enough applied will in time cause it to disappear. The other answer is apt to be hopelessly involved and complex—to indicate no simple panacea, and to end in a somewhat hopeless—There it is; what can we do? Both of these sorts of answers have something of truth in them: the Negro problem looked at in one way is but the old world questions of ignorance, poverty, crime, and the dislike of the stranger. On the other hand it is a mistake to think that attacking each of these questions single-handed without reference to the others will settle the matter: a combination of social problems is far more than a matter of mere addition,—the combination itself is a problem. Nevertheless the Negro problems are not more hopelessly complex than many others have been. Their elements despite their bewildering complication can be kept clearly in view: they are after all the same difficulties over which the world has grown gray: the question as to how far human intelligence can be trusted and trained; as to whether we must always have the poor with us; as to whether it is possible for the mass of men to attain righteousness on earth; and then to this is added that question of questions: after all who are Men? Is every featherless biped to be counted a man and brother? Are all races and types to be joint heirs of the new earth that men have striven to raise in thirty centuries and more? Shall we not swamp civilization in barbarism and drown genius in indulgence if we seek a mythical Humanity which shall shadow all men? The answer of the early centuries to this puzzle was clear: those of any nation who can be called Men and endowed with rights are few: they are the privileged classes—the well-born and the accidents of low birth called up by the King. The rest, the mass of the nation, the *pöbel*, the mob, are fit to follow, to obey, to dig and delve, but not to think or rule or play the gentleman. We who were born to another philosophy hardly realize how deep-seated and plausible this view of human capabilities and powers once was; how utterly incomprehensible this republic would have been to Charlemagne or Charles V or Charles I. We rather hasten to forget that once the courtiers of English kings looked upon the ancestors of most Americans with far greater contempt than these Americans look upon Negroes—and perhaps, indeed, had more cause. We forget that once French peasants were the "Niggers" of France, and that German princelings once discussed with doubt the brains and humanity of the *bauer*.

Much of this—or at least some of it—has passed and the world has glided by blood and iron into a wider humanity, a wider respect for simple manhood unadorned by ancestors or privilege. Not that we have discovered, as some hoped and some feared, that all men were created free and equal, but rather that the differences in men are not so vast as we had assumed. We still yield the well-born the advantages of birth, we still see that each nation has its dangerous flock of fools and rascals; but we also find most men have brains to be cultivated and souls to be saved.

And still this widening of the idea of common Humanity is of slow growth and to-day but dimly realized. We grant full citizenship in the World Commonwealth to the "Anglo-Saxon" (whatever that may mean), the Teuton and the Latin; then with just a shade of reluctance we extend it to the Celt and Slav. We half deny it to the yellow races of Asia, admit the brown Indians to an ante-room only on the strength of an undeniable past; but with the Negroes of Africa we come to a full stop, and in its heart the civilized world with one accord denies that these come within the pale of nineteenth-century Humanity. This feeling, widespread and deep-seated, is, in America, the vastest of the Negro problems; we have, to be sure, a threatening problem of ignorance but the ancestors of most Americans were far more ignorant than the freedmen's sons; these ex-slaves are poor but not as poor as the Irish peasants used to be; crime is rampant but not more so, if as much, as in Italy; but the difference is that the ancestors of the English and the Irish and the Italians were felt to be worth educating, helping and guiding because they were men and brothers, while in America a census which gives a slight indication of the utter disappearance of the American Negro from the earth is greeted with ill-concealed delight.

Other centuries looking back upon the culture of the nineteenth would have a right to suppose that if, in a land of freemen, eight millions of human beings were found to be dying of disease, the nation would cry with one voice, "Heal them!" If they were staggering on in ignorance, it would cry, "Train them!" If they were harming themselves and others by crime, it would cry, "Guide them!" And such cries are heard and have been heard in the land; but it was not one voice and its volume has been ever broken by counter-cries and echoes, "Let them die!" "Train them like slaves!" "Let them stagger downward!"

This is the spirit that enters in and complicates all Negro social problems and this is a problem which only civilization and humanity can successfully solve. Meantime we have the other problems before us—we have the problems arising from the uniting of so many social questions about one centre. In such a situation we need only to avoid underestimating the difficulties on the one hand and overestimating them on the other. The problems are difficult, extremely difficult, but they are such as the world has conquered before and can conquer again. Moreover the battle involves more than a mere altruistic interest in an alien people. It is a battle for humanity and human culture. If in the hey-dey of the greatest of the world's civilizations, it is possible for one people ruthlessly to steal another, drag them helpless across the water, enslave them, debauch them, and then slowly murder them by economic and social exclusion until they disappear from the face of the earth—if the consummation of such a crime be possible in the twentieth century, then our civilization is vain and the republic is a mockery and a farce.

But this will not be; first, even with the terribly adverse circum-

stances under which Negroes live, there is not the slightest likelihood of
their dying out; a nation that has endured the slave-trade, slavery, reconstruction, and present prejudice three hundred years, and under it
increased in numbers and efficiency, is not in any immediate danger of
extinction. Nor is the thought of voluntary or involuntary emigration
more than a dream of men who forget that there are half as many
Negroes in the United States as Spaniards in Spain. If this be so then a
few plain propositions may be laid down as axiomatic:

1. The Negro is here to stay.

2. It is to the advantage of all, both black and white, that every
Negro should make the best of himself.

3. It is the duty of the Negro to raise himself by every effort to the
standards of modern civilization and not to lower those standards in
any degree.

4. It is the duty of the white people to guard their civilization
against debauchment by themselves or others; but in order to do this it
is not necessary to hinder and retard the efforts of an earnest people to
rise, simply because they lack faith in the ability of that people.

5. With these duties in mind and with a spirit of self-help, mutual
aid and co-operation, the two races should strive side by side to realize
the ideals of the republic and make this truly a land of equal opportunity for all men.

The Duty of the Negroes

That the Negro race has an appalling work of social reform before it
need hardly be said. Simply because the ancestors of the present white
inhabitants of America went out of their way barbarously to mistreat
and enslave the ancestors of the present black inhabitants gives those
blacks no right to ask that the civilization and morality of the land be
seriously menaced for their benefit. Men have a right to demand that
the members of a civilized community be civilized; that the fabric of
human culture, so laboriously woven, be not wantonly or ignorantly destroyed. Consequently a nation may rightly demand, even of a people
it has consciously and intentionally wronged, not indeed complete
civilization in thirty or one hundred years, but at least every effort and

213

sacrifice possible on their part toward making themselves fit members of the community within a reasonable length of time; that thus they may early become a source of strength and help instead of a national burden. Modern society has too many problems of its own, too much proper anxiety as to its own ability to survive under its present organization, for it lightly to shoulder all the burdens of a less advanced people, and it can rightly demand that as far as possible and as rapidly as possible the Negro bend his energy to the solving of his own social problems—contributing to his poor, paying his share of the taxes and supporting the schools and public administration. For the accomplishment of this the Negro has a right to demand freedom for self-development, and no more aid from without than is really helpful for furthering that development. Such aid must of necessity be considerable: it must furnish schools and reformatories, and relief and preventive agencies; but the bulk of the work of raising the Negro must be done by the Negro himself, and the greatest help for him will be not to hinder and curtail and discourage his efforts. Against prejudice, injustice and wrong the Negro ought to protest energetically and continuously, but he must never forget that he protests because those things hinder his own efforts, and that those efforts are the key to his future.

And those efforts must be mighty and comprehensive, persistent, well-aimed and tireless; satisfied with no partial success, lulled to sleep by no colorless victories; and, above all, guided by no low selfish ideals; at the same time they must be tempered by common sense and rational expectation. In Philadelphia those efforts should first be directed toward a lessening of Negro crime; no doubt the amount of crime imputed to the race is exaggerated, no doubt features of the Negro's environment over which he has no control, excuse much that is committed; but beyond all this the amount of crime that can without doubt rightly be laid at the door of the Philadelphia Negro is large and is a menace to a civilized people. Efforts to stop this crime must commence in the Negro homes; they must cease to be, as they often are, breeders of idleness and extravagance and complaint. Work, continuous and intensive; work, although it be menial and poorly rewarded; work, though done in travail of soul and sweat of brow, must be so impressed upon Negro children as the road to salvation, that a child would feel it a greater disgrace to be idle than to do the humblest labor. The homely virtues of honesty, truth and chastity must be instilled in the cradle, and although it is hard to teach self-respect to a people whose million fellow-citizens half-despise them, yet it must be taught as the surest road to gain the respect of others.

It is right and proper that Negro boys and girls should desire to rise as high in the world as their ability and just desert entitle them. They should be ever encouraged and urged to do so, although they should be taught also that idleness and crime are beneath and not above the lowest work. It should be the continual object of Negroes to open up better industrial chances for their sons and daughters. Their success here must of course rest largely with the white people, but not entirely. Proper co-operation among forty or fifty thousand colored people ought to open many chances of employment for their sons and daughters in trades, stores and shops, associations and industrial enterprises.

Further, some rational means of amusement should be furnished young folks. Prayer meetings and church socials have their place, but they cannot compete in attractiveness with the dance halls and gambling dens of the city. There is a legitimate demand for amusement on the part of the young which may be made a means of education, improvement and recreation. A harmless and beautiful amusement like dancing might with proper effort be rescued from its low and unhealthful associations and made a means of health and recreation. The billiard table is no more wedded to the saloon than to the church if good people did not drive it there. If the Negro homes and churches cannot amuse their young people, and if no other efforts are made to satisfy this want, then we cannot complain if the saloons and clubs and bawdy houses send these children to crime, disease and death.

There is a vast amount of preventive and rescue work which the Negroes themselves might do: keeping little girls off the street at night, stopping the escorting of unchaperoned young ladies to church and elsewhere, showing the dangers of the lodging system, urging the buying of homes and removal from crowded and tainted neighborhoods, giving lectures and tracts on health and habits, exposing the dangers of gambling and policy-playing, and inculcating respect for women. Day-nurseries and sewing-schools, mothers' meetings, the parks and airing

215

places, all these things are little known or appreciated among the masses of Negroes, and their attention should be directed to them.

The spending of money is a matter to which Negroes need to give especial attention. Money is wasted to-day in dress, furniture, elaborate entertainments, costly church edifices, and "insurance" schemes, which ought to go toward buying homes, educating children, giving simple healthful amusement to the young, and accumulating something in the savings bank against a "rainy day." A crusade for the savings bank as against the "insurance" society ought to be started in the Seventh Ward without delay.

Although directly after the war there was great and remarkable enthusiasm for education, there is no doubt but that this enthusiasm has fallen off, and there is to-day much neglect of children among the Negroes, and failure to send them regularly to school. This should be looked into by the Negroes themselves and every effort made to induce full regular attendance.

Above all, the better classes of the Negroes should recognize their duty toward the masses. They should not forget that the spirit of the twentieth century is to be the turning of the high toward the lowly, the bending of Humanity to all that is human; the recognition that in the slums of modern society lie the answers to most of our puzzling problems of organization and life, and that only as we solve those problems is our culture assured and our progress certain. This the Negro is far from recognizing for himself; his social evolution in cities like Philadelphia is approaching a mediaeval stage when the centrifugal forces of repulsion between social classes are becoming more powerful than those of attraction. So hard has been the rise of the better class of Negroes that they fear to fall if now they stoop to lend a hand to their fellows. This feeling is intensified by the blindness of those outsiders who persist even now in confounding the good and bad, the risen and fallen in one mass. Nevertheless the Negro must learn the lesson that other nations learned so laboriously and imperfectly, that his better classes have their chief excuse for being in the work they may do toward lifting the rabble. This is especially true in a city like Philadelphia which has so distinct and creditable a Negro aristocracy; that they do something already to grapple with these social problems of their race is true, but they do not yet do nearly as much as they must, nor do they clearly recognize their responsibility.

Finally, the Negroes must cultivate a spirit of calm, patient persistence in their attitude toward their fellow citizens rather than of loud and intemperate complaint. A man may be wrong, and know he is wrong, and yet some finesse must be used in telling him of it. The white people of Philadelphia are perfectly conscious that their Negro citizens are not treated fairly in all respects, but it will not improve matters to call names or impute unworthy motives to all men. Social reforms move slowly and yet when Right is reinforced by calm but persistent Progress we somehow all feel that in the end it must triumph.

The Duty of the Whites

There is a tendency on the part of many white people to approach the Negro question from the side which just now is of least pressing importance, namely, that of the social intermingling of races. The old query: Would you want your sister to marry a Nigger? still stands as a grim sentinel to stop much rational discussion. And yet few white women have been pained by the addresses of black suitors, and those who have easily got rid of them. The whole discussion is little less than foolish; perhaps a century from to-day we may find ourselves seriously discussing such questions of social policy, but it is certain that just as long as one group deems it a serious *mésalliance* to marry with another just so long few marriages will take place, and it will need neither law nor argument to guide human choice in such a matter. Certainly the masses of whites would hardly acknowledge that an active propaganda of repression was necessary to ward off intermarriage. Natural pride of race, strong on one side and growing on the other, may be trusted to ward off such mingling as might in this stage of development prove disastrous to both races. All this therefore is a question of the far-off future.

To-day, however, we must face the fact that a natural repugnance to close intermingling with unfortunate ex-slaves has descended to a discrimination that very seriously hinders them from being anything better. It is right and proper to object to ignorance and consequently to ignorant men; but if by our actions we have been responsible for their

ignorance and are still actively engaged in keeping them ignorant, the
argument loses its moral force. So with the Negroes: men have a right
to object to a race so poor and ignorant and inefficient as the mass of
the Negroes; but if their policy in the past is parent of much of this
condition, and if to-day by shutting black boys and girls out of most
avenues of decent employment they are increasing pauperism and vice,
then they must hold themselves largely responsible for the deplorable
results.

There is no doubt that in Philadelphia the centre and kernel of the
Negro problem so far as the white people are concerned is the narrow
opportunities afforded Negroes for earning a decent living. Such discrimination is morally wrong, politically dangerous, industrially waste-
ful, and socially silly. It is the duty of the whites to stop it, and to do
so primarily for their own sakes. Industrial freedom of opportunity has
by long experience been proven to be generally best for all. Moreover
the cost of crime and pauperism, the growth of slums, and the perni-
cious influences of idleness and lewdness, cost the public far more than
would the hurt to the feelings of a carpenter to work beside a black
man, or a shop girl to stand beside a darker mate. This does not con-
template the wholesale replacing of white workmen for Negroes out of
sympathy or philanthropy; it does mean that talent should be rewarded,
and aptness used in commerce and industry whether its owner be black
or white; that the same incentive to good, honest, effective work be
placed before a black office boy as before a white one—before a black
porter as before a white one; and that unless this is done the city has
no right to complain that black boys lose interest in work and drift into
idleness and crime. Probably a change in public opinion on this point
to-morrow would not make very much difference in the positions occupied by Negroes in the city: some few would be promoted, some few
would get new places—the mass would remain as they are; but it would
make one vast difference: it would inspire the young to try harder, it
would stimulate the idle and discouraged and it would take away from
this race the omnipresent excuse for failure: prejudice. Such a moral
change would work a revolution in the criminal rate during the next
ten years. Even a Negro bootblack could black boots better if he knew

he was a menial not because he was a Negro but because he was best fitted for the work of being a boot black.

We need then a radical change in public opinion on this point; it will not and ought not to come suddenly, but instead of thoughtless acquiescence in the continual and steadily encroaching exclusion of Negroes from work in the city, the leaders of industry and opinion ought to be trying here and there to open up new opportunities and give new chances to bright colored boys. The policy of the city to-day simply drives out the best class of young people whom its schools have educated and social opportunities trained, and fills their places with idle and vicious immigrants. It is a paradox of the times that young men and women from some of the best Negro families of the city—families born and reared here and schooled in the best traditions of this municipality have actually had to go to the South to get work, if they wished to be aught but chambermaids and bootblacks. Not that such work may not be honorable and useful, but that it is as wrong to make scullions of engineers as it is to make engineers of scullions. Such a situation is a disgrace to the city—a disgrace to its Christianity, to its spirit of justice, to its common sense; what can be the end of such a policy but increased crime and increased excuse for crime? Increased poverty and more reason to be poor? Increased political serfdom of the mass of black voters to the bosses and rascals who divide the spoils? Surely here lies the first duty of a civilized city.

Secondly, in their efforts for the uplifting of the Negro the people of Philadelphia must recognize the existence of the better class of Negroes and must gain their active aid and co-operation by generous and polite conduct. Social sympathy must exist between what is best in both races and there must no longer be the feeling that the Negro who makes the best of himself is of least account to the city of Philadelphia, while the vagabond is to be helped and pitied. This better class of Negro does not want help or pity, but it does want a generous recognition of its difficulties, and a broad sympathy with the problem of life as it presents itself to them. It is composed of men and women educated and in many cases cultured; with proper co-operation they could be a vast power in the city, and the only power that could successfully cope with many phases of the Negro problems. But their active aid cannot be gained for purely selfish motives, or kept by churlish and ungentle manners; and above all they object to being patronized.

Again, the white people of the city must remember that much of the sorrow and bitterness that surrounds the life of the American Negro comes from the unconscious prejudice and half-conscious actions of men and women who do not intend to wound or annoy. One is not compelled to discuss the Negro question with every Negro one meets or to tell him of a father who was connected with the Underground Railroad; one is not compelled to stare at the solitary black face in the audience as though it were not human; it is not necessary to sneer, or be unkind or boorish, if the Negroes in the room or on the street are not all the best behaved or have not the most elegant manners; it is hardly necessary to strike from the dwindling list of one's boyhood and girlhood acquaintances or school-day friends all those who happen to have Negro blood, simply because one has not the courage now to greet them on the street. The little decencies of daily intercourse can go on, the courtesies of life be exchanged even across the color line without any danger to the supremacy of the Anglo-Saxon or the social ambition of the Negro. Without doubt social differences are facts not fancies and cannot lightly be swept aside; but they hardly need to be looked upon as excuses for downright meanness and incivility.

A polite and sympathetic attitude toward these striving thousands; a delicate avoidance of that which wounds and embitters them; a generous granting of opportunity to them; a seconding of their efforts, and a desire to reward honest success—all this, added to proper striving on their part, will go far even in our day toward making all men, white and black, realize what the great founder of the city meant when he named it the City of Brotherly Love.

Index

225

DATE DUE			